Sons of East Tennessee

Sons of East Tennessee
Civil War Veterans Divided and Reconciled

JACK BRUBAKER

Foreword by JACK NEELY

McFarland & Company, Inc., Publishers
Jefferson, North Carolina

LIBRARY OF CONGRESS CATALOGUING-IN-PUBLICATION DATA

Library of Congress Cataloging-in-Publication Data

Names: Brubaker, John H., III, 1944– author. | Neely, Jack, writer of foreword.
Title: Sons of East Tennessee : Civil War veterans divided and reconciled / Jack Brubaker ; foreword by Jack Neely
Other titles: Civil War veterans divided and reconciled
Description: Jefferson, North Carolina : McFarland & Company, Inc., Publishers, 2022 | Includes bibliographical references and index.
Identifiers: LCCN 2021057642 | ISBN 9781476684147 (paperback : acid free paper) ∞
ISBN 9781476644301 (ebook) ∞
Subjects: LCSH: Bernard, Reuben Frank, 1832-1903. | McCorkle, William Alexander, 1830-1910. | Bernard, John Jay, 1872-1898—Death and burial. | McCorkle, Henry Leftwich, 1867-1898—Death and burial. | McCorkle family. | Bernard family. | United States—History—Civil War, 1861-1865—Influence. | United States—History—Civil War, 1861-1865—Veterans. | Veterans—Tennessee—Biography. | Tennessee—Biography. | Knoxville National Cemetery (Tenn.)—History. | BISAC: HISTORY / United States / Civil War Period (1850-1877) | HISTORY / United States / State & Local / South (AL, AR, FL, GA, KY, LA, MS, NC, SC, TN, VA, WV)
Classification: LCC F435 .B75 2022 | DDC 976.8/040922—dc23/eng/20211130
LC record available at https://lccn.loc.gov/2021057642

BRITISH LIBRARY CATALOGUING DATA ARE AVAILABLE

ISBN (print) 978-1-4766-8414-7
ISBN (ebook) 978-1-4766-4430-1

© 2022 John H. Brubaker III. All rights reserved

No part of this book may be reproduced or transmitted in any form or by any means, electronic or mechanical, including photocopying or recording, or by any information storage and retrieval system, without permission in writing from the publisher.

Front cover image: Memorial Day, 1899—three veterans under one flag, Udo J. Keppler, 1872–1956, artist (Library of Congress)

Printed in the United States of America

McFarland & Company, Inc., Publishers
  Box 611, Jefferson, North Carolina 28640
  www.mcfarlandpub.com

To Christine

May the soldiers' children never prove unworthy of their fathers' name; may they grow up into true heroism and love of their native land, and, as did their fathers, let them be willing to shed their blood, to lay down their lives, for the sake of their country.
—The Rev. Henry Ward Beecher praying at the dedication of the Soldiers' National Monument in the national cemetery at Gettysburg, Pennsylvania, July 1, 1869

Once more the blood of North and South has been poured out together—no longer beneath contending standards in the bitterness of war between the States, but beneath one flag, to the glory of one country. These dead, at least, belong to us all. The last hateful memory that could divide our country is buried with them. About their grave kneels a new nation, loving all her children everywhere the same.
—Former Confederate Lieutenant General Stephen D. Lee reading from a report at a United Confederate Veterans' reunion in Charleston, South Carolina, May 10, 1899

Table of Contents

Foreword by Jack Neely	1
Preface	5
Prologue: Nashville, Tennessee (Memorial Day, 1899)	11
1. Reuben Bernard (1832–1865)	21
2. Wartime East Tennessee (1861–1865)	31
3. William McCorkle (1830–1865)	46
4. Post-War East Tennessee (1865–1868)	56
5. Separating the Dead (1865–1868)	66
6. Memorializing the Dead (1868–1898)	77
7. Monuments to the Dead, Reunions for the Living (1868–1898)	89
8. Reuben Bernard and William McCorkle (1865–1898)	104
9. Henry McCorkle (1867–1898) and John Jay Bernard (1872–1898)	115
10. Preparing for War (Winter 1898)	126
11. Sailing from Tampa to Cuba (Spring, 1898)	138
12. The Battle at El Caney (July 1, 1898)	149
13. Burial and Memorial (July 1898–Winter 1899)	162
14. Reburial and Reconciliation (April 2, 1899)	174
Epilogue: Knoxville, Tennessee (Memorial Day, 1899)	184
Chapter Notes	199
Bibliography	213
Index	221

Foreword
by Jack Neely

This is a dramatic war story of national resonance little remembered even in the hometown of its protagonists. It's a story about a terrible coincidence. Two army lieutenants who died at nearly the same instant are buried alongside one another in Knoxville's National Cemetery, one of the nation's oldest formal military cemeteries. The street that forms its northern border is named Bernard, the last name of one of the soldiers. But in the twenty-first century, perhaps no one who passes along that street, in a car or on foot, can offer any clues about any soldier of that name, in a long-ago war forgotten by most.

I admit I knew nothing about John Jay Bernard and Henry McCorkle myself, even after thirty years as a Knoxville historian with a special interest in the Victorian era. I had never run across the accounts of how my own alma mater, the University of Tennessee, had conducted a rather elaborate memorial to these two fellow alumni.

Part of the reason was that despite an attraction to graveyards nurtured in childhood, it took me a long time to find a reason to explore National Cemetery. It was designed during the Civil War, as the occupying Union Army braced for a Confederate siege. Most of its first 4,000 burials were enlisted men, people whose names are not well known to history, and about a third of those are inscribed with the terrible adjective "Unknown." You don't expect to find famous people here. But the cemetery was unusual then as now in that it was designed in concentric circles. From the road, you won't guess at that fact. Across the stone wall, the cemetery looks clean and orderly, without much to charm or intrigue, the qualities that make other historic cemeteries appealing to the curious. From a distance, the lawn is perfectly green, and the graves are perfectly white, uniform in size and shape.

Foreword by Jack Neely

The cemetery appears to be in perfect military order, as if awaiting inspection.

A research project for my nonprofit Knoxville History Project sent me wading deeper into the cemetery, where I found a few surprising irregularities not obvious from the road. I discovered that after the economic exigencies of the Civil War—but before the War Department's military regimentation that came with the massive losses of the two World Wars—there was another period, an interim of sorts that was distinctly different, a period of variation. The high Victorian era, which produced such elaborate gravestones in private cemeteries, happened to coincide with an unexpected conflict, brief but violent, called the Spanish-American War.

That period produced hundreds of new standard military stones, but there were also several others, more elaborate markers placed around the periphery of the circular center. Of those nonstandard stones, closest to the center are the graves of Lieutenants Bernard and McCorkle, elaborate Victorian markers side-by-side. Distinctly different from the sea of uniform graves around them, they are also different in design from one another—but equivalent in size and dimensions, so much so that they seem like a set. And they both feature references to a Cuban battlefield little-remembered today—El Caney—and they feature an identical inscription: a death date, July 1, 1898.

I had never noticed this pair before, but the oddity prompted me to look up their story, of how they had both attended the University of Tennessee, but at different times, and how they had both volunteered to fight, but in different regiments. How McCorkle grew up on a farm in a remote section of East Tennessee, and how Bernard grew up in the Wild West, among the army forts where his father, General Reuben Bernard, was stationed. They would seem to have little in common but their alma mater, their rank—and the fact that they died in battle at almost the same moment.

I wrote two or three paragraphs about it, and it became an unexpected part of a small book about the history of the cemetery that the Knoxville History Project produced for the federal department known as Veterans Affairs.

In what may be an even more unlikely coincidence than two simultaneous deaths on a battlefield, it was only weeks after I first noticed the graves of McCorkle and Bernard that I received a letter from a writer in Lancaster, Pennsylvania. I had never met Jack Brubaker, but from a

Foreword by Jack Neely

distance he had learned the story of these same two fellows who had just recently intrigued me.

It's not unusual to hear from writers who say they're working on a book. I do try to help, especially when the subject is of interest to me. But I typically never hear from them again, and after an email or two they go silent. I assume they discovered something that many of us have learned the hard way: that writing a book is hard, especially when it's a book based on facts concerning people who died more than a century ago. Brubaker is more resourceful as a researcher, more talented as an author, and endowed with more patience for a complex story than most writers who assail a project of this scope. As a result, he learned much more depth to the story than I did, connecting Bernard and McCorkle to the national reconciliation that seemed to come only thirty-three years after the Civil War, when sons of Union and Confederate families fought alongside each other in a common struggle.

Resentment had remained fresh in the South for a generation. Home to many prominent Unionists, Knoxville was no typical "Southern" city, and as soon as the Confederates left, Knoxville celebrated patriotic holidays like Decoration Day and the Fourth of July with enthusiasm. However, large parts of the former Confederacy remained bitter about rejoining the nation that had invaded, and for decades declined to participate in its annual patriotic rites. That seemed to change with the Spanish-American War.

By some accounts, a key agent of change was General Joseph Wheeler, one of the Confederacy's youngest and most colorful cavalry generals during the Civil War. Among his many daring exploits, which earned him fame but also three battlefield wounds, "Fightin' Joe" Wheeler led a raid at the beginning of the rebel siege of Knoxville in 1863. Thanks to Union General Ambrose Burnside's deft defenses, Wheeler never set foot in the city. Remarkably, though, thirty-five years later, the same legendary Confederate commander volunteered to lead U.S. troops in combat with Spanish forces in Cuba, capturing the imagination of the South. The old rebel hero's new victories on the battlefield wearing a blue uniform may have signaled to many recalcitrant Confederate sympathizers that the War Between the States was finally over, and it was time to rally around the red, white, and blue again.

But perhaps more telling and enduring were the reconciliations symbolized by younger men of lower ranks, men like McCorkle and Bernard, who were too young to remember the Civil War, but who

Foreword by Jack Neely

represented families who fought and suffered in opposition to each other in that divisive earlier era.

No soldiers in that war were mourned in the same way as those young lieutenants. Their twin deaths prompted an extraordinary ceremony hosted by University of Tennessee President Charles Dabney. The Virginia-born son of a Presbyterian minister had studied in Europe to become a professor of chemistry and mineralogy; he had recently served in Washington as a cabinet official for the Cleveland administration. The cannonball-scarred university had suffered the strain of partisan divisions for years after the Civil War; Dabney may have seen an opportunity to bring everyone together with an emotional public gesture.

Through years of research, in which he connected with descendants and traveled to archival libraries, Jack Brubaker discovered private sources previously unknown to the public, including personal letters. In the process, he has accomplished an impressive feat, learning more about Bernard and McCorkle than most of their contemporaries knew, and brings vivid light to this forgotten story, which is both a dual family tragedy and a story of dramatic reconciliation. I'm grateful he has shared it with us.

Jack Neely, a graduate of the University of Tennessee, worked for 30 years as a newspaper columnist and has written more than a dozen books, most of them about Knoxville's complex past. Since 2014 he has been executive director of the Knoxville History Project.

Preface

Like many American young men who came of age during the Civil War's centennial in the early 1960s, I was obsessed with the bloody battles. I frequently toured the turning-point battlefield at Gettysburg, not far from my home in Lancaster County, Pennsylvania. I read stacks of books on First Manassas and the Atlanta Campaign, on Robert E. Lee and Abraham Lincoln. I overstuffed four scrapbooks with magazine and newspaper clippings related to the war and the centennial. I was the youngest member of the local Civil War Round Table. Eventually, I learned how to fire a musket and became a Union re-enactor. When other college students drove nonstop to Florida beaches for spring break, two buddies and I toured every major Civil War battlefield. I was passionately devoted to that war.

I enthusiastically agreed with Robert Penn Warren's comment in his meditation on the centennial that the Civil War is "our only 'felt' history—history lived in the national imagination." Even when my intellectual interest in the Civil War and war in general began to wane in later years, my emotional investment remained intact. So, searching for a topic for a new book several years ago, I naturally turned to an aspect of the war that I had not explored. I had often wondered how veterans, who had been dedicated for four years to killing anyone who wore an enemy uniform, had reunited and reconciled their differences following the war. I soon found that historians had created a modest library answering that question in various ways. What I did not find was a book on reconciliation that, at its core, focused on specific veterans.

Caroline E. Janney's insightful book, *Remembering the Civil War: Reunion and the Limits of Reconciliation*, briefly referred to such a singular story. Janney proposed that men from the North and South who died in the Spanish-American War symbolized a reunited nation of reconciled veterans. She provided several examples. One of them: "From

Preface

Tennessee came the story of two fathers, one a Union veteran, the other a Confederate, meeting at the graves of their sons who had fallen on San Juan Hill [actually on the nearby battlefield of El Caney]. Men who had once fought against each other now mingled their tears over sons who had sacrificed their lives on the same altar of patriotism."

That is all Janney wrote, but her end note led me to the information I needed to track down the fathers—General Reuben Bernard and Dr. William McCorkle—and their sons—Lieutenants John Jay Bernard and Henry Leftwich McCorkle. When I traced these families' stories—outlined in newspaper accounts, their own letters, comments of their contemporaries, and recollections of their descendants, I knew I had a solid example of veterans who, at least for a day, set aside any old grievances when forced to face their sons' mortality. When I realized that their stories played out largely in East Tennessee, an unusually fractured section of the nation during the Civil War, I knew I had a compelling tale to tell.

This book explores the lives of those fathers and sons within the context of veteran reconciliation. The narrative runs from just before the Civil War began in 1861 until just after the Spanish-American War ended in 1898. It proceeds chronologically, with chapters about the fathers and sons alternating with chapters about events occurring in East Tennessee and elsewhere. The settings range from Knoxville, Rogersville and other locations in East Tennessee to battlefields in Virginia, Arizona, and Cuba. The book begins and ends in national cemeteries, because this story is about death as well as reconciliation.

Three major themes run through the book: separation, reunification, and reconciliation. These themes are developed primarily in East Tennessee, but often with national associations.

By separation I mean not only the Confederacy's secession from the union of states, but East Tennessee's separation from the rest of Tennessee because of the severe Union/Confederate fracture in the region. Beyond these schisms, another separation is not so well known: tens of thousands of soldiers' remains lie in distinct cemeteries. By design, the federal government established national cemeteries in Knoxville and elsewhere, North and South, for Union casualties alone. Only if Confederates died while prisoners or as patients in Union hospitals were they buried in national cemeteries, and then in separate sections. That partitioning of the dead required Confederates to establish cemeteries of their own, at their own expense. So the separation by war of over thirty-one million people living in the United States in 1860 culminated

Preface

in the separation of as many as three-quarters of a million soldiers in that population who died during the war. This division of the dead, along with separate cemetery monuments and separate Decoration Days, presented a substantial early obstacle to reunification and reconciliation.

Basic reunification occurred rapidly following the Civil War. With the surrender of Confederate armies in the field, the secessionist government fell apart and there was no viable choice but to reunite the country. Tennessee's road to reunification, at least on paper, was the shortest in the Confederacy. After being the last state to secede in 1861, it was the first to rejoin in 1866.

A more complex reunification process involved formal rules for renewed citizenship of Confederate veterans and readmission of the rest of the rebellious states to the union. It also featured a decade of U.S. army–enforced Reconstruction in Southern states that seemed obligatory to Northerners intent on preventing the Confederacy from rising again but punitively restrictive to ex-Confederates, especially those who lost political power. However, following the end of Reconstruction in 1876 and certainly by the 1880s, reunification for most Civil War veterans was a settled issue. People who elected the same president, paid taxes to the same government, traded essential goods with each other, and traveled to formerly alien parts of the country on business or as tourists recognized that the sections were reunited, practically if not politically.

Veteran reconciliation was a far more difficult process, especially for Southerners who had not only lost a war but, in many cases, a way of life. Northerners also had reservations about reconciling their differences with the other side, especially if former Confederates refused to modify beliefs they had advocated before the war. But most Americans who fought each other at Shiloh or Chancellorsville or Chickamauga eventually did forgive their former enemies. They did this, many of them, without abandoning their opinion of which side had fought for the right cause. They did this, some of them, without modifying the bitterness they felt about the loss of so many relatives and friends. All but the most recalcitrant veterans reconciled, finally, when their generation and their sons' generation fought and died together in the Spanish-American War. As William Blair put it in *Cities of the Dead*, that cooperative foreign venture "provide[d] the exclamation point to sectional reconciliation."

Reconciliation ultimately occurred because veterans on both sides

Preface

decided that their common bond as Americans outweighed their differences over slavery and secession before or after the war. It also occurred because white veterans—actively in the South, more passively in the North—agreed that black Americans would not be included as full participants in a reunited democracy. Those two decisions seemed to resolve major conflicts for many veterans; but they also virtually guaranteed that succeeding generations, who were not bonded by wartime service and sacrifice, would contend with continuing sectional and racial issues that have undermined reconciliation into the twenty-first century.

One of Eugene O'Neill's forlorn characters in *A Moon for the Misbegotten* says, "There is no present or future—only the past happening over and over again—now. You can't get away from it." This book's Epilogue examines why the nation's emotional story of separation and reunification and the ongoing efforts to reconcile differences over secession and slavery and states' rights and civil rights remains something we can't get away from.

✥✥✥

It took a while to pull together the varied elements of this tale. As a Yankee who lived for five years in southern Virginia but knew little about neighboring East Tennessee before taking on this project, I needed substantial help. McCorkle and Bernard descendants, now scattered throughout the United States, contributed generously to the project.

Most significant, the southern branch of Dr. William McCorkle's family held a reunion for my benefit at a superb bed and breakfast in Mooresburg, Hawkins County. Priscilla Rogers, a descendant of the Leftwiches, Dr. McCorkle's wife's side of the family, runs the B&B. She has lived all of her life in the McCorkles' hometown and explained the lay of the land. Pat Talty, a direct descendant of the McCorkles from Birmingham, Alabama, provided a poignant letter the doctor wrote to his sister following Henry McCorkle's death in Cuba. Tom Shelton, of Hampstead, Maryland, and Joe Santen of Mooresville, North Carolina, both descended from Leftwiches, told family stories.

At her home in Stone Ridge, New York, Marian McCorkle Beckerman, another direct descendant but representing a northern branch of the McCorkles, shared a significant bundle of family correspondence. These papers include the detailed letters Henry McCorkle wrote to his wife in the days before he was killed in Cuba. Marian's brother, Maynard

Preface

McCorkle, of Topsham, Maine, described and photographed items he had inherited that had been found on Henry McCorkle's body after he was shot.

Collecting information about General Reuben Bernard's family proved more difficult because his son, John, had no descendants who could hold a reunion or provide much information. Clayton Bernard, a collateral descendant of Lakewood, Colorado, enthusiastically discussed details of Reuben Bernard's battles with American Indians. Austin Dopman, a great-grandson of Reuben Bernard who lives in Fort Myers, Florida, contributed photographs of Reuben and a letter concerning the birth and early travel of his eighth child. John Hale, a Bernard family descendant who lives in Williamsburg, Virginia, contributed genealogical information.

Several libraries, museums, and other institutions provided essential materials.

In Knoxville, the Calvin M. McClung Historical Collection at the Knox County Library was my best source for newspapers, documents, and photographs of the period; Jeanie Watts helped me retrieve some of these materials. At the University of Tennessee's Hodges Library, archivist Alesha Shumer provided Henry McCorkle's and Jack Bernard's transcripts and yearbooks, as well as copies of University President Charles Dabney's correspondence with the McCorkles and Bernards following the death of the two lieutenants. Barb Wiest, an administrator at Knoxville's First Presbyterian Church, retrieved an audiotape of a 2015 reconciliation sermon. In Rogersville, the staff of Rogersville's H.B. Stamps Memorial Library turned me loose in the local history room. Rogersville bookseller George Webb provided access to several McCorkle family documents. In Nashville, the Tennessee State Library and Archives provided military service and pension records and useful information on East Tennessee in the nineteenth century.

Outside Tennessee, the National Archives in Washington provided military service records. Lisa McCown and Brian Faidley, of special collections and archives at Washington & Lee University's Leyburn Library, located William McCorkle's meager student records and his birthplace. The archives at the University of Colorado at Boulder produced a file of information on Reuben Bernard. The William L. Clements Library at the University of Michigan provided a brief description of the reburial of Union soldiers in Knoxville National Cemetery.

I did much of my reading in the archives of the U.S. Army Military

Preface

Heritage and Education Center in Carlisle, Pennsylvania. There I sifted through Reuben Bernard material collected by the Order of Indian Wars of the United States, as well as regimental histories and other military records. For general reading, the Shadek-Fackenthal Library at Franklin & Marshall College in Lancaster provided a comprehensive collection of books on the Civil War, the Spanish-American War, and the late nineteenth century. Thanks to the collection of digitized newspapers at Newspapers.com, I uncovered stories about the Bernards, the McCorkles, and the period between the wars, especially in Knoxville, that I otherwise would not have known existed.

This would be a lesser book if several people had not graciously agreed to review an early draft of the manuscript. Jack Neely, executive director of the Knoxville History Project, stayed up one night poring over an early version of the manuscript. He suggested significant adjustments, then agreed to write the Foreword. Historian James Marten read the work and made penetrating comments. Historian Nina Silber read parts of the manuscript and provided additional sources. My longtime friend, the late historian David Schuyler, suggested a crucial addition. My versatile friend Leslie Stainton, a writer and university lecturer, recommended new ways of looking at structural elements. My creative niece, Jennifer Besse, a teacher of the Classics and a budding novelist, persuaded me to rethink and reconstruct the Prologue.

My editor at McFarland, Dylan Lightfoot, encouraged me to expand the original manuscript—a process that compelled me to reconsider several important issues in greater depth and add useful details throughout. He also guided me through the sometimes tedious, sometimes serendipitous process of turning a manuscript into a book with photographs and an attractive cover and all of the other elements that help make a historical work friendly to readers.

My steadfast and patient spouse, Christine Conant Brubaker—teacher, conservationist, and cheerleader—accompanied me on research trips to Tennessee and regularly reminded me, with her own special enthusiasm, that there is more to life than the past happening over and over again.

Prologue

*Nashville, Tennessee
(Memorial Day, 1899)*

Knoxville Mayor William Rule addressed the holiday crowd with confidence born of passion and repetition. In the war with Spain, he said, the sons of Civil War veterans "went forth to battle under one flag the blue, and under the same flag the gray, united and harmonious, sectional lines obliterated, the fires of patriotism burning brightly in all hearts." Rule had traveled to Nashville on Memorial Day 1899 to proclaim what he believed many Civil War veterans believed: most Northerners and Southerners had reunited and had reconciled their differences, in large part because of their common cause in the Spanish-American War that had begun and ended so swiftly the previous year.

As the day's keynote speaker, the former Union army officer had prepared remarks acceptable to Union and Confederate veterans throughout Tennessee, a state whose residents had been divided explosively by the Civil War nearly four decades earlier. He explained that he would not argue the question of which side had been right. "Both were right. Both were honest," he said. "If it be true that actions speak louder than words, then it is not for me to say that the Confederate soldiers who fought so valiantly on so many bloody fields and endured so much suffering for four long years with so much fortitude were not sincere."

Well into his second term as mayor, the sixty-year-old editor of the *Knoxville Journal and Tribune* paused to look over his audience. Somber men and women and subdued children had wedged themselves among rows of identical white marble tombstones. They had come in a crush on a warm spring day to Nashville National Cemetery just northeast of the city to honor the remains of more than sixteen thousand Union soldiers. Many had brought flowers to decorate graves and to mourn the loss of

Prologue

a father or a son, a brother or a neighbor. Some had arrived by carriage or streetcar. Others had ridden on a special excursion of the Louisville & Nashville Railroad, a line that split the cemetery in half. Most had entered the cemetery by way of the main entrance on the Gallatin Road and arranged themselves on uneven terrain on the far side of the elevated rail line.

Here and there, among the mass of residents dressed in holiday clothes, Rule spotted a Union veteran still able to fit into his old uniform. Rule also noticed groups of younger men wearing newer, brighter blue uniforms. Spanish-American War soldiers eager to play their part as the nation's newest veterans had come to honor men who had died in Cuba.

On the speakers' platform, an array of local Grand Army of the Republic (GAR) officials waited their turns to praise the bravery of both Union and Confederate soldiers. Former Union Brigadier General Gates Thruston, now a sixty-three-year-old Nashville businessman and amateur archaeologist, and George N. Tillman, a U.S. marshal and leading

One of five upright seacoast cannons stands among thousands of Union graves in Nashville National Cemetery. In the background, a freight train passes through the graveyard. Burials were made on either side of the Louisville & Nashville line, which began operating seven years before the cemetery opened in 1866 (photograph by Christine Brubaker).

Nashville, Tennessee (Memorial Day, 1899)

Nashville Republican, led a contingent of aging officers of the Nashville and Tennessee State units of the GAR.

A cluster of singers from Nashville's Fisk University Glee Club sat to the side of the platform. These performers were the successors of Fisk's original Jubilee Singers, former enslaved Africans who had entertained audiences around the world with their renditions of Negro spirituals following the Civil War. The all-black Glee Club contrasted sharply with the predominantly white crowd.

Rule, whose white hair and Van Dyke beard softened his formal dark attire, glanced at his notes and resumed his address on the theme of national reunification. He said Southerners would have joined Northerners to fight a common foe at any time after the Civil War, but the occasion for mutual combat did not occur until 1898. "Then," he said, "the sons of the veterans who fought in both armies fell promptly into line, ready to do or to die."

He provided an illustrative anecdote.

"A few weeks ago two fathers stood before two open graves in the national cemetery in Knoxville, into which were tenderly lowered two caskets, containing the remains of two Tennessee boys," he said. These young soldiers, sons of officers who had fought on opposite sides during the Civil War, had died leading their troops in battle at El Caney, Cuba. They had been buried hastily where they fell on July 1, 1898. They had been reburied ceremoniously, side-by-side, at Knoxville on April 2, 1899. This is the memorial service Rule described.

"Both were lieutenants in the regular army," he explained. "Both were Tennessee boys, who attended the same Tennessee university, and each had poured out his life's blood following the same flag on the same battlefield, and now their fathers—one who wore the blue, the other who wore the gray—mingled their tears over the biers of their precious boys who had sacrificed their young lives on the same altar of patriotism in defense of the same flag and the same country."

"Ah!" Rule continued. "Tell me not, in the presence of such a scene as that, that Americans are not Americans, even though they may have radically differed in the past...! The time is at hand," he concluded, "when we are indeed and in truth one people, with a common interest, a common ambition, a common purpose, a common destiny."[1]

Rule did not name the "Tennessee boys" or their fathers who had prompted this spirited tribute to reunion. Perhaps he thought his listeners knew their names. One of the fathers had become a prominent

Prologue

army general, and newspapers in Tennessee and elsewhere had reported extensively on the deaths and reburials of the sons.[2] Possibly, Rule did not name the lieutenants because he intended to elevate this story into a parable of reconciliation. What greater signal of the altered order of things than that fathers, once opponents in battle, would now mourn together at the graves of their warrior sons?

The dapper William Rule, Knoxville's mayor and a Union veteran, addressed the Memorial Day crowd at Nashville National Cemetery in 1899. He mentioned two East Tennessee Civil War veterans who had fought on opposite sides and met at the graves of their Spanish-American War sons (Knox County Two Centuries Photograph Project, McClung Historical Collection, Knox County Public Library).

Second Lieutenant John Jay Bernard, Fourth U.S. Infantry, and First Lieutenant Henry Leftwich McCorkle, Twenty-fifth U.S. Infantry, were born several years after the Civil War to fathers in their late thirties. Reuben Frank Bernard, a brevetted colonel of the First U.S. Cavalry during the Civil War, concluded his lengthy army career as an Indian fighter and brevetted brigadier general. Dr. William Alexander McCorkle. a major and surgeon of the Confederate Second Tennessee Cavalry from 1861 to 1865, served as a community physician following the war.

Both families had settled in Hawkins County, about seventy-five miles northeast of Knoxville. Reuben Bernard was born in the Beech Creek region in 1832. His son, John, known more familiarly as "Jack," was born at a frontier post in California in late 1872, but spent many of his early years in East Tennessee. William McCorkle was born in Virginia in 1830, but moved to Mooresburg, Hawkins County, and practiced medicine there before and after the Civil War. His son, Henry, was born on the doctor's Mooresburg farm in 1867.

Nashville, Tennessee (Memorial Day, 1899)

Both families had ties to the University of Tennessee at Knoxville. Henry McCorkle graduated from Tennessee in 1889 and Jack Bernard in 1893. Although they just missed being enrolled at the same time, they reportedly became friends when McCorkle remained in the area following graduation and most likely renewed ties as their regiments prepared to fight in Cuba. In addition, two of Jack Bernard's younger brothers had attended the university.

East Tennessee newspapers reported the story of the Bernards and the McCorkles in 1898. William Rule and others retold the story in 1899. The university kept the tale alive on campus by memorializing the two lieutenants on several occasions in the early 1900s. But then the story seems to have been buried with its principal characters. Today historians in East Tennessee know little about General Bernard, less about Dr. McCorkle, and nothing about their sons. The most genealogically and historically astute McCorkle and Bernard descendants knew nothing about the two young officers dying on the same battlefield and being interred together. The idea that the fathers' tearful meeting at their sons' graves had served as an example of post–Civil-War reconciliation came as news to all. Most family members were intrigued when introduced to the story. Some said it might make an interesting book.

※※※

The Bernard-McCorkle association appears to be unique. No other officers who fought on opposite sides during the Civil War lost their officer sons on the same Spanish-American War battlefield and met for the first time at their adjacent graves. But other reconciliation stories have a similar theme. While serving as superintendent of West Point Military Academy in the early 1880s, Major General Oliver O. Howard hosted two fathers from New York and Georgia who were enrolling their sons as cadets. Discussing their war experiences, the men found that they had been wounded while fighting on opposite sides on the same part of the battlefield at Malvern Hill, Virginia. The men reportedly parted "the closest of friends."[3]

Other officers who had opposed each other renewed friendships following the war's end in 1865. Reunification of West Point's Northern and Southern graduates was a primary reason for forming the Association of Graduates of the United States Military Academy in 1869. All alumni did not board the reunion train, but many did.

Union General and later President Ulysses S. Grant and

Prologue

Confederate Lieutenant General James Longstreet were best friends at West Point and served in the same regiment before the war. Afterwards, they renewed their friendship. The president made Longstreet U.S. Minister to Turkey in 1880. After Grant died five years later, Longstreet wrote a touching essay about their friendship for the *New York Times*. He concluded: "Why do men fight who were born to be brothers?"[4]

General Joseph E. Johnston and the man to whom he surrendered the Confederate Army of Tennessee, Union Major General William T. Sherman, corresponded and dined together frequently following the war. When Johnston served as an honorary pallbearer at Sherman's funeral on a cold and rainy day in February 1891, he refused to wear his hat while honoring the dead general. He subsequently caught a cold and died of pneumonia.[5]

There are numerous well-documented stories of warm reunions of a more general nature. In 1885, for example, the Society of the Army of the Potomac held a reception at Baltimore for Richmond's Robert E. Lee Camp No. 1, the first permanent Confederate veterans' organization. Former Union General H.W. Slocum told the assembled veterans that the genial gathering proved "there is nothing so makes men respect one another as standing up in the ranks and firing at one another."[6]

By the end of the century, many spokesmen for Union and Confederate veterans periodically announced that reunification, and even reconciliation, had been achieved. It is difficult to determine whether a majority of veterans actually believed this. Caroline Janney maintains that former enemies might remain silent on divisive issues when they greeted each other on formal occasions, but otherwise "veterans tended to maintain that their cause was the virtuous one."[7] We have no idea what Reuben Bernard and William McCorkle thought about reconciliation; they, along with most veterans, left no records mentioning the subject.

Still, descriptions of many commemorative events depict a misty-eyed reunion of former enemies. The Memorial Day 1899 gathering in Nashville prompted a second, similar reference. After Mayor Rule told the crowd that fathers Bernard and McCorkle had wept over their sons' graves, George Tillman, Nashville's U.S. marshal, paid his tribute to veterans. The *Nashville Tennessean* reported that Tillman's reference to "the union of the Confederate and Federal soldiers and their descendants in the Spanish war, fighting side by side under one glorious banner, the flag of the Union, brought tears, mingled with joy, to the eyes of the many assembled."[8]

Nashville, Tennessee (Memorial Day, 1899)

Confederate, left, and Union veterans shake hands with a young Spanish-American War veteran in this Memorial Day 1899 cover of *Puck*, the satirical political magazine. Many Americans viewed the Spanish-American War as accelerating the reconciliation of Civil War veterans by joining "Three Veterans Under One Flag" (Library of Congress).

Prologue

The dam that divided the nation cracked gradually during the years following the Civil War, then seemed to rupture in 1898. The united front that North and South presented during the Spanish-American War, as Nina Silber maintained in *The Romance of Reunion*, "provided a culminating point for much of the patriotic and reunion-oriented ideology that had been building in the preceding years."[9] As the troops assembled to go to war, many sources reported a widespread urge to reunite without reservation. The chorus was not unanimous but calls for the reunion of North and South under one battle flag were an essential aspect of patriotic propaganda.

Brigadier General John Wilder, a New York native who settled in East Tennessee after the war, praised the bravery of the Union soldiers buried in Knoxville National Cemetery on Memorial Day 1898—a year before Mayor Rule spoke in Nashville. He commended veterans of both sides for reuniting the nation by preparing for a new conflict. Flushed with patriotism, he concluded, "Now we see the hosts of blue and former gray and the sons of both massing and rallying in generous and hearty rivalry under the flag of our country, marching in solid phalanx under common leaders to the relief of the oppressed of the isles of the summer ocean...."[10]

Following the brief war, Walter Hines Page, the journalist and diplomat who edited the *Atlantic Monthly*, explained the process of reunification: "We have recovered our own national feeling. Four months ago, we were a great mass of people rather than a compact nation conscious of national strength and unity. By forgetting even for this brief time our local differences, we have welded ourselves into a conscious unity such as the Republic has not felt since its early days."[11]

On a goodwill tour of the South in December 1898, President and former Union General William McKinley told the Georgia legislature that sectional lines had been erased from the map of the United States. "Sectional feeling no longer holds back the love we bear each other," he said in Atlanta. "Fraternity is the national anthem, sung by a chorus of forty-five States and our Territories at home and beyond the seas. The Union is once more the common altar of our love and loyalty, our devotion and sacrifice. The old flag waves over us in peace, with new glories which your sons and ours have this year added to its sacred folds."[12]

During a Confederate reunion in Charleston, South Carolina, in May 1899, former Confederate Lieutenant General Stephen D. Lee, quoting from a report of the United Confederate Veterans' (UCV)

Nashville, Tennessee (Memorial Day, 1899)

historical committee, represented eloquently how shared bloodshed had forged new ties. "Once more the blood of North and South has been poured out together," he said, "no longer beneath contending standards in the bitterness of war between the States, but beneath one flag, to the glory of one country. These dead, at least, belong to us all. The last hateful memory that could divide our country is buried with them. About their grave kneels a new nation, loving all her children everywhere the same."[13]

Subsequent events have shown that "the last hateful memory" of the war can never be buried with the corpses it created, but the bitterest feelings of most combatants in the nation's bloodiest conflict had largely dissipated by the 1890s. Leaders of veteran organizations chose to emphasize the bravery of white soldiers on both sides rather than the causes or the horrors of a four-year bloodbath. Therefore, most sons of veterans did not inherit lingering animosity from their fathers. They went to war determined to prove their mettle on new fields of battle.

This was true even of young soldiers from East Tennessee, where their fathers had fought for the Union and the Confederacy in nearly equal numbers, and where the loyalties of families and neighbors were often divided during the war and remained divided afterwards. While some East Tennesseans continued to cultivate these divisions, they were of little consequence to most of the young men fighting side-by-side in Cuba.

They were of no consequence at all when bodies of the dead were returned to the United States for reburial. As historian John R. Neff explained in *Honoring the Civil War Dead*, "In addition to fighting together, Northern and Southern sons died together and were then buried together. The staunch separation of Union and Confederate soldiers had no counterpart in the interment of fatalities from the Cuban campaign."[14] That is why two fathers who had been Civil War opponents became emblematic of national reunion and reconciliation when they buried their soldier sons side-by-side.

1

Reuben Bernard (1832–1865)

The hills and hollows of the Appalachian Highlands where he grew up were as isolated as any part of the eastern United States. His family scratched out a living in impoverished soil. He experienced little, if any, formal education. But the boy had the backbone to escape the back country of East Tennessee and pursue a lifelong military career against American Indians of several tribes and Confederate armies in New Mexico and Virginia. He enlisted as a private and retired as a brigadier general in an army not inclined to advance teenage recruits to high command.

Reuben Frank Bernard was born October 14, 1832, in the Van Hill community along Beech Creek, Hawkins County, not far south of the Virginia border. Bernard's parents, John and Mary Morelock Bernard, probably had migrated from Pittsylvania, a Virginia county a couple hundred miles to the east. No one today knows precisely where the Bernards built their Tennessee home in a wooded area that remains sparsely populated. The fertile Bernards filled that house with twelve children who survived infancy. Reuben was the second born and the oldest son.[1]

The future general's neighbors (Hales, Lights, Simpsons, Morelocks, other Bernards—many of whom intermarried) called him "Rube." They meant no disparagement and the nickname did not accompany him when he left Van Hill. His early life demanded hard hoeing in rock-pocked fields that grew little more than tobacco and corn. He also toiled for a time as a blacksmith.

In the summer of 1854, when he was nearly twenty-two, Bernard abruptly abandoned the backwoods. Beaumont Bonaparte Buck, a son-in-law who became a major general himself, provided a lively description of why Bernard left home: "While a young man he had hay fever dreadfully, and being raised on a farm, it fell to his lot to plough

[sic] and hoe corn. Now, when the corn began to tassel the pollen made his hay fever so bad that it drove him almost crazy. So, one bright, hot morning when he was hoeing in the cornfield and the pollen showered down every time his hoe touched a stalk, he threw the hoe down and 'lit out' on foot to Knoxville without a word to anyone."[2]

Bernard's most direct route to Knoxville would have crossed several high ranges between Van Hill and Rogersville, the county seat to the west. As a crow might fly, the distance is about twelve miles, but climbing up and down the hills must have made it seem twice that far. Many years later he recalled his first view of Rogersville as he crossed the last mountain. "I came over the Academy Hill just as the sun was setting on a newly tinned roof," he said. "That was the most beautiful sight I have ever seen. To a boy shut in the mountains, it was a glorious sight."[3]

Walking Rogersville's unpaved Main Street for the first time, Bernard would have passed the state's second-oldest county courthouse, John Rogers' well-known tavern, and other substantial inns and homes built along one of the nation's major stage routes. He probably stayed in town overnight while waiting for a stagecoach running southwest to the principal town of East Tennessee.

Knoxville photographed in 1859, four years after Reuben Bernard arrived. East Tennessee's largest town doubled its population from 1850 to 1860 and increased business and industry in kind. This photograph was taken from the cupola of the Knox County Courthouse (McClung Historical Collection, Knox County Public Library).

1. Reuben Bernard (1832–1865)

Knoxville was booming in the 1850s. The East Tennessee and Georgia Railroad, which recently had extended its tracks to Knoxville, was largely responsible for more than doubling the town's population to 5,300 between 1850 and 1860. Knoxville enjoyed many of the amenities available to small American towns. Workmen had paved several streets with cobblestones from the Tennessee River. The town had built a modest brick market house on Market Square. Gas lights were on the way. But Knoxville also was known as a wild river town. It contained more taverns than churches. Gambling and prostitution were as popular as tippling. Riverboats transported a steady stream of travelers looking for fun before traveling on. One of the area's periodic cholera epidemics stole some of the steam from the city when it reached Knoxville a few weeks after Bernard.[4]

The young man began working for a new blacksmith. As he learned more about the trade, he became intimately familiar with horses, a crucial requirement for a man who would spend much of his life in the cavalry. In February 1855, several months after he arrived in Knoxville, Bernard encountered an army recruiter. The recruiter wondered if the young man wanted to become a horse soldier.

According to *One Hundred and Three Fights and Scrimmages: The Story of General Reuben F. Bernard*, Don Russell's 1936 biography, this recruiter also informed the impressionable young man that he could fight in one hundred battles.[5] This quoted number may have been a Bernard or Russell concoction. It is hard to believe that an army recruiter in the mid–1850s could predict that a soldier would engage in so many battles—most of which would be fought during an unexpectedly elongated Civil War six years in the future.

But, in fact, Bernard would participate in three more than one hundred fights, by his own meticulous count—from major battles of the Civil War to relatively minor skirmishes with Apaches, Modocs, and other tribes. Western historian Gregory Michno suggested that Bernard "compiled an amazing record, and in terms of number of engagements he may be the winner." For his part, Don Russell said other officers might have been able to claim as many or more battles, "but most of them lost count, while Bernard had the evidence."[6] Whether by skill or by luck, the cavalryman survived all of these battles with one minor wound.

The 1855 enlistment register indicates that the brown-eyed, black-haired Bernard stood five feet, nine inches, or about an inch taller than the average Civil War soldier. In his introduction to a reissue of

Sons of East Tennessee

Russell's biography, Edwin Sweeney said the future cavalryman weighed 180 muscular pounds. Even when Bernard was sixty years old, Sweeney said, "the wife of a fellow officer would describe him as 'so big and so strong. He looked like a great Norseman.'"[7] Allowing for some hyperbole, Bernard was, by all accounts, a physically powerful man.

Bernard spent eight months drilling in Missouri and Kansas. In September 1855, the army assigned him to Fort Craig on the west bank of the Rio Grande in New Mexico. He would serve with Company D, First Dragoons, the oldest cavalry regiment in the army. His commander appointed him company blacksmith the next month. But that was a part-time job. He was and always would be a fighting cavalryman.

The heart of Apache country provided a quick opportunity for the young soldier to notch the first of his battles to suppress western tribes. In the spring of 1856, elements of the First Dragoons, including Bernard's company, attacked Chiricahua Apaches near the Gila River. They killed several Apaches and recovered stolen livestock. A week later, the detachment fired on peaceful Apaches, killing a woman and wounding four women and children. Bernard counted the second action as another skirmish, although the enemy did not return fire and the attackers acknowledged they had made a mistake.

That summer, Company D moved to a post at Tucson, Arizona, and Bernard was promoted to corporal. Over the next three years, from Tucson and subsequent Arizona posts, Bernard pursued outlaws, protected mail carriers, and participated in a campaign against the Pinal and Aravaipa Apaches.

In March 1859, Company D returned to New Mexico—this time to Fort Fillmore—where Bernard was promoted to first sergeant, apparently because of his brawn. Richard S.C. Lord, the second lieutenant of Bernard's company, reportedly was having trouble disciplining his troops. A fellow officer recommended that Bernard "will straighten things out.... What you need is Bernard's fists. They're the biggest in the regiment."[8]

At the end of the year, Bernard reenlisted at Fort Buchanan, Arizona, and in the summer of 1860 he returned home on furlough. With radical forces, North and South, propelling the nation toward war, Bernard tended to wear civilian clothes in East Tennessee, where neighbors could have strong disagreements. Visiting friends in Knoxville, he also donned a stovepipe hat, similar to the headpiece favored by Abraham Lincoln, the Republican candidate in the upcoming election. On a

1. Reuben Bernard (1832–1865)

dare, Bernard wore the hat to a meeting of Democrats. This attracted the attention of a large, inebriated man, who smashed the hat down over Bernard's eyes and ears. Bernard had trouble removing the hat, at last tearing it to pieces. Then he tore into the Democrat. "The drunk kept his feet long enough to receive blow after blow, and to return some of them with interest," Russell reported, "but at last he went down for a clean knockout. It was the only Republican victory in Tennessee in 1860."[9]

Bernard returned to Arizona, where the Apache leader Cochise was about to begin a decade-long war with the U.S. Army. Russell cast the sergeant in a central role in what has become known as the "Bascom Affair," although there is no record that Bernard had anything to do with the matter.

Cochise tangled with Second Lieutenant George N. Bascom and the Seventh Infantry at Apache Pass in early February 1861. Bascom believed Cochise had taken a boy hostage, so he invited Cochise, his brother, and two nephews to his tent to talk. After Cochise arrived, Bascom said he would hold him prisoner until the boy was returned. Feeling betrayed, Cochise cut his way out of the tent and escaped. He took several prisoners and offered to exchange them for the members of his family that Bascom still held. Bascom refused. Cochise tortured and killed his prisoners and Bascom hanged the Apaches.[10]

Russell inserted Bernard into this affair, claiming that the sergeant had argued for the hostage exchange so vigorously that Bascom charged him with insubordination. Almost in passing, Russell mentioned that Bernard was acquitted at his court-martial. In fact, according to Edwin Sweeney, who wrote several books about Cochise and the Chiricahuas, Bernard was not involved and was never tried at a court-martial. Records indicate that the sergeant first arrived in the area with a relief force more than a week after Cochise's escape. If Bernard had been there during the hostage killings, Sweeney argued, he would have noted the incident among his list of skirmishes.[11]

Confederate forces in Charleston, South Carolina, fired the opening shots of the Civil War that April. As the federal government realized that the rebellion of Tennessee and ten other Southern states would require the service of a substantial counter force of regular and volunteer troops, it turned its primary attention in the West from Apaches and other tribes to Confederate insurgents. As part of this shift in focus, the army reorganized all mounted troops into one branch, to be called cavalry. Bernard's First Dragoons became the First Cavalry. Company D

Sons of East Tennessee

and Company G were assigned to the Department of New Mexico under Colonel Edward R.S. Canby. Canby made Bernard acting second lieutenant of Company D, now commanded by Richard Lord, who had been elevated to captain.

Canby's opponent, Confederate Brigadier General Henry H. Silbey, had assembled a sizable force of Texas troops and opposed Canby at Valverde, a crossing of the Rio Grande, in February 1862. Following a pitched battle involving infantry and cavalry, Canby withdrew to Fort Craig and Silbey toward Albuquerque and Santa Fe. Canby assigned part of his force, including Bernard's company, to prevent Silbey from capturing Fort Union to the northeast.

Company D, with fifty men and horses, set out separately for another Rio Grande crossing and reached the river ahead of Silbey. Thawing ice filled the high water. Captain Lord decided not to risk a crossing and to surrender when the larger enemy force arrived. Bernard disagreed and led all of the men into the frozen water. Russell recounted what happened: "Soon the tired horses were fighting for their lives, swimming in the swirling water, buffeted by crumbling ice cakes, many of them cut by the sharp edges of the floes leaving quickly-washed-away traces of blood in the water, plunging, but with heads kept up by expert riders who swam beside them. Bernard

This is a photograph of a portrait of Reuben Bernard that was painted from an original photograph taken when Bernard was a captain in the First U. S. Cavalry at Walla Walla, Washington, about 1878. Bernard spent most of his military career fighting Indian tribes in the West before and after serving in the Civil War (courtesy Austin Dopman, Reuben Bernard's great-grandson).

1. Reuben Bernard (1832–1865)

reached the other shore and turned to help those who were in trouble.... Not a man was lost."[12]

Although Lord considered arresting Bernard for insubordination, the soldiers had more pressing business. They surprised and captured a small Confederate force at Tejaras Pass and moved on to Fort Union.

Shortly afterwards, Colonel John P. Slough brought his Colorado Volunteers into Fort Union and led a combined force, including Bernard's company, in a strike against the enemy near Santa Fe. This army of thirteen hundred men fought and defeated Silbey's troops twice in late March 1862. The battle of Apache Canyon was fought March 28 and the battle of Glorietta, or Pigeon's Ranch, March 30.

Somehow Reuben Bernard found time between his twelfth and thirteenth battles to write a letter to future President Andrew Johnson, a fellow East Tennessean and Southern Unionist who recently had been appointed military governor of Federally occupied Tennessee. Bernard asked Johnson to transfer him to a Tennessee regiment. "New Mexico is a place of slow operations and is Filled with Traitors and Cowards," Bernard wrote. "I will move in one Hower [sic] agains [sic] the Enemy under a Drunken commander. Such is the Management of this Department.... We air [sic] placed in a very bad position at presant [sic] tho it may all come right yet if we git [sic] our Troops all together which will be a scratch if we do it[.] Do something for me if you can[.]"[13]

Bernard returned to Fort Union. Lord had been assigned to another company, and Bernard took command of Company D. He also was appointed acting assistant quartermaster and assistant commissary of subsistence—duties that required considerable attention to detail. His troops remained in northeastern New Mexico for more than a year, seeing little action. More than likely, Bernard was itching for a fight.

In the summer of 1863, Bernard was commissioned first lieutenant and was dispatched at last to the Eastern Theater of the Civil War. The soldiers of Companies D and G of the First Cavalry arrived days after the Battle of Gettysburg in early July and moved to nearby Carlisle, Pennsylvania, where they drilled until October. Then they joined the full regiment at Camp Buford, Maryland, as part of the Second Brigade, First Division, of the Army of the Potomac's Cavalry Corps. Reassigned to Company I, Bernard began his most intensely active period as a soldier.

From late 1863 through the surrender of the Army of Northern Virginia to the Army of the Potomac in April 1865, Bernard participated in sixty-five actions—from massive, multi-day battles to hit-and-run

Sons of East Tennessee

skirmishes. Along with many other officers in the enlarged Union army, he was rapidly brevetted up the ranks—from lieutenant to colonel—in recognition of his leadership ability as well as to replace casualties.

Russell embellished an anecdote "based upon an indication in Bernard's record," that may illustrate how Bernard reached the top ranks by being aggressive off the battlefield as well as on. Companies D and G had reported to Camp Buford without horses. As acting assistant quartermaster, Bernard took responsibility for obtaining five hundred mounts for these companies and other horseless soldiers. He initially could not obtain the horses he needed from army officials. Russell claimed that Bernard talked directly to Secretary of War Edwin M. Stanton, who somehow found time in his frenetic schedule of running a war on several fronts to find the horses.[14]

The lieutenant fought his first Civil War skirmish near Culpeper, Virginia, on November 5. During the last seventeen months of the war, Bernard was involved in most of the major battles in Virginia, including the Wilderness; Spotsylvania Court House; Cold Harbor; Winchester,

Kurz & Allison lithograph of fighting near Todd's Tavern during the Battle of the Wilderness, in Virginia, May 6, 1864. Cavalry officer Reuben Bernard was lightly wounded during the battle (Library of Congress).

1. Reuben Bernard (1832–1865)

Smithfield, and other encounters in the Shenandoah Valley; Five Forks; and Sailor's Creek.

More specifically, Bernard commanded Company I during a major action against General J.E.B. Stuart's Confederate cavalry in the Wilderness in early May 1864. At Todd's Tavern on May 6, the First Cavalry suffered forty-five casualties, including one-third of its eighteen officers. Bernard was one of the lightly wounded. For his service at Todd's Tavern, Bernard received his first brevet promotion, to captain, for "gallant and meritorious service." Despite his wound, he was back in his saddle the next day during a skirmish preliminary to the Battle of Spotsylvania Court House. Several days later, he engaged in fighting at Yellow Tavern, where Stuart was mortally wounded. During the latter days of May, the entire Cavalry Corps, commanded by General Philip Sheridan, rode around Richmond. The soldiers participated in almost daily skirmishes leading to the Battle of Cold Harbor. There they seized the field, dismounted, and used their repeating carbines to check the enemy until Union infantry regiments arrived.[15]

In late summer, the First Cavalry moved with Sheridan to the Shenandoah and fought almost continuously until the army left the Valley. At New Town on August 11, the regiment helped drive the enemy for several miles until encountering a large force of Confederate infantry. The Federal cavalry abandoned horses and charged on foot across an open, plowed field to drive the Confederates from a wooded area. Heavy flank fire forced the dismounted soldiers to take cover behind rail barricades. They defended the line against repeated Confederate attacks.[16]

At Smithfield, on August 28, 1864, Bernard was brevetted to major for his service during a battle in which the First Cavalry charged with sabers to beat back an attack by a full brigade of Confederates using firearms. At Winchester on September 19, Union troops won their first large victory in the Shenandoah. The First and Second Cavalry captured two hundred prisoners—but they paid a high price: the First Cavalry alone counted thirty-seven casualties.[17]

The First Cavalry suffered greater losses than any other Union cavalry regiment during the war. It had opened the spring campaign of 1864 with seven hundred men. That number had been reduced to two hundred by the winter of 1864–65. So few officers were available that Bernard temporarily commanded the regiment after it rejoined the Army of the Potomac.[18] He received a double brevet—to lieutenant colonel and colonel—on March 13, 1865, less than a month before the war's end.

Sons of East Tennessee

The First Cavalry was among the regiments that blocked Confederate General John Gordon's desperate effort to cut through the Union line at Appomattox Court House on April 8.[19] Colonel Bernard assembled with thousands of Union soldiers the next day to accept the surrender of the Army of Northern Virginia. Scores of colonels stood on that field, but few had progressed so rapidly through the ranks. Bernard was thirty-two years old.

2

Wartime East Tennessee (1861–1865)

Following the surrender of Confederate armies, Reuben Bernard's regiment marched in the Army of the Potomac's Grand Review in Washington before joining the occupation forces in New Orleans. After months of relentless warfare in Virginia, Bernard must have welcomed the summer assignment in oppressively humid but relatively placid Louisiana. Union forces had captured New Orleans in the spring of 1862; after three years, the area reluctantly had learned to live under Federal control.

In September, Bernard took a two-month leave and returned to Hawkins County. His homecoming would have been awkward.

Four Bernard brothers went to war. Only Reuben fought with the Union army. The military service and death records of his three Confederate brothers are incomplete. It is possible, but seemingly impossible to verify, that at least two died during the war.[1]

Jonathan Bernard, two years younger than Reuben, enlisted at Rogersville in March 1862. Most of the recruits in Company G, Thirty-first (later Thirty-ninth) Tennessee Infantry, came from Hawkins County and they elected Jonathan first lieutenant. Jonathan was a sickly soldier: his service record indicates that he returned home several times to recuperate from illness. After spending well over a month in defensive trenches surrounding Vicksburg, Mississippi, he was captured and paroled with the rest of the Confederate forces there in July 1863. He resigned the next February. A regimental surgeon had declared him disabled because of chronic hepatitis, chronic diarrhea, and other ailments. Genealogical records at Ancestry.com suggest that Jonathan survived the war and that he and his wife, Eleanor Light Bernard, had seven children, the last born the year before Jonathan died in 1870.

Sons of East Tennessee

Samuel Bernard enlisted as a private in the Ninth Tennessee Cavalry. His spare Confederate service record lists him as a 23-year-old prisoner of war who signed a deserter's oath of amnesty in Union-occupied Memphis in June 1864.[2] Then he disappears from all records.

John Bernard, who was about seventeen when the war began, also enlisted as a private in the Ninth Tennessee Cavalry. He appears on the muster roll for Company C in November and December of 1862. There his service record and any other information about him end.

Whatever became of these brothers, Reuben Bernard's homecoming as a career officer in the U.S. cavalry probably stirred emotions among relatives and neighbors who had fought for or sympathized with the Confederate cause.

In most sections of the Confederacy, it was rare for members of one family to fight on opposing sides. But in Hawkins County, Knoxville, and other areas of East Tennessee, family splits were not unusual. For example, two brothers who lived on a farm just east of Rogersville were killed while fighting on opposite sides. William Merrimon first served in Company B of the Confederate Sixtieth Tennessee Mounted Infantry. He was captured in battle and released in early 1864. For unknown reasons, he decided to return to service as a Union soldier and died, at age twenty-five, just a month before the war ended. His younger brother, James Peyton Merrimon, had served with the Confederate army and was killed, at age twenty-one, at the Battle of Drewry's Bluff, Virginia, in the spring of 1864.[3]

Similar situations occurred in the greater Knoxville area. Knoxville physician Digby Gordon Seymour recounted a poignant divided-family story in his history of the Knoxville battle of Fort Sanders. A chaplain with a Pennsylvania regiment was foraging for canteen water prior to the initial assault on Knoxville in September 1863. He passed two brothers with the Third East Tennessee Artillery. One brother said he would like to see his mother. The chaplain said all soldiers felt this way but that he would have "to go a thousand miles to see my mother."

"I would not have to go two miles," said the brother.

"Well, that alters the case," the chaplain replied. "If I were that near to my mother I would certainly see her."

"Maybe not," the soldier responded, "for our family is equally divided. My mother, my brother here, and myself are for the Union, and my father and two brothers are on the other side, and we may meet in battle."[4]

2. Wartime East Tennessee (1861–1865)

If the war divided family members, the press rushed to report and the public eagerly read the details. The possibility that relatives would physically encounter each other on a battlefield was remote but, when it occurred, was viewed as one of the chief tragedies of civil conflict. Border states and areas such as East Tennessee with divided loyalties naturally experienced more incidents involving "brother against brother." For example, at least five soldiers in Company F, Twenty-fourth Tennessee Union Regiment, chiefly from DeKalb County, said they had brothers in the Confederate army. One of these pairs of brothers reportedly met twice in combat—an unusually rare coincidence.[5]

Robert McKenzie Jr. analyzed hundreds of families who resided in Knoxville during the war. In *Lincolnites and Rebels: A Divided Town in the American Civil War*, he documented only one nuclear family in which brothers fought on opposite sides. James C. Luttrell, Knoxville's mayor throughout the war, had three sons. One died fighting for the Confederacy. The second also served in a Confederate unit, but the third joined a Federal cavalry regiment. McKenzie found inter-generational conflict more common: fathers in six families took up arms against their sons.[6]

McKenzie cited numerous examples of non-combatant Knoxvillians whose relatives or close friends fought on the opposite side. The Rev. Thomas Humes, an Episcopal minister who refused to pray for Confederate President Jefferson Davis and eventually lost his pulpit, was the uncle of Confederate Brigadier General and Memphis lawyer William Young Conn Humes. William Cogswell Hazen, son of Gideon Morgan Hazen, a Union-supporting paper manufacturer and a former Knoxville mayor, rode with Confederate General John Hunt Morgan. Union supporter Frederick S. Heiskell, a prominent Knoxville publisher and politician, was dismayed when a son, stepson, and son-in-law joined the Confederate army. Another son, Joseph P. Heiskell, of Rogersville, served in the Confederate Congress until he was captured at Nashville and imprisoned until the end of the war.[7]

McKenzie determined that neighbors were more likely to be divided than families. With the exception of one Knoxville neighborhood, clearly delineated Unionist or Confederate sections of the city did not exist. People of opposing views often lived next to each other. These neighbors, McKenzie said, waged "a civil war within the Civil War."[8]

The dividing line seems to have been more clearly determined in Hawkins County. North of the Holston River, which runs south of

Rogersville after flowing in horseshoe loops from the northeast, was largely Confederate territory. South of the river was predominantly Union ground, except for one section termed "disputed land." This area lay just west of Van Hill, Reuben Bernard's birthplace. Considerable conflict occurred in that middle ground.[9]

These local clashes were more common in East Tennessee than elsewhere in the Confederacy—and most common in Knoxville, the most divided of all Southern cities—because of the nature of the region's population. East Tennessee was the largest section of a seceded state in which a majority of residents continued to support the Union. In fact, Knoxville, Knox County, and surrounding counties maintained a seat in the U.S. Congress for the duration of the war. The most comparable Unionist area in a Southern state was West Virginia, which seceded from Virginia in order to rejoin the Union.[10]

Tennessee was the last state to join the Confederacy, on June 8, 1861, in large part because East Tennessee was far more divided over the question of secession than western and central Tennessee. In February 1861, Tennesseans voted on whether to call a convention to consider secession. West Tennessee voted by nearly three to one for a convention; Middle Tennessee was almost evenly divided; and East Tennessee voted heavily against a convention. At the June 8 election, only thirty-one percent of East Tennesseans voted to secede, while eighty-six percent of all other Tennesseans voted to lead the state out of the union. Dissatisfied East Tennessee Unionists meeting in Greeneville in mid–June resolved to seek legislative consent for the eastern counties to establish a separate state. The Tennessee Legislature denied the request.[11]

Scott County, a remote, mountainous area on the Kentucky border, led the way in voting against secession with 95 percent opposition. Rather than ask the state legislature for permission to create a separate state, Scott simply cut ties with Tennessee and formed the "Free and Independent State of Scott." The county never joined the Confederacy and did not formally dissolve its independent status until it applied for readmission to the state of Tennessee in 1986.[12]

East Tennesseans voted differently on secession for numerous reasons. Among the most significant were topography (removed from the rest of the state by the Appalachian Range, East Tennesseans developed different economic and cultural characteristics); political party (they were far more likely to be Republicans than Democrats); and slavery (with mostly small mountain farms, not large plantations, they did not

2. Wartime East Tennessee (1861–1865)

own nearly so many slaves as other Tennesseans). A federal government map created in September 1861 illustrates the distribution of the slave population in all counties of the Southern states. Only 16.6 percent of the residents of Knox County were enslaved, compared with nearly double that percentage (32.3 percent) in Davidson County, which includes Nashville. Scott County's percentage was 1.7, lowest in the state.[13]

In an 1899 memoir designed to vindicate Tennessee Unionists, Knoxville attorney, judge, and historian Oliver P. Temple explained how the process of deciding which side to join played out in East Tennessee: "In December, 1860, the question was whether there was a sufficient cause for dissolving the Union. In February following, the question was, shall Tennessee secede? In May, it was, what shall I, as an individual, do? Shall I go with my state into secession, or shall I remain true to the old government? So, with each stage of the great revolution, new questions arose for the solution of each individual."[14]

Area residents warmly debated these issues during the early months of 1861. Flags representing the United States of America and the fledgling Confederate States of America flew near each other on Knoxville's Gay Street. Partisans sometimes held simultaneous rallies at the flagpoles, as they did on the night of April 27, 1861, when then–U.S. Senator and anti-secessionist Andrew Johnson addressed Unionists while Confederate troops marched from their flagpole toward the Union rally. Knoxville attorney and secessionist William McAdoo observed before one of these Union rallies, "We are but a step removed from civil war amongst ourselves in East Tennessee."[15]

During another Unionist rally the next month—with both flags still flying on Gay Street—Charles Douglass, a Union man who enjoyed his liquor, argued vehemently with secessionist Major Washington Morgan. Morgan drew his pistol and fired at Douglass, wounding him slightly and killing a passerby. A few days later someone again shot Douglass, this time mortally. Both Unionists and secessionists attended his funeral. Peace was barely maintained.[16]

And yet, as McKenzie has pointed out, East Tennesseans largely remained united on every point except secession. Most of those who chose to support the Union, as well as those who chose to dissolve it, remained committed to maintaining slavery and white supremacy; they believed that Southern rights had been violated before the war; they rejected extremism on either side; they opposed Lincoln's presidency;

Sons of East Tennessee

Samuel Bell Palmer, a young Knoxville resident who would join the Confederate army, made this pencil sketch of simultaneous rallies on Knoxville's Gay Street on April 27, 1861. Supporters of secession gather around their flagpole, upper right, while Unionists assemble beneath an American flag. Orators fulminated and tempers flared before Tennessee seceded in June (courtesy Richard P. W. Williams).

and they hoped their disagreement over one fundamental issue would not lead to war.[17]

But Tennessee did secede in June and the fratricidal war soon overwhelmed all other concerns. Each side quickly recognized the vital importance of East Tennessee to its overall strategy. If the Union controlled the region, it could sever the rail connection between Virginia and the Mississippi Valley. Acknowledging this possibility, some Southern strategists boosted the region as the "Keystone of the Confederate Arch." On the other hand, President Davis often chose to ignore the area because of its substantial and belligerent pro–Union population. For that reason, one historian has termed East Tennessee "the Confederacy's madman in the attic"—an embarrassment to the Confederate cause that the government preferred not to acknowledge.[18]

Although a minority of East Tennessee's residents supported the

2. Wartime East Tennessee (1861–1865)

Confederacy, approximately twenty-five thousand of the region's men joined Confederate regiments. (An incensed Confederate in Greeneville claimed that East Tennessee alone, of all sections of the Confederacy, had failed to furnish its quota of troops.) In opposition, an estimated twenty thousand to thirty thousand East Tennesseans fled to Kentucky or other Northern states and enlisted to fight for the Union. That was more men than the other twelve Confederate states contributed together to the Union army. And thousands of Union sympathizers remained in East Tennessee to harass Confederate soldiers and residents.[19]

Tennessee Governor Isham G. Harris, an ardent secessionist, ordered Confederate troops to suppress East Tennessee's Unionists in July 1861. Thousands of soldiers traveled to the region from western Tennessee and other Southern states. Many of them did not relish policing an area they believed was populated largely by Union sympathizers and backward mountaineers. "East Tennessee is an enemy's country," observed Confederate Major General Edmund Kirby Smith, the first of a series of commanders of the District of East Tennessee. After examining the country and people, Alabama soldier Basil Manly told his parents in the summer of 1862 that he was "thoroughly disgusted [with] East Tennesseans, a more spiritless and degraded a race I hope it will never be my lot to see."[20]

Confederate troops displeased with their assignment regularly oppressed citizens loyal to the Union. Simeon Dawson, a Knoxville carpenter, said Confederates abused him for being "a damn Lincolnite." Unionist John Griffin said Confederate soldiers "molested" him on a Knoxville street. VIPs were hardly immune. *Knoxville Whig* editor and Methodist minister William G. "Parson" Brownlow, a fiery Unionist, claimed Confederate harassment drove him to bankruptcy. He was arrested and eventually banished to Union territory near Nashville in February 1862.[21]

The Confederate crackdown in East Tennessee escalated after Union men, anticipating a Federal invasion from Kentucky that never occurred, burned several railroad bridges between Bristol and Chattanooga in November 1861. Confederate authorities hanged five men from Knoxville and Greeneville for burning the Lick Creek Bridge in western Greene County. Then they arrested, imprisoned, and burned the homes of hundreds of Union sympathizers throughout East Tennessee.[22]

Local groups of home guards and guerrillas enforced the first Confederate military draft in April 1862 with as much enthusiasm as they

Sons of East Tennessee

Harper's Weekly cover for March 29, 1862, depicts Colonel David Fry, left foreground, and others pledging allegiance to the Union. They were preparing to burn a bridge in East Tennessee in November 1861. The Union presence remained strong throughout the region during the war (Library of Congress).

2. Wartime East Tennessee (1861–1865)

harassed Unionists. Guerrillas threatened and sometimes killed civilians if they tried to evade military service. "Voices of the Land," a permanent exhibit at the Museum of East Tennessee History in Knoxville, includes a bloody shirt pierced by bullet holes. Alfred Greene was wearing that shirt when he was shot in the chest and killed by Confederate guerrillas on July 26, 1863. Greene had tried to evade the draft by hiding in the mountains near his home in Hancock County, immediately west of his native Hawkins County. Three Confederates from a neighboring family, which had been feuding with the Greenes for years, discovered and shot him during one of the bloodiest inter-family squabbles in Appalachia.[23]

Confederate home-guard units in the far eastern counties killed so many Union men on the Carter-Sullivan County border that local residents referred to it as the "boneyard." The home guard shot John Smith, Henry Archer, and John Blevins there when they refused to volunteer for the Confederate army. They also had accused Blevins of "bushwhacking" on behalf of Unionists. When he protested his innocence, his accusers told him that "if you have told us the truth, you need not be afraid to die." They shot him three times in the chest and left him dead where he fell.[24]

Thousands of Unionist East Tennesseans fled to Kentucky to evade the Confederate draft and join Union regiments. They traveled through rough terrain, generally at night, following "pilots" who guided them away from Confederate bushwhackers waiting in ambush. Union recruiters channeled potential recruits to these guides. Recruiters took risks to lure more men into blue uniforms, and some were killed when Confederates discovered their activities. For example, Captain Spencer Deaton, on a recruiting mission to East Tennessee, was charged with being a spy and hanged in Richmond.[25]

William Rule, the former Union officer who eulogized Henry McCorkle and John Jay Bernard at Nashville National Cemetery in 1899, recognized the danger. A recruiter for the Sixth Tennessee Infantry, Rule narrowly escaped from Confederate forces in the autumn of 1862. He traveled on foot to his father's home near Knoxville. Before he could sign up anyone, a squad of Confederate cavalry located the house and asked Rule's sister where he was. "While they were talking with her, I was thinking rapidly," Rule wrote later. "Being well armed, I had determined that I would not be arrested to be taken to a Southern prison—perhaps to the gallows...." Rule hid in the house while his sister did some fast talking and sent the squad on its way.[26]

Sons of East Tennessee

Meanwhile, Union sympathizers actively opposed the Confederate occupation of East Tennessee. In early 1862, the Unionists who overwhelmingly predominated in Scott and Morgan counties killed several secessionists, threatened to kill more, plundered and burned Confederate homes, and took control of county offices. In response, General Edmund Kirby Smith dispatched nearly a thousand troops to restore order. Unionist guerrillas fired on Smith's soldiers along their route and both sides suffered casualties. The Confederates dispersed the guerrillas but were called away to more pressing duties and Unionists took control of those counties once more.[27]

After Confederate troops ransacked Unionist farms in Fentress County in January 1862, David Beatty organized his fellow farmers into a Unionist guard to patrol Fentress and neighboring Overton County. Beatty's home guard fought several battles with Confederates in the area. The fighting accelerated as Federals advancing into Tennessee late that year supplied Beatty's forces with munitions.[28]

On a larger scale, the Confederate catastrophe at Vicksburg in early July 1863 proved to be the end of the war for many wearing gray uniforms. Half of the soldiers in Tennessee's Thirty-ninth Regiment, captured and paroled at Vicksburg, never returned to the army: they included Jonathan Bernard. Deserters increased rapidly after that summer: Samuel Bernard was among them.[29]

Union cavalry commanded by Colonel (soon-to-be Brigadier General) William P. Sanders raided the outskirts of Knoxville in June 1863. With limited forces, the Confederates decided they could not defend both Knoxville and Chattanooga. In early September, Brigadier General Simon Bolivar Buckner, then commanding the Department of East Tennessee, abandoned Knoxville and marched south to reinforce the Army of Tennessee at Chattanooga. Major General Ambrose E. Burnside and the Army of the Ohio soon entered Knoxville without resistance. The North greeted the news that East Tennessee had been "liberated" with jubilation. "The day of deliverance has dawned at last," commented the *New York Times*, "and the chains are riven from the limbs of the noblest people that ever breathed God's air. Free at last! Free as their own mountain air."[30]

A number of former Confederate sympathizers eagerly joined the liberators. Joseph Mabry, Jr., a wealthy Knoxville businessman who had spent hundreds of thousands of dollars supplying Confederate units, reoriented his resources and offered to supply Burnside's army

2. Wartime East Tennessee (1861–1865)

Union Major General Ambrose E. Burnside and the Army of the Ohio "liberated" Knoxville on September 3, 1863. An etching on the cover of the October 24, 1863, *Harper's Weekly* depicted local Unionists enthusiastically greeting Burnside's fifteen thousand troops (McClung Historical Collection Knox County Public Library).

with whatever it needed. Burnside rejected the offer, but Mabry and other Knoxvillians suddenly disenchanted with the Confederate cause remained Unionists.[31]

Following the Confederate victory on the Chickamauga battlefield near Chattanooga in late September, the Confederate army began making plans to prevent Burnside's troops from moving south to reinforce the defeated but still formidable Army of Tennessee. In early November, Confederate General James Longstreet began moving north from Chattanooga to Knoxville. In reaction, Burnside ordered his troops to fortify the city. Engineers designed multiple defensive forts, redoubts and batteries to withstand an extended siege. One of the most substantial earthen forts was located on a hill just north of the campus of the University of Tennessee, which had closed during the war. The fort was named for General Sanders, who had been killed in a preliminary action with Longstreet's troops in mid–November. Union officers viewed the fort, at the northern end of the line of defense, as a probable point of attack.

As Longstreet laid siege to the city, the fort's 440 defenders, ex-slaves, and other laborers strengthened Sanders with two bastions, substantially raising the height of walls at the northwest and southwest corners. Then they dug a deep, wide ditch, with vertical sides, beneath both bastions. About eighteen feet separated the bottom of the ditch from the top of the parapets constructed on the bastions. In the ground in front of the fort, the laborers sank sharpened oak limbs as an abatis pointed at the enemy. They strung telegraph wire and piled up cut brush, stumps, rocks, and other obstacles throughout the approaches to the fort. They also carefully positioned artillery pieces and stored excess firearms at strategic places inside the fort so they could keep firing without stopping to reload. They particularly buttressed the fort's vulnerable northwest bastion, which was defended by the "Highlanders," the battle-hardened troops of the 79th New York Regiment.[32]

The Confederates finally struck on November 29. Artillery exchanged fire before dawn. Then Longstreet sent three thousand troops, with fixed bayonets but without scaling ladders, to attack the northwest bastion. They marched through a dense fog that filled the lowlands between the opposing armies. As they strained to see and fire on the advancing Confederates, the Highlanders shouted "Give it to them boys! Remember James Island! Remember James Island!"—a reference to the regiment's failed attack on a Confederate fort. After making

2. Wartime East Tennessee (1861–1865)

"Battle of Fort Sanders," an 1891 oil painting by N. Jordan, depicts the disastrous attack on Fort Sanders on November 29, 1863. Confederate forces are making their way through an obstacle course of abatis, telegraph wire and other impediments in front of the Union fort (from the permanent collection of the East Tennessee Historical Society).

their way through the wires, abatis, and continuous shooting and shouting by the Highlanders, Longstreet's troops reached the ditch, which became a trap. Hundreds of soldiers died or were maimed there as the Highlanders fired volleys and tossed artillery shells with short fuses into the mass of Confederates. Despite the impediments, Confederate soldiers twice clawed to the top of the parapet. On the second attempt, they planted three flags, only to see them fall quickly as Union reinforcements arrived.

After forty minutes of combat, half of it in the ditch and atop the bastion, Confederate survivors returned, demoralized, to their lines. They had lost 813 men: 129 killed outright, 458 wounded, and 226 missing. Several of the dead were high-ranking officers, targeted by the fort's defenders. The missing included scores of men captured in the ditch as the battle ended. Federal losses were relatively light: twenty men killed and injured inside the fort, several of them Highlanders, and another thirty by artillery outside.[33]

On December 4, with twenty-five thousand Union troops moving toward Knoxville following a major Union victory at Chattanooga on November 25, Longstreet abandoned the city and retreated northeast toward Rogersville. The two armies fought subsequent battles in Grainger and Hawkins counties, notably at Bean's Station on the Holston River. By the time Union forces and a severely cold winter forced the Confederate army to leave East Tennessee in early 1864, significant portions of the region had been depleted by fighting and foraging soldiers from both armies. A Union commissary sergeant reported: "We have drained the country around of everything that can be eaten, and the citizens are as destitute as we are.... Between us and the rebels the country is ruined."[34]

With the Union army in permanent control of Knoxville, William Brownlow, the exiled newspaper editor, returned to the city. He quickly facilitated retribution against Southern sympathizers. In February 1864, he published the names of seventy-two Blount County men who had voted for secession in June 1861, in order that "our soldiers and officers may appreciate the patriotism of these men when found." Two months later, when a Unionist was killed by men Brownlow suspected of being Confederate guerrillas, he published their names as well. "We tell the world that such men can't live in East Tennessee," Brownlow wrote. "They must die if they ever return to this country. Let Union men kill them like dogs if they ever meet with them."[35]

Confederates who did return and refused to pledge their allegiance to the United States were arrested and imprisoned, or forcibly banished to another Southern state. Often, Unionists confiscated their property. Other Confederate sympathizers voluntarily fled to Georgia, North Carolina, or Virginia. At the same time, exiled Unionists were returning from Kentucky and other Northern and border states, creating a volatile shift in the population.[36]

Vigilante violence escalated as the uniformed war wound down. Union bushwhackers took advantage of a new freedom to beat or kill Confederate sympathizers. One gang of sixty-five men raided Mill Bend in Hawkins' disputed land in the winter of 1865. They plundered homes, killed two Confederate sympathizers, and stole all of the clothing of another man, including his sleeping attire. Other men barely escaped the melee. Within six days, Confederate soldiers tracked several members of the gang to Greene County and killed them in a cave.[37]

William O. Sizemore and his Unionist guerrillas were notorious for raiding Confederate homes in Rogersville and vicinity. Eliza Fain, whose husband and five sons fought for the Confederacy, lived on a 200-acre

2. Wartime East Tennessee (1861–1865)

farm two miles east of Rogersville. She kept a diary throughout the war. On April 5, 1865, she recorded her relatively good fortune that Sizemore's raiders only took the contents of her house without destroying it. Later that day, the guerrillas rode into Rogersville and terrorized the population before killing five men four miles southwest of town.[38]

Unionist newspapers blared news of the faltering Confederacy and the evacuation of Richmond. "Babylon the Great, the Mighty, has Fallen," exclaimed the *Knoxville Whig*. Union sympathizers celebrated with fireworks and dancing. A brass band and a detachment of the Fortieth U.S. Colored Infantry paraded through Knoxville, followed by the town's black residents. When the news reached town that Lee had surrendered at Appomattox, Knoxville residents celebrated again. Jubilation continued through the spring.[39]

While the victors danced and the band played, William McCorkle and other defeated Confederate veterans began making their way home. More violence awaited them.

3

William McCorkle
(1830–1865)

William McCorkle's service in the Confederate army followed a resolute family military tradition. His great-grandfather, John McCorkle, enlisted as an ensign in Captain James Gilmore's Rockbridge County (Virginia) "Rifles" in the summer of 1778. Promoted to lieutenant, he was wounded in the foot three years later at the Battle of Cowpens, South Carolina; he eventually died of lockjaw associated with his wound. William's grandfather, Alexander McCorkle, served as a captain in the War of 1812. William's father, Thomas J. McCorkle, also carried the title "captain," although his military service is uncertain.[1]

The Scots-Irish Presbyterian MacCorkles had emigrated to America in the early 1700s. They settled in Lancaster County, Pennsylvania, then followed the Great Wagon Road to Virginia. The family thrived in Rockbridge: there seem to have been more MacCorkles/McCorkles in the county than members of any other family, at least into the nineteenth century.[2]

Born May 24, 1830, William Alexander McCorkle was the first of nine children of Thomas and Susan Alexander McCorkle. His childhood was remarkably different from Reuben Bernard's. He grew up at Westwood, one of Rockbridge County's substantial antebellum homes. The Federal–style brick residence with impressive white columns stands just northwest of Lexington, one of the premier communities in the Shenandoah Valley. McCorkle's grandfather and father owned substantial plantations. Most members of the McCorkle family were well educated and had succeeded in a number of professions. The family expected William McCorkle to extend this record.

He attended schools near his home and went on to Washington College, later Washington & Lee University, in Lexington. Just as

3. William McCorkle (1830–1865)

Rockbridge was the home county of many McCorkles, Washington was the McCorkles' preferred college. All four of William McCorkle's brothers who lived to maturity also graduated from Washington. As of the 1920s, MacCorkles and McCorkles composed the largest connected family of Washington alumni.[3]

Washington & Lee's records are incomplete, but McCorkle first enrolled in 1849 and apparently graduated in 1852. He was a member of the Washington Literary Society, a student literary and debating club. He took part in a debate sparked by one of the primary political questions of the 1850s: "Has Congress the right to legislate on the subject of slavery in the territories?" He borrowed frequently from the society's library, including books of history, literature, and the classics, as well as treatises on social issues of the time. McCorkle enjoyed poetry and was "a constant student of Shakespeare," according to a tribute written many years later.[4]

McCorkle earned his medical degree from the University of Virginia Medical School in 1853. The university's M.D. Program, second oldest in the South, was more thorough than most. While many schools, South and North, provided only a four- or five-month series of lectures leading to a medical degree, Virginia's Medical School required a nine-month course. McCorkle also attended lectures at the University of Pennsylvania Medical School in 1855. This was at a time when most doctors did not attend medical school but were tutored by older doctors. McCorkle was among a small minority of physicians with advanced training when American medical standards remained mediocre.[5]

In 1857, McCorkle married Susan Leftwich, of Bedford County, Virginia. The couple and Susan's parents soon moved to Mooresburg, Tennessee. Why they moved there is unknown, but a logical reason would be McCorkle's profession. He was one of the first doctors in the small community, nestled in the valley of Clinch Mountain, fourteen miles west of Rogersville and just north of the Holston River. His residence there explains his enlistment in a Confederate regiment from Tennessee, whereas his brothers and other relatives served in units organized in Virginia.

McCorkle joined the Army of Tennessee in the summer of 1861 at nearby Cumberland Ford, Kentucky. He began as a private/surgeon in Company E, First (later Second) Tennessee Cavalry. The regiment was commonly called "Ashby's" for its commander, Colonel Henry Ashby, a Chattanooga businessman who was visiting Knoxville when the war began. Company E's recruits came from Hawkins and nearby counties. Several enlistees may have been related to McCorkle by marriage. They included four Leftwiches, five Moores and a Galbraith. McCorkle soon became acting surgeon and then surgeon of the regiment and was promoted to major by the end of the war.[6]

There is no known photograph of Major McCorkle, but he must have cut an imposing figure. His military records describe him as six feet, four inches tall, with dark hair, hazel eyes and a "sandy" complexion. His exceptional height would have been an advantage when overseeing the chaos of a field hospital.

McCorkle served with the Army of Tennessee throughout the war, primarily in Tennessee and farther south. Therefore, it is doubtful that McCorkle and Reuben Bernard, who fought Confederates in New Mexico and Virginia, ever occupied the same field of battle. Even if they had, it would have been extremely unlikely that they would have encountered each other. Both were in cavalry regiments, but the surgeon ordinarily

Kurz & Allison lithograph of the Battle of Stones River (Murfreesboro), Tennessee, fought December 31, 1862, and January 2 and 3, 1863. William McCorkle served as surgeon of the Second Tennessee Cavalry during one of the bloodiest battles of the war (Library of Congress).

3. William McCorkle (1830–1865)

would have operated well behind the firing line. McCorkle owned a copy of William J. Hardee's *Rifle and Light Infantry Tactics*, the bible for commissioned officers, but his interest in that book would have been more academic than practical.

McCorkle provided a terse report of his battlefield experiences in his 1909 pension application. He said he was engaged in the battles of Fishing Creek, Kentucky (a Confederate disaster in January 1862); Murfreesboro, Tennessee (a bloodbath for both sides as 1862 turned to 1863); and "all the battles from Dalton to Atlanta, Ga." The Second Tennessee wintered with the rest of the Army of Tennessee's cavalry at Dalton, North Carolina, and fought as General Joseph E. Johnston retreated through Georgia that spring and summer until Atlanta fell to Union forces in September 1864. The battles in between included Resaca, Kenesaw Mountain, Brown's Mill, and Jonesborough. The Second Tennessee surrendered when the rest of the Army of Tennessee laid down arms at Durham, North Carolina, in late April 1865. Ashby's regiment actually was then at Charlotte, where McCorkle was paroled and sent home on May 3.[7]

The doctor may have served with the regiment in other battles (for example, Shiloh, Corinth, and Perryville in 1862), but he did not mention them in his pension request. While Reuben Bernard meticulously maintained a list of his sixty-five cavalry engagements during the war, William McCorkle was satisfied to provide the names of two battles and one lengthy campaign.

McCorkle's pension application does not reveal that he was out of commission entirely for about eight months after being captured following a Confederate cavalry raid into central Kentucky in March 1863. Union forces routed the invaders at Somerset. McCorkle remained behind the retreating army to care for the wounded and all were taken prisoner. According to McCorkle's service record, he was held at Camp Chase, Ohio; Fort Norfolk, Virginia; and Fort McHenry, Maryland. He was paroled to Washington, D.C., in June under the condition that he would "do no act of hostility either by word, writing or otherwise" against the United States. He was exchanged as part of a swap of surgeon POWs the following November and returned to his regiment.[8]

The family story is that McCorkle was embittered by his imprisonment as a POW, as well as by the war in general. He practiced medicine in the prison camps, apparently treating fellow prisoners, but he must have been frustrated to have been cut off from his regimental duties. Beginning in June 1862, both sides agreed that captured medical officers, as non-combatants, should not be detained, but should be "immediately and unconditionally discharged" so they could return to doctoring their units. But this agreement broke down in the summer of 1863; McCorkle was not released until its terms were reinstated in November.[9]

Conditions in prison camps deteriorated during this time as both armies held increasing numbers of men. Overcrowding often led to insufficient food and shelter and more disease and death. Writing about Camp Chase many years after the war, a Confederate POW observed that "a constant want of necessary, healthy food to sustain life fast filled those graves. The weak went first, and the unfortunate ones who contracted diseases next; while strong men, inured to hardship and short rations, wore on."[10]

If McCorkle ever wrote about his wartime medical experiences or his imprisonment, nothing has survived. But other doctors kept records, so the work of Confederate surgeons is well documented.

Southern doctors seem to have been as well trained as their Northern counterparts during what is now considered medicine's relative infancy. Germ theory was virtually unknown, and few doctors understood the value of maintaining antiseptic operating areas. Especially during a battle, with wounded men arriving by dozens at medical stations, surgeons rarely had time to wash their hands, let alone disinfect instruments and make sure bandages were clean. Gangrene commonly resulted. Doctors freely administered chloroform to patients who required amputation or suffered from internal injuries. If chloroform or ether were not available, whiskey often was. Doctors rarely had more than a few moments to diagnose a wound, anesthetize the patient and go to work.

No one was prepared for the massive medical mayhem of the Civil War. Confederate surgeon Joseph Jones estimated that, on average, the approximately six-hundred thousand men who served in the Confederate army suffered from wounds or disease an astounding six times during the war, making for a constant flow of patients. In many regiments, disease killed twice as many soldiers as battle wounds. A 1908 federal record of deaths of white Union soldiers from Tennessee indicated an even more dramatic ratio. Of 6,777 deaths, only 11 percent resulted from battle wounds. In some instances, a violent death may have seemed preferable to chronic disease. By the end of the war, the

3. William McCorkle (1830–1865)

Title page from the *Confederate States Medical & Surgical Journal*, published from January 1864 to February 1865. As a regimental surgeon, William McCorkle would have read the journal's reports on wound treatment, developments in prosthetics, and other medical matters (U. S. National Library of Medicine).

sick rate for diarrhea and dysentery—twin scourges of both armies— was a debilitating 995 per thousand.[11] Jonathan Bernard may have been sicker than most with those infectious ailments, but he had plenty of company. A quarter or more of any unit's soldiers might have been on sick call at any one time.

Attrition was relentless. The Confederate Nineteenth Tennessee Infantry mustered over one thousand East Tennessee men at Knoxville in the spring of 1861. Those soldiers went on to fight and sicken themselves to tatters, assembling only seventy-eight men when the regiment surrendered four years later. Hundreds of soldiers died in battle and as furious waves of dysentery, typhoid, tuberculosis, and other diseases swept through their camp throughout the war. Seven men, including Hawkins County farmer Thomas McLain, died before they ever left Knoxville.[12]

Of seventeen men in Company F of McCorkle's Second Tennessee who died during the war, all but one expired from disease, including two from chronic diarrhea. Only Private Samuel Henderson died in battle, at Murfreesboro, where McCorkle would have coordinated treatment of the wounded following an attack on Federal cavalry December 30, 1862.[13]

Most Southern regiments employed a surgeon and an assistant surgeon, along with a nurse, steward, and cook for each company. Surgeons were responsible not only for caring for wounded and ill soldiers during and between battles, but also for sending the worst cases to general hospitals removed from the battle area. In some cases, they had to maintain a record of deaths of soldiers while in their care. They also were in charge of maintaining sanitary camps, an almost impossible task under wartime conditions.[14]

During the turmoil of battle, doctors established field hospitals as close as they could safely move toward the fighting. Those soldiers who were not killed outright by musket and rifle fire or blasted to pieces by artillery found their own way to these stations or were carried there by litter. Surgeons and their assistants tried to stop the bleeding, splinted broken bones, and moved the most severely injured soldiers to larger division hospitals, by ambulance if available. Surgeons at both field and general hospitals used saws and knives to amputate severely wounded arms and legs. They disposed of these appendages on gory piles that later would be buried or, alternatively, tossed them into "limb pits" that could be covered with dirt.[15]

During calmer periods between battles, regimental surgeons and other officers dealt with the distress of soldiers who suffered not only physical ailments but psychic stress. What is today termed "battle fatigue" or "post-traumatic stress disorder" was known as "soldier's heart" during the Civil War. Acute anxiety prompted depressed soldiers to desert. Some lost the ability to function; others committed suicide.[16]

More elementally, soldiers often were deprived of basic daily necessities. A South Carolina surgeon summed up these challenges: "Continued exposure and fatigue, bad and insufficient food, salt meat, indifferent clothing, want of cleanliness, poor shelter, exposure at night to sudden changes of temperature, infected tents and camps, form a combination of causes which explains the fatality of an army in the field."[17]

Soldiers who had served in McCorkle's regiment expressed similar complaints in recollections near the end of their lives. James Nicely,

3. William McCorkle (1830–1865)

of Company B, wrote that the cavalrymen "lived poorly in camps, wore bad cloths [,] we had a little mule meet [sic]—and fly soup and I was exposed to cold and hunger." Rufus Ireland, of Company D, said the soldiers "lived mighty hard in camp. We half naked. Slept on ground. Poor beef and corn bread. Exposed to cold all times hungry many times. In hospital had nothing to eat." James Nail, of Company F, also complained about bad food, sparse clothing and exposure to the elements. But he said he was "in no hoss pittle [sic]. Hired my own docter [sic]."[18]

As the war progressed and doctors learned more about the prevention and treatment of infectious diseases, anesthetics, and the primitive beginning of modern surgical practices, deaths from disease and amputations began to decline. McCorkle, along with most other surgeons on both sides, never received recognition for this achievement. They endured the same long marches, limited rations and exposure to disease and battle as the men they treated, but they rarely were rewarded by promotions or even grateful comments by field commanders.

After suffering four years of war, trying to save lives but often watching men die in agony, McCorkle returned to his young family and former patients in Mooresburg. Meanwhile, he had absorbed the havoc the war had inflicted on members of his first family in Lexington. One of his brothers had been killed. Two other brothers and two brothers-in-law had survived Confederate service. But the war had disrupted the lives of the entire McCorkle family.

John Baxter McCorkle died in his early 20s. Born in 1840, a decade after William, he had graduated from Washington College in 1860 and worked as a teacher before joining the Rockbridge Artillery and becoming a second lieutenant. He distinguished himself at Second Manassas in August 1862 by capturing a mounted Federal soldier, armed with a Colt revolver and a cavalry saber, while McCorkle had only a sword. At Fredericksburg in December 1862, the young man was serving with the battery when a large piece of shell struck his right side. He died instantly. His horse had been killed at Winchester the previous May, and his father spent years unsuccessfully attempting to collect compensation from the government for the horse and his son's back pay.[19]

Alfred Leyburn McCorkle, born two years after William, graduated from Washington College in 1854 and the University of Virginia Medical School in 1856. Like his older brother, he attended the University of Pennsylvania Medical School, where he earned a second medical degree in 1857. He moved with his family to Carrollton, Missouri. After serving as a surgeon with an unknown Missouri regiment, he practiced in Carrolltown.[20]

Thomas Edward McCorkle, the second of William McCorkle's brothers to join the Rockbridge Artillery, was seventeen when he enlisted in March 1862. He served as a private until his parole at Appomattox, although he often was absent from his company because of sickness. He became a lawyer and served as mayor of Lexington.[21]

William McCorkle's oldest sister, Sarah, married John Rice McNutt, also a Washington graduate. Company H, Fourteenth Virginia Cavalry, elected him captain at the company's organization in the spring of 1861. A few months later, he was arrested for unknown reasons. The company replaced him as captain in May 1862. That is where McNutt's official service record ends. However, he apparently reenlisted in the Rockbridge Senior Reserves as a private in 1864. Following the war, he worked as a farmer and merchant in Carroll County, Missouri, and in Rockbridge County.[22]

William McCorkle's second oldest sister, Susan, married William Madison Sterrett. Sterrett enlisted shortly after the war began and eventually was promoted to second lieutenant. Wounded at the battle of Cedarville in the Shenandoah Valley late in 1864, Sterrett recovered in time to be captured at Dinwiddie Court House on April 1, 1865. He was released that June and returned to Rockbridge County, where he, like McNutt, labored as a merchant and farmed.[23]

Several of these men would oppose Reuben Bernard's cavalry on Virginia battlefields. Bernard was at Appomattox Court House when Thomas McCorkle surrendered with the rest of Lee's army. The Rockbridge Artillery had lost several cannons and men during the flight from Richmond and Petersburg to Appomattox. The company mustered only 101 men at the end.[24]

Returning home following the surrender, the defeated veterans would have found the vast majority of the local population depressed by the war's outcome. Rockbridge County had been relatively slow to join the secession movement, but once President Lincoln called for seventy-five thousand Federal volunteers, residents quickly approved separation from the Union.[25] Like most Virginians—loyal West Virginians being the exceptional example—they chose state over country.

While most McCorkles found sympathetic neighbors in Rockbridge County, William McCorkle returned to live in a land of widespread antagonism, on both sides, in Hawkins County. The war had

3. William McCorkle (1830–1865)

even divided members of the founding family of Mooresburg, according to Moore family history. Early in the conflict, a young Moore woman who was a strong Union sympathizer hoisted an American flag over her home. Her father passed by the house shortly afterward and shot down the flag. Someone asked why he had done that. "For the love of my country," he said, "and the contempt I have for that flag."[26]

Such disagreements, within and between families, would persist.

4

Post-War East Tennessee (1865–1868)

Following their surrender, many Confederate veterans struggled to get back to East Tennessee. Most came home on foot, often sleeping outside or in barns and begging for food. Hawkins County soldiers had typical experiences. W.H. Wetzel, of the Twenty-ninth Virginia Infantry, slowly made his way alone to Surgoinsville. "I had to sleep in the barns on my way back," he reported, "and had very little to eat." William G. Taylor and other veterans of William McCorkle's Second Tennessee Cavalry were told they could keep their horses and sidearms when they surrendered at Athens, Georgia. But on their way to Morristown, Taylor's group "met with federal soldiers and others that robbed us of our horses and everything of value."[1]

Other returning Confederates encountered worse fates than robbery. East Tennessee suffered the most sustained violence in the former Confederacy. Unionists murdered or assaulted dozens of returning Confederates before they could reach their homes. A Union veteran described the situation succinctly on his return to Tennessee: "Union men and Rebels cannot live together." Federal soldiers reportedly killed several veterans from the Army of Northern Virginia as they came back to Knoxville. Union men killed four ex-Confederate soldiers and severely beat others in Rhea and Washington counties. Fourteen Unionists encountered James Harris on his return to Blount County, threatened him with a pistol, and hit him with a two-handed brush. Confederates returning to Grainger County and Dandridge in Jefferson County also were assaulted.[2]

Physical attacks and intimidation did not always succeed. A large contingent of the Fifth Tennessee Cavalry maintained ranks while returning to Rhea County. The soldiers encountered a sizable force of

4. Post-War East Tennessee (1865–1868)

partisans, many of them deserters from the Confederate army. Their commander, Colonel George W. Kirk, demanded that the Confederate cavalrymen surrender their weapons and horses. Colonel George W. McKenzie, the Confederate commander, refused. His fourteen remaining officers had retained their pistols and he called them forward. McKenzie told Kirk to order his force to step aside "or somebody would be killed." Kirk's partisans parted and the regiment's remnant passed.[3]

If they got home safely, Confederate veterans sometimes found that multiple members of their families had been killed. W.D. Van Dyke, of Athens and later Chattanooga, served with Brigadier General John C. Vaughn throughout the war. He alone of four brothers survived. Other returning veterans discovered that their buildings had been burned and farm fields scavenged by foraging soldiers and bands of guerrillas. Many wondered what to do next. Upon returning to Rogersville, J.C. McCarty, a soldier in the Sixtieth Tennessee Infantry and later Rogersville's city marshal, reported that he "did nothing. We had nothing to do with. I had only what clothes I had on. It had all been carried off and ruin stalked the land."[4]

William McCorkle had a professional service to provide to his neighbors, but most veterans had been farmers and returned to ravished properties, impoverished families, and few prospects for improvement. Soldiers who had suffered the humiliation of defeat also had received grossly insufficient monetary compensation for their time in the field. Many could not revive their farms or businesses: some had lost workers as war casualties; others had their work forces emancipated. Veterans who had been wounded or afflicted by major illness rarely recovered their previous ability to make a living. Many women had worn themselves and their clothes ragged coping with children and properties by themselves. Assistance from other family members, churches, and benevolent individuals often was insufficient.[5]

Union veterans also faced challenges. Many of their properties had been damaged or destroyed when Confederates controlled the area. Most veterans returned to mixed neighborhoods where continuing conflicts seemed inevitable. As William Rule explained in his history of Knoxville, "The ugly wounds made by the hands of 'grim-visaged war' in this section healed slower, and unsightly scars were visible longer, than in other parts of the country, where the people were either all for the Union or all for the rebellion." Fellow Unionist Oliver Temple, the Knoxville attorney who had defended Union sympathizers on trial during the early years of the war, had a different recollection. "Often the Union soldier and the Confederate soldier settled side by side," he wrote in his history of the war in East Tennessee. "Each had chosen his side from honest convictions. When they returned they respected each other, and met as old friends."[6]

Although Rule and Temple published their books at about the same time, just after the Spanish-American War, the former provided a realistic assessment of the depressed and partisan climate of East Tennessee in 1865, whereas the latter seems to have embraced the enthusiasm for reconciliation that peaked in the 1890s and projected it onto the 1860s. Some neighbors who fought for opposing sides met again as "old friends" in 1865; but other veterans, especially Union men, carried home the "ugly wounds" of war and sought vengeance.

East Tennesseans were not alone in recognizing their unusual predicament. On a tour of the South following the war, journalist Whitelaw Reid visited Knoxville in the autumn of 1865. Unionists "who had been driven from their homes or half-starved in the mountains, or hunted for with dogs, were not likely to be very gentle in their treatment of the men who persecuted them," he wrote, "and one readily believed what all observers said, that in no place through the South had the bitterness of feeling, engendered by the war, been so intense or the violence so bloody in its consequences."[7]

The situation in East Tennessee was as atypical of the South following the war as during it. In most Southern states, former Confederates harassed the relatively few residents who had remained loyal to the Union, as well as Northern carpetbaggers, and, unrelentingly, the newly-emancipated black population. The Ku Klux Klan, organized at Pulaski in 1866 and officially reorganized as a terrorist group at Nashville in 1867, often led these attacks. But the KKK never made much headway in East Tennessee, and former Confederates found themselves members of a sizable but despised and often oppressed minority.[8]

Ex-Confederates who had played the most prominent roles in the rebellion were prime targets. In May 1865 Robert Johnson, son of Andrew Johnson, who had served as president for just over a month, said that "Union men will not permit the leaders, and others that persecuted their families to live in this section." Unionists in Washington County issued notices to secessionists to leave or suffer violence. A Rogersville woman said a "mob" of Unionists had conspired to deny

4. Post-War East Tennessee (1865–1868)

Confederates access to schools, churches, and employment in an effort to drive them out of the area.[9]

The secessionist flight began immediately. A Knoxville resident listed thirty-one prominent Confederate families who had left or been expelled by federal authorities by July 1865. In August, John Crozier Ramsey, Knox County's district attorney when Confederates controlled Knoxville early in the war, reported that "no prominent Southern men [from Knoxville] have returned and those who are there are making arrangements to leave." David T. Patterson, Andrew Johnson's son-in-law, testified to Congress that by early 1866 few Confederates remained in East Tennessee.[10]

Union troops played a large role in persuading Confederate veterans and sympathizers to leave the area by subduing pockets of resistance. In late April and May 1865, the Ninth Tennessee Cavalry moved to pacify Knoxville and counties north of it, arresting nine men suspected of bushwhacking in the Rutledge area. The Fourth Tennessee Mounted Infantry repressed secessionists in more rural counties. Orders to shoot bushwhackers and guerrillas on sight crushed most opposition.[11]

Union soldiers acting independently or as vigilante bands carried out some of the deadliest attacks. They targeted not only Confederate veterans but anyone known to have supported the rebellion. In Knoxville, a Southern-sympathizing druggist reported that he had received "a thorough cowhiding" by a Union officer, while another Unionist gave "a good cudgeling" to a Confederate sympathizer and then threw stones at him as he chased him down the street. Mrs. E.C. Caswell wrote to her son from Knoxville: "A great many southern men have been severely used by the soldiers." One had been "terribly cowhided." Another "had his skull broken." A third had been "beaten all most to death."[12]

Unionist Isham Alley murdered Robert West after West returned to Knoxville. Several years earlier, West had beaten Alley for broadcasting his hostility to the Confederacy, according to *Knoxville Whig* editor William Brownlow. Therefore, Brownlow determined, West received "Just Retribution." Discharged Union soldiers killed John Kincaid outside the Knox County courthouse, although he had taken a loyalty oath. Brownlow thought this murder also was just because Kincaid was "a bitter, thorough, and unrelenting rebel" and "injured, insulted and oppressed Union men will redress their own wrongs...."[13]

Union veterans repeatedly threatened soldiers who had served with

General John Vaughn, of Monroe County. Vaughn had raised Tennessee's first Confederate infantry regiment and his troops had oppressed Union sympathizers while Confederates controlled East Tennessee. In apparent retaliation, Unionists shot and killed one of Vaughn's paroled veterans, Deen Anderson, after he returned to Knoxville. Anderson died despite assurances by local officials that paroled Confederate soldiers would be protected.[14]

Ellen Renshaw House chronicled one particularly brutal slaying in her Knoxville diary on August 16, 1865: "This morning a man (southern) named Cox was in Tooles store when a Lincolnite named Foster came in [,] shook hands with him, inquired after his health and just as Cox turned round shot him in the back first [,] then in three other places."[15]

For a long time, it seemed that the violence would not end, that the oppression of the war's losers by its winners—the effort to kill, exile, or at least silence all former Confederates—would become a permanent way of life in East Tennessee. Beyond launching physical attacks, Unionists harassed secessionists by suing them for financial losses they allegedly had suffered. Again encouraged by William Brownlow, they filed damage suits against Confederate officers who had enforced the draft, encouraged the arrests of Unionists, or supplied vital information to Confederate authorities. While Unionists initially won many court actions, as time passed and cases clogged the courts, juries became less sympathetic. Ultimately, conservative Union lawyers forcefully represented secessionists and reversed some decisions.[16]

Unionists were even less successful in bringing criminal suits for murder, assault, or robbery committed during the Confederate occupation. Many men were imprisoned, but juries found few guilty. In an exceptional case, four men who had served on the court-martial that had found A.C. Hawn guilty of being one of the bridge burners of 1861 were charged with his execution. Many observers anticipated a guilty verdict, but the four men were found not guilty by a "decidedly Union" jury in a Knox County Circuit Court trial in late 1865.[17]

While Unionists harassed former Confederates in East Tennessee communities, they had a strong ally in Nashville. In April 1865, Republican William Brownlow had succeeded Democrat Andrew Johnson as Tennessee governor following a brief caretaker appointment. Brownlow quickly prodded the Tennessee Assembly into voting to disenfranchise the most prominent Confederates for fifteen years and the rest

4. Post-War East Tennessee (1865–1868)

for five. The new governor also led an effort to confiscate the property of Confederate veterans who had fled the state or the country. And he promoted continuing treason trials, which had begun in the spring of 1864 and continued well after the war ended. Most of these actions failed when a defendant produced a copy of a signed amnesty oath or pardon from the president.[18]

Not everyone approved of the persistent physical and legal attacks on former Confederates. Some Unionists had urged reconciliation immediately after formal hostilities ended. "Let us display towards the thousands of our fellow citizens who were engaged in the recent rebellion ... the same magnanimous spirit which our Government has exhibited," wrote a correspondent of the *Knoxville Whig* in June 1865.

"Parson" William Gannaway Brownlow, *Knoxville Whig* editor, Methodist minister, staunch Republican, anti-secessionist, and scourge of Confederates, served as post-war governor of Tennessee and later as U.S. senator (Library of Congress).

That August, in an extraordinary gesture of good will, two Union men in Madisonville, well south of Knoxville, invited "all that had been rebels" to attend a party to "restore good feelings among the young folks." The Republican *Greeneville New Era* urged restraint in September 1865. "Those of our Union citizens who have been aggrieved (and there are many such) by the acts and outrages of the rebels," wrote the editor, "will do well to exercise a philosophic and magnanimous forbearance toward their late vile persecutors."[19]

But some secessionists did not want to reconcile with their Unionist neighbors, especially if the Union men remained hostile. In Hamilton County, Confederate veterans demanded that the courts order Unionists to stop trying to drive them out of the region. In Sullivan County, former Confederates beat up a justice of the peace who attempted to prosecute veterans. In Jonesborough, Confederate veterans unsuccessfully attempted to burn the office of the *Union Flag* newspaper. A group of former Confederate soldiers published an open letter to Brownlow in September 1865. They called for protection and demanded justice for those committing crimes against former Confederates. "We have forbore with a certain class until forbearance has ceased to be a virtue," they wrote, and declared that "we have sworn to put an end to them" if they did not stop the oppression.[20]

Many women who had supported the Confederacy continued to despise Unionists. They had stayed home and despaired as their families disintegrated and properties were destroyed. They often were as bitter as combat veterans. Ellen Renshaw House, the Knoxville diarist, felt more hostile toward the Union as the war turned sour and remained resolutely rebellious well after it was over. On September 1, 1865, House penned her opinion of the soldiers and politicians who had taken over East Tennessee. "Now we are slaves," wrote this young woman whose family actually had enslaved black Africans, "slaves to the vilest race that ever disgraced humanity."[21]

Five days later, Eliza Fain wrote in her diary at her home outside Rogersville with similar disdain for the Unionists who had taken over in Hawkins County: "My poor heart has this day been wrung with anguish. I do feel all things are so much greater trials now than when war fierce, yea terrible war was everywhere abroad in the land.... Men of the lowest character stalk through the land with the most lordly air defying God and his children."[22]

During the week House and Fain chronicled their resentfulness in defeat, one of the most violent post-war incidents shocked East Tennessee. Abner Baker, formerly a private in Company I of the Second Tennessee Cavalry, killed a Union veteran in downtown Knoxville and was summarily lynched.

The event that seems to have precipitated the violence had occurred more than two years earlier, in June 1863. Dr. Harvey Baker, Abner's father, sympathized with his son's cause. When he heard that Colonel William Sanders' Union cavalry, then just entering the area, was traveling toward his house on the Kingston Pike in western Knox County, he took up his rifle to meet them. He exchanged shots with Union skirmishers, who pursued him into his house and killed him.

In apparent retaliation, following two years of festering resentment,

4. Post-War East Tennessee (1865–1868)

Abner Baker rode to the Knox County Courthouse on September 4, 1865, and killed Will Hall, deputy clerk of the circuit court and a Union veteran. Some former Confederates viewed the encounter otherwise, claiming that the considerably larger Hall had been the aggressor and that Baker had shot Hall in the brain in self-defense. In any case, authorities immediately arrested and jailed Baker. Unwilling to let the sun set on Hall's killing, a mob of Federal soldiers hauled Baker out of jail and hanged him from a nearby tree. No one was charged with this killing. Outraged friends of Abner Baker raised a substantial obelisk at his grave site in the cemetery of Knoxville's First Presbyterian Church. The inscription claims his death was "an honor to himself, but an everlasting disgrace to his enemies."[23]

Home on leave in Van Hill at the time, Reuben Bernard probably would have lost no sleep over the killing of a Confederate veteran. It is doubtful, however, that he shared the anger against his rebellious neighbors that some Unionists felt. As a career army officer who had fought Apaches as well as Confederates and soon would return to the Indian wars, he likely had a different mindset about war in general. Besides, his brothers had worn gray uniforms. He would have spoken carefully about their comrades.

William McCorkle, reviving his medical practice in Mooresburg, would have been more disturbed by the hanging of a soldier who had served in his regiment, as well as by other Union reprisals that occurred with regularity throughout 1865 and 1866.

Meanwhile, Republican politicians, many of whom were Union veterans or sympathizers, pushed Tennessee to rejoin the United States. With Brownlow leading the way, the state adopted the Thirteenth Amendment to the Constitution in April 1865 and the Fourteenth Amendment in July 1866. The state that had been the last to leave the Union became the first to rejoin on July 24, 1866. Thereby, Tennessee avoided most aspects of the Military Reconstruction program imposed on the rest of the South by the Republican-led Congress in 1867.

Union-Confederate feuding in East Tennessee had eased considerably by then as most people on both sides decided to get on with their lives. But political disputes that had their roots in the war continued. One of East Tennessee's worst episodes of violence in the post-war era occurred nearly one year after the state rejoined the union. Republican factions rioted in Rogersville, leaving one man dead and several wounded.

Tennessee's Conservative Unionists nominated Emerson Etheridge to oppose the radical Republican Brownlow in the 1867 election. Etheridge, a former Republican congressional representative from western Tennessee, had opposed emancipation and supported the restoration of voting rights for Confederates following the war. As a result, he drew support from conservative Republicans as well as ex-Confederates. On July 23, 1867, he was scheduled to debate U.S. Representative Horace Maynard, a Brownlow supporter, in downtown Rogersville. Maynard's supporters included both blacks and whites.

Etheridge presented his side of the debate to a largely sympathetic audience and then left the area. Maynard's forces, who had jeered Etheridge throughout his presentation, then began a loud demonstration for Brownlow. Someone from the Brownlow contingent fired a weapon at the Etheridge crowd. That prompted volleys on both sides, during which an Etheridge supporter, a Union veteran, was killed. Over a period of some hours, the confrontation continued, abated, and was renewed, with the result that nine men were wounded, some severely. At least five hundred men, including a number of Confederate veterans, took part in the fight, which, according to the court record, produced multiple "noises, tumults and disturbances" that terrorized the citizenry.[24]

While political partisan bickering continued, the worst of the animosity among veterans was over by the late 1860s. Here and there, individual feuds still simmered and, sporadically, flared. In the summer of 1868, William McCorkle must have been shocked to learn of the death of his regimental commander at the hands of an enraged former Union officer.

Radical Unionists did not forget Colonel Henry Ashby's real or perceived transgressions when he returned to Knoxville following the war. He was the object of multiple indictments for larceny and robbery, although Unionists dropped or settled most of those charges before trial. Ashby's enemies particularly cited his treatment of 421 Union men captured while attempting to cross into Kentucky during the second year of the war. They said Ashby's soldiers murdered some of these men and abused others while escorting them back to Knoxville on their ultimate way to imprisonment in Georgia in the spring of 1862.

In 1866, Eldad Cicero Camp, a former Union Army major and Knox County's prosecuting attorney, sued Ashby for his mistreatment of prisoners and for treason against the state. Ashby promptly left town, returning to Knoxville only after the courts dismissed the treason indictment. Ashby and Camp encountered each other several times. They quarreled

4. Post-War East Tennessee (1865–1868)

and engaged in at least one physical altercation, with Ashby wielding a cane and Camp an umbrella. On the afternoon of July 10, 1868, Ashby went to Camp's office and demanded that they settle the dispute. The men walked out to the street and continued to argue. Camp drew a pistol and shot Ashby three times in the head and chest. The colonel, who also had drawn his pistol but had not fired, died instantly.[25]

Rival Knoxville newspapers reported this event in predictably partisan ways. "Since Cain slew Abel no human being has committed homicide under circumstances more justifiable than those under which the bully Ashby lost his life," reported the *Knoxville Whig*. The *Knoxville Press and Herald* countered that Camp was "a man of no character.... He belongs to that low order of 'shysters' that frequent the Police Courts of Chicago and New York."[26]

Confederate Colonel Henry M. Ashby commanded William McCorkle's regiment. Following the war, Eldad Cicero Camp, a Union veteran and Knox County's prosecuting attorney, sued Ashby for treason and drove him from the state. After Ashby returned to Knoxville, Camp shot and killed him (Library of Congress).

Knoxville authorities charged Camp with Ashby's murder, but the Knox County coroner, a Unionist and a Brownlow supporter, determined that Camp had fired in self-defense. Deciding that he could not obtain a conviction, the prosecutor dropped the case. Camp eventually became U.S. District Attorney for East Tennessee, and a respected coal tycoon and philanthropist.[27] This was only one of many equivocal resolutions of disputes during the contentious years immediately following the war. The outcome of the case may have distressed the Second Tennessee's former surgeon as much as the killing itself.

5

Separating the Dead (1865–1868)

Both Confederate Colonel Henry Ashby and Union Major Eldad Camp are buried in Old Gray, an antebellum garden cemetery adjacent to Knoxville National Cemetery about a mile north of downtown Knoxville. Other notable men who supported opposite sides in the war also are buried there. They include Union captain and Knoxville mayor William Rule and Confederate-turned-Union wartime merchant/opportunist Joseph Mabry, Sr. Many Knoxville families buried veterans who died after the war in Old Gray, so wartime enemies often are closer in death than they had been in life. In striking contrast, most Union and Confederate soldiers who died during the war were buried in separate cemeteries by deliberate, nearly inflexible, design.

"The initial motivations governing the creation of national cemeteries were born of the hostility of the war," John Neff has observed. "No Confederates who died while under arms opposing the Union were interred in any of the national cemeteries." Similarly, Union soldiers were not buried in Confederate cemeteries throughout the South. "The segregation," noted Neff, "was complete."[1]

If Reuben Bernard had died in battle in Virginia and had been buried where he fell, as most soldiers were, he no doubt would have been reburied in a national cemetery. (He eventually was buried at Arlington National Cemetery in northern Virginia.) If William McCorkle had died and been buried on a battlefield, he would not have been reburied in a national cemetery. His body would have been removed to a private cemetery set aside strictly for the Confederate dead or to the church cemetery in Mooresburg where he eventually rested.

Civil War historian Earl Hess suggested that the division of the dead had even greater significance in Knoxville. In addition to the

5. Separating the Dead (1865–1868)

Federally mandated separation of the dead, he said, Knoxville's cemeteries "reflect the divided loyalties of the city during the Civil War."[2] In Knoxville National Cemetery, the oldest graves hold the remains of men who died fighting for the Union between 1863 and 1865. East of town, in lushly landscaped Bethel Cemetery, lie most of the Knoxville area's Confederates who died during the war. A similar separation occurred in hundreds of cemeteries, North and South, but not commonly in the same city. This division of the dead, especially during the first years after the war, restrained efforts to reunite the living.

There was no grand plan for this radical separation at the beginning of hostilities. No one knew that as many as 750,000 men—one in every ten white men of military age—would die and require substantial tracts of land for burial. No one thought that major battles would produce thousands of dead who would be buried in place and then reburied somewhere else. No one anticipated that nearly half of these men would be so stripped of identification, so decomposed, so mutilated—some literally blown to fragments by artillery shells—that their remains could only be labeled "Unknown." No one expected that even more thousands would die in prison camps and in hospitals, requiring scores of additional graveyards or sections of graveyards beyond fields of battle. And no one considered that a visceral hatred of the living enemy would compel absolute segregation of the dead.

The requirement of moving hundreds or thousands of corpses underground as quickly as possible following a battle explains in part why enemies originally were buried separately and differently. The victors in any fight dealt with their dead first, taking care to place bodies in individual graves well covered with earth. If there was time before moving on, the victors might bury the enemy dead, too, but in a separate location, often in a pit or ravine that could be turned into a mass grave. Occasionally, as following the Battle of Fort Sanders in Knoxville, the two sides would announce a truce during which each side would collect its dead soldiers and bury them in graves at separate locations.[3]

If names and units were known, they would be inscribed on wood headboards, especially over officers' graves. But this, too, was done primarily by the winners of the field. The enemy dead remained largely anonymous. A victorious army might provide religious rites. But victors weary from fighting and possibly preparing to follow the retreating enemy did not have time to do much more than dig graves and cursorily mark them. The purpose of battlefield interment was basic: to shield the

Sons of East Tennessee

bodies of lost comrades from the elements, wild hogs and other hungry animals, and, if they were in enemy territory, human vandals.[4]

Sometimes the dead were too numerous and the armies were moving too quickly to bury anyone—friend or foe. In those cases, bodies decomposed in place, leaving skeletons to greet soldiers returning to fight on the same ground months later. Frank Oakley, an officer in Wisconsin's Seventh Regiment, found skeletons from the First Battle of Manassas when he fought the second battle on the Virginia battlefield in August 1862, more than a year later. Similarly, Union soldiers fighting in Virginia's Wilderness in 1864 saw human bones left behind following the battle of Chancellorsville a year earlier.[5]

From the first pitched battles until well after all fighting ended, both sides treated the enemy dead with indifference, if not loathing.

At the end of 1861, the U.S. Congress formed the Committee on

This Alexander Gardner photograph shows a Union soldier examining a common Civil War scene. "A contrast!" reads the caption. "Federal buried, rebel unburied, where they fell at the Battle of Antietam." The buried soldier is First Lieutenant John A. Clark, Company D, 7th Michigan Infantry. Customarily, the army that held the field did not bury enemy soldiers (Library of Congress).

5. Separating the Dead (1865–1868)

the Conduct of the War to investigate early Union losses at First Manassas and Ball's Bluff in Virginia. Among the committee's investigations was "the barbarous treatment by the rebels at Manassas of the remains of the officers and soldiers of the United States killed in battle there." Testimony included allegations that Confederates stripped the bodies of Union soldiers of all clothing and possessions before burying them face down in "the negro burying ground" as a show of disrespect. Following the battle of Shiloh in southwestern Tennessee in the spring of 1862, Union soldiers were buried in individual graves all over the battlefield, but most Confederates were interred in twelve mass graves, only five of which can still be located.[6]

While both sides universally condemned mistreatment of their own dead when their graves were separated and disrespected, many observers were equally indignant when graves were commingled. A Union colonel reportedly expressed outrage when he found that military hospitals buried the dead together following the battle of Antietam, without "distinction between the graves of our Brave men who have died for our cause, and the grave of the worthless invaders of our soil." This concern persisted following the war. In 1866, a Union woman visiting the national cemetery at Arlington, said she hoped "no rebel will ever set his accursed foot within these sacred precincts."[7]

The federal government began the national cemetery system primarily to show respect for the men who fought and died for the Union; but the system had a secondary purpose of assuring that the nation as a whole would pay no similar respect to the Confederate dead. In July 1862, Congress authorized President Lincoln to purchase land and establish burial grounds on behalf of the United States, not the Confederate States. The United States established fourteen cemeteries by the end of that year, not only to bury but to memorialize the dead.[8]

Throughout the war, national cemeteries were established at Gettysburg in Pennsylvania; Antietam in Maryland; at Knoxville, Chattanooga, and Stones River in Tennessee; and at other sites as Union forces occupied Confederate territory. This effort accelerated following hostilities and became one of the largest federal projects undertaken in the nineteenth century. The Confederacy's primary goal had been to separate itself from the union of states; one of the Union's goals was to separate the dead who had worn blue uniforms from those who had worn gray. Samuel Weaver, a Gettysburg physician who supervised the recovery and reburial of the dead in Gettysburg National Cemetery, reported that "in no instance was a body allowed to be removed which had any portion of rebel clothing on it." He claimed "infallible accuracy," asserting that "there had not been a single mistake made ... by taking a rebel for a Union soldier."[9]

Two initiatives helped to ensure that most of the Union dead would be found, reburied, and remembered, if possible, by name. As the war ended in the spring of 1865, Clara Barton, the resolute nurse who later founded the American Red Cross, originated a service with the remarkably elongated title of Office of Correspondence with the Friends of the Missing Men of the United States Army. When she closed that office in 1868, she had secured information on 22,000 missing soldiers from thousands of letters provided by relatives and friends. Undertaking a more comprehensive effort, U.S. Quartermaster General Montgomery Meigs in July 1865 ordered Union commanders to report the location of all Union interments registered during the war. Listed interments totaled 101,736 men—fewer than one-third of estimated casualties. The others were soldiers buried at unknown sites.[10]

In 1867, Congress enacted the first National Cemetery Act appropriating funds to construct stone or iron fencing around all cemeteries, mark every grave site with a headstone, and hire cemetery superintendents. Graves were arranged in concentric circles around a central flagpole, as at Knoxville, or in a variety of other geometric or free-style layouts. The massive national reburial program, which lasted until 1870, discovered three-hundred thousand remains of Union soldiers and removed them to seventy-three national cemeteries throughout the country, many of them in the former Confederate states and far from home.[11]

The tedious, back-breaking labor of locating and transferring these Union remains to national cemeteries began in the spring of 1866 when Meigs ordered officers and work crews to begin searching for all possible Union graves. He divided the country into sections. Captain Edmund Burke Whitman, who was serving as chief quartermaster of the District of Tennessee at the end of the war, took charge of the national cemeteries and mortuary records for the same district in 1866. As had Barton, he asked for information about missing Union soldiers. He surveyed surviving witnesses of burials, former regimental surgeons, chaplains, and other army officers. He published notices in hundreds of newspapers and periodicals. As had Barton, he received thousands of responses. Then he traveled thirty thousand miles through Tennessee,

5. Separating the Dead (1865–1868)

Kentucky, Georgia, and Alabama searching for graves and asking directions to obscure sites. He and his men often encountered still-rebellious, uncooperative residents.[12]

Whitman inspected battlefields, older cemeteries, and former hospital and prison sites. The process was systematic (Whitman described how he and his ten-man crew spaced themselves before carefully crossing the battlefield at Shiloh) and specific to the Union dead. Similar to the operation on the Gettysburg battlefield, Whitman and those in charge of locating graves in other regions disinterred and reinterred only Union bodies.[13]

Before he left the quartermaster's office in 1869, Whitman presided over "a Harvest of Death" that relocated over 114,560 Union bodies. Later in life, he said the experience revealed that "the entire country over which the war had extended its ravages, was one interminable grave-yard." He reburied the bodies in twenty national cemeteries, each one in a coffin with name and military unit if known.[14]

Each cemetery collected bodies from a large circular area surrounding it. Whitman reported that Knoxville National Cemetery contained remains from 174 separate locations, Nashville from 252, Shiloh from 565, and Marietta, Georgia, from 1,970. Whitman oversaw all of these reburials, making certain that graves were dug and marked in accordance with established procedures. He maintained detailed accounts of his activities. For example, in late July 1866, he met with the officer in charge of reburying soldiers in Knoxville's cemetery. He offered a long list of suggestions for improvement, among them that "the graves he had put in were too near by half—and did not correspond with the previous burials—that the graves were too shallow by a foot" and that the temporary wood headboards would have to be repositioned. The officer agreed to make all changes.[15]

The process of collecting and reburying dead soldiers in Knoxville is representative of what happened at most national cemeteries. The melancholy and tedious task of consolidating the Union dead changed the landscape of towns and battlefields throughout the country.

Before locating the bodies to fill these cemeteries, of course, the government had to acquire the land. Shortly after he took over Knoxville in September 1863, General Ambrose Burnside essentially confiscated both the fourteen-acre Old Gray Cemetery and the nearly ten acres that would become the national cemetery. Union troops were dying in skirmishes near Knoxville and Burnside thought the vacant tract on higher ground along Old Gray's northern border would provide a proper central location for burial. Private Orville Hosford of the 2nd Ohio Cavalry had participated in Colonel William Sanders' raid on Knoxville that June and was one of the cemetery's first interments. Gravediggers removed Hosford's remains from a temporary plot in the Knox County burial ground, a Potter's Field for indigent residents.

Hosford soon was joined by members of the 79th New York Volunteers, the Highlanders who had died defending Fort Sanders from the Confederate attack in November 1863. Hugh Young, a member of the regiment and a stone cutter by trade, carved a small memorial stone near the center of the cemetery in March 1864. "Sacred to the memory of deceased soldiers of the 79th N.Y. Vols. 'Highlander,'" it declares, and

This 1864 print from a sketch of Knoxville National Cemetery made by a member of the Seventy-ninth New York Volunteers, the "Highlanders," shows the regiment's memorial and individual tombstones at center foreground. A member of the regiment carved the memorial to his fellow soldiers who died defending Fort Sanders in November 1863 (Library of Congress).

5. Separating the Dead (1865–1868)

"By all the thousands that have died for thee, O loved Republic, be thou just and free!" The monument is surrounded by tombstones of members of the regiment. Other early burials included Union soldiers who died in a hospital located near the cemetery.[16]

Within a year, 1,475 bodies had been buried in the "National Soldiers' Cemetery," according to a Union military newspaper. By May 1867, twenty-six hundred men lay buried in the cemetery, according to the *Knoxville Whig*. The *Whig* praised recent improvements to the grounds and concluded with one of William Brownlow's partisan blasts: "National Cemeteries are a sad comment on the wicked men of the rebellion." By 1868, according to a government report, the number of burials had increased to 3,153, all marked by wooden planks. Only 2,079 of the graves contained named soldiers; the rest were "unknown." Unlike many cemeteries, North and South, Knoxville National Cemetery was not segregated by race: U.S. Colored Troops from the Civil War era are buried throughout the graveyard. Most of these bodies, white and black, had been reburied from their original grave sites elsewhere in E.B. Whitman's territory.[17]

According to the *Whig*, "the memory of these noble heroes, whose forms repose beneath the sod, who sacrificed their life for the good of their country, should always be cherished and venerated by all true patriots." Not every citizen subscribed to that opinion. Under the heading "Disgraceful and Infamous," the *Whig* reported that a well-known Knoxvillian, J.C. Passmore, walked through the cemetery with another man and remarked that "there was a goodly number of Yankee soldiers there, but not half as many as he desired to see." Brownlow believed Passmore deserved to be "spurned from decent society."[18]

Many former Confederates who shared Passmore's view about buried Yankees had a very different opinion about their own dead. With its government dissolved, the former Confederacy had no central authority to organize a reburial program. But Southerners felt strongly that men who had given their lives in a failed effort to secede from the union should be treated honorably. Responding to the federal proposal for a national cemetery system in April 1866, the *Richmond Examiner* called on Richmond's churchwomen to do something similar for Virginia's dead. If the Confederate soldier was not part of the national burden of war, the newspaper said, "he is *ours*—and shame be to us if we do not care for his ashes." The editor pursued the subject on May 5, 1866, noting that while the "Nation's Dead ... are abundantly cared for by their

Government ... the nation contemns [sic] our dead. They are left in deserted places to rot into oblivion."[19]

Two days earlier, a group had founded the Hollywood Memorial Association of the Ladies of Richmond. The women began repairing the thousands of graves at Hollywood Cemetery along the James River. The Ladies' Memorial Association for the Confederate Dead of Oakland soon took on the same project for another large cemetery on the eastern edge of Richmond. Women throughout the South replicated this grassroots effort, not only to honor the dead but to reserve for themselves some power in the post-war South and as a passive way to counter Reconstruction.[20]

Women's groups, which generally took the name Ladies' Memorial Association (LMA), led the effort because Confederate veterans had pledged upon signing their paroles not to do anything to encourage further resistance to the United States. Men often played an important role in the background, especially in fund-raising efforts. Meanwhile, Southern women became the primary custodians not only of cemeteries but of Memorial Day commemorations and, later, the construction of Confederate monuments in those cemeteries.[21]

These women always considered the proper burial of the dead as their primary duty, and they often felt their response was insufficient. After surveying the national cemeteries around Petersburg, Virginia, the local LMA president commended them in the autumn of 1867. "They are adorned, so neatly and tastefully arranged," she said, "that it makes one sad to look upon them and think how the bones of Southern men and soldiers lie scattered among the weeds."[22]

The process of locating bodies and moving them to Confederate cemeteries was similar to the National Cemetery operation, but with local LMAs, rather than a governmental agency, as organizers. The LMAs collected funds contributed by private individuals and states to pay for transporting corpses from Gettysburg and other distant locations. The LMA initiative differed from the federal project in that most cemeteries deliberately reburied soldiers in sections by state. That division occurred in large part because individual states often financed reburial programs for their own dead. It also underscored the South's unvanquished belief in states' rights. The women attempted to identify as many men as possible, but, with fewer official records to consult, erected a larger number of headboards and stones engraved "Unknown" and created separate sections for them.[23]

5. Separating the Dead (1865–1868)

LMAs actually inherited a process that was well underway before the end of the war. Organizers of those early efforts, also women, were just as concerned as Northerners about keeping their "cities of the dead" free from the taint of an enemy body. For example, the Georgia Memorial Association in Marietta gathered three thousand bodies from nearby battlefields. A local Union man suggested burying these men in the Marietta National Cemetery, which opened in 1866. The women of the memorial association rejected that idea, insisting that the Confederate dead should remain where they were and be "protected from a promiscuous mingling with the remains of their enemies."[24]

Most of Knoxville's Confederate dead were buried or reburied in the cemetery on Bethel Avenue, about two miles east of the National Cemetery. Many of the cemetery's interments date to 1861–1863, the period of Confederate occupation. Cemetery caretakers maintained a register of those interred, but names are not attached to individual bodies. The number buried there eventually totaled about sixteen hundred, including the 129 soldiers who died in the assault on Fort Sanders and dozens more who died during the siege of Knoxville and at various other places in Knox County and the surrounding area. About fifty Union soldiers who died while prisoners of war also were buried there.[25]

Immediately following the war, Knoxvillians neglected what soon became known as Bethel Cemetery. The *Knoxville Whig* expressed its disgust at the condition of the graves. Of those who died at the fort, the newspaper reported in 1867, "the hogs are occasionally disinterring their bodies" and "sights are sometimes seen there which cause humanity to shudder and sicken." The *Whig* suggested that "some of the wealthy rebels of Knoxville" might take better care of the graves of "men who fought the battles of the slave lords of the South—who met death like heroes, though in a wicked cause."[26]

In the spring of the next year, the *Knoxville Daily Press and Herald*, a Democratic newspaper, hoped that the local LMA would find a way to take better care of the area's Confederate dead. The paper suggested that the Confederates could be moved to ground next to the National Cemetery so that "the dead might rest under one flag, acknowledging one country in whose cause the living might, if necessary, fight gallantly side by side as those dead soldiers once fought...."[27]

That proposal might have been acceptable three decades later, but in 1868 the wounds of war were too fresh to consider burying enemies in adjacent graveyards. Taking better care of the Confederate dead was another matter. A Knoxville businessman began advertising for information on any Confederate graves outside Bethel. That September, a group of men met to consider ways to assist the LMA in its fledgling efforts "to gather into a suitable cemetery, the Confederate dead of East Tennessee." These men included both Democrats and Republicans and former Confederate and Union officers, including the ever-present William Rule. In October, the Knoxville LMA took over the project. The stated objective was to fence and beautify the cemetery's grounds. The foundational purpose was to honor Confederate soldiers from the region who had no place in America's national cemeteries.[28]

6

Memorializing the Dead (1868–1898)

After Americans buried their war dead in separate cemeteries, they memorialized them each spring in separate ceremonies. In the North, Decoration Day, later known as Memorial Day, became a national holiday almost as revered as Independence Day. Southerners initiated individual Confederate Decoration Days in their own graveyards with a similar sense of veneration. While much of the South virtually ignored traditional Memorial Day services held in national cemeteries, East Tennesseans acknowledged both Northern and Southern commemorations. In Knoxville, where memorial services were held on separate days in the National Cemetery and in Bethel Cemetery, some veterans attended both ceremonies.

In 1868, former Union Major General John A. Logan, commander of the GAR and a Republican representing Illinois in Congress, formalized May 30 as the first national Decoration Day. He set aside the date exclusively to honor Union soldiers. At memorial services that spring, hundreds of thousands of loyal Americans spread flowers over Union graves in national cemeteries and private burial grounds.[1]

Residents of several Southern towns had begun decorating Confederate graves two years earlier—on various dates in the spring of 1866—and those towns today claim to have begun the Memorial Day tradition. Alternatively, some historians believe that formerly enslaved black South Carolinians and white Northern abolitionists held the first Memorial Day services even earlier. On May 1, 1865, residents of Charleston honored 257 dead Union soldiers who had been buried in a mass grave at a Confederate prison camp.[2]

There is no question about who held the first Decoration Day ceremony in Knoxville. Following General Logan's directive, Union veterans and more than three thousand civilians assembled in Knoxville National Cemetery on May 30, 1868. The Knoxville Brass Band; a company of the Fifth Cavalry; and citizens on foot and horseback and in carriages paraded the mile-long route from downtown to the cemetery. Area women, assisted by the dismounted cavalry, covered the graves with sprays of flowers and wreaths. The Rev. Thomas W. Humes, pastor of St. John's Episcopal Church, prayed for an end to malice and the beginning of reconciliation. The band played a dirge. Oliver P. Temple, then a judge of the Knoxville Chancery Court, presented a brief address, which was not reported.

The Democratic *Knoxville Press and Messenger* editorialized on the proceedings: "We were gratified to note among the spectators many of those who wore the gray, and we were no less gratified to hear an expression from a number of federal officers of both [political] parties, that they would gladly assist the friends of the Confederate soldiers in paying a similar tribute of respect to the graves of their dead. We are all one people and the animosities of the war must die out...."[3]

Former Confederates in Knoxville delayed initiating formal memorial services while they relocated the bodies of Confederate soldiers and brought order to the graveyard. The Knoxville LMA, with organizational and financial assistance from prominent men of the area, held the first Confederate Decoration Day ceremonies on June 10, 1870. Knoxville attorney H.T. Taylor presented the memorial address. The *Press and Herald* did not report Taylor's remarks but suggested that "the decorative ceremonies are happy auguries of a future, when our citizens shall mingle together ... cemented in the bonds of an everlasting brotherhood."[4]

The service drew nearly two thousand spectators, including veterans of both sides.

Reported the *Knoxville Chronicle*, a Republican newspaper: "There mingling together were the young and the aged, the ex-Confederate and his whilom antagonist of the Federal army, and fair women, those ministering angels of beauty and love, each animated by the same spirit—a testimonial on the shrine of valor."[5]

Memorial Day services in other parts of the country, especially during the first years after the war, were not always so conciliatory or reported with rhetoric as flowery as Knoxville's decorated graves. Former Union and Confederate soldiers did not customarily mingle. Many early Memorial Day ceremonies in the solidly Union or Confederate

6. Memorializing the Dead (1868–1898)

sections of the nation commemorated only the dead of their own side, in their own cemeteries, for their own reasons.

"We are met to-day ... to strew flowers upon and fittingly decorate the graves of those who died in defense of their country," said Henry L. Burnett, a former Union brigadier general, on Cincinnati's first Memorial Day in 1868. Veterans, soldiers in the regular army, and a large crowd gathered to hear Burnett and to beflower Union graves at Spring Grove Cemetery. Burnett clearly described the war as a "conflict between the idea that man should be free, against the idea that man should be enslaved."[6]

A few early Union ceremonies emphasized reconciliation. GAR Post 19 of Philadelphia issued a remarkable advance statement on decorating graves for Memorial Day, 1869: "Wishing to bury forever the harsh feelings engendered by the war, Post 19 has decided not to pass by the graves of the Confederates sleeping in our lines, but to divide each year between the blue and grey the first floral offerings of a common country. We have no powerless foes. Post 19 thinks of the Southern dead only as brave men."[7]

In Southern states, the federal Memorial Day atmosphere was very different. Arlington National Cemetery included one of those small Confederate sections where only enemy soldiers who had died in Federal custody were isolated. As visitors spread flowers on Union graves at Arlington on Memorial Day 1869, Union veterans stood guard to prevent anyone from decorating Confederate graves. After a woman tossed a small bouquet onto a Confederate grave, a Federal lieutenant quickly trampled the flowers. Then he brandished his bayonet and threatened anyone who objected.[8]

Shortly after that Memorial Day, the GAR released orders clearly stating its position on decorating graves. "We strew flowers on the graves of our comrades," the orders read, "and prevent them from being strewn in the national cemeteries at the same time on the graves of such rebel dead as may be buried therein, not because we cherish any feelings of hate or triumph over our individual foes, but because we seek to mark the distinction and manner the feelings with which the nation regards loyalty and treason."[9]

Many Southerners at first ignored the federal Memorial Day and shunned national cemeteries. They concentrated on their own burial grounds. "These are not the 'nation's dead,'" said a Virginian surveying Confederate graves at the University of Virginia in May 1866. "They are

Sons of East Tennessee

Mourners from Richmond, Virginia, gathered on Confederate Decoration Day in 1867 to decorate the graves of soldiers in Hollywood Cemetery. This wood engraving was made from a drawing by William Sheppard, a professional artist who had served with the Richmond Howitzers in the Army of Northern Virginia (Library of Congress).

'our dead.'" Extending that sentiment, some Confederate Decoration Day services in the first years after the war were bitterly anti–Union and anti–Reconstruction. Following the 1868 Decoration Day commemoration in Petersburg, Virginia, a local newspaper argued against celebrating Independence Day, fuming that "with the heel of the oppressor on our necks, we have no use for a day of rejoicing now; but rather a day of mourning and humiliation." A speaker at an 1869 Decoration Day service in Putnam County, Georgia, hoped for eventual vindication. He said, "Here let us look away from the gloom of political bondage and fix our vision upon a coming day of triumph, when principles, born of truth and baptized in the blood of our brothers, shall outlive the persecution of a merciless enemy and the treachery of unhallowed ambition."[10]

As Reconstruction brought more Union observers into the South, Confederates generally constrained their Decoration Day activities. Ex-Confederates in many Southern states were not permitted, on Decoration Day or at any other time, to wave Confederate flags, wear gray uniforms, carry weapons, march, or speak on behalf of the Confederate

6. Memorializing the Dead (1868–1898)

cause in public addresses. To act otherwise would have invited a charge of treason—not that veterans always obeyed these rules.[11]

As Reconstruction wound down, Northern officials relaxed these rules and Southern orators had more freedom to speak favorably of secession and to lament what quickly became known as the "Lost Cause." As early as the first Confederate Memorial Day in 1866, speakers began charging the South's loss primarily to the North's superior numbers. By the end of Reconstruction, defenders of the Confederate faith were holding forth on Northern aggression and Southern sacrifice in all parts of the former Confederacy.[12] Still, Memorial Day was always primarily a day of mourning, and that tended to tone down partisan rhetoric as the 1870s progressed.

Observance of the nation's centennial in 1875 and 1876 prompted Memorial Day speakers, North and South, to emphasize conciliatory themes. Paul Buck described a remarkable observance at Little Rock, Arkansas, in 1875. A joint Memorial Day service commemorated Confederate and Union veterans who lay in adjoining cemeteries. The speakers' platform extended over both cemeteries so that a Northerner could speak from the Confederate cemetery side and a Southerner from the Union cemetery side. At the end of the service, a Confederate veteran buried a hatchet in the Union cemetery and a Union veteran did the same in the Confederate.[13]

As time passed, leading spokesmen on both sides began placing less emphasis on who was right or wrong while focusing on respect for soldiers of any stripe. Most veterans—including certainly the career soldier Reuben Bernard and, probably to a lesser extent, the wartime surgeon William McCorkle—understood that their military service set them apart from civilians. Veterans often included battlefield enemies as well as comrades in this special group. Many Memorial Day orators celebrated this fraternity of warriors.

On Memorial Day 1874, the Rev. Cyrus Augustus Bartol presented a sermon entitled "The Soldier's Motive" to a local camp of the GAR at Boston's West Church. Bartol praised a soldier's devotion to duty and unquestioning obedience, no matter what the cause. This blind faith, he said, "is the all-surpassing reason for our approval and love." Oliver Wendell Holmes, Jr., a Union veteran who had been wounded three times, repeatedly refined this proposition over the next two decades. The future Supreme Court justice entitled his Memorial Day address at Harvard University in 1895, "The Soldier's Faith." He said: "The faith is true and adorable which leads a soldier to throw away his life in obedience to a blindly accepted duty, in a cause which he little understands, in a plan of a campaign of which he ... does not see the use."[14] This argument seemed to assign all who wore a uniform of any color to a dedicated brotherhood of automatons.

Whether the soldiers buried in Knoxville's divided cemeteries died out of blind devotion to duty or passionate devotion to a cause, veterans and residents marched by the thousands each spring to memorialize them. In the nineteenth century, Memorial Day ordinarily was honored on May 30 as a federal holiday. Confederate Decoration Day, as it was called until the 1890s when it became Confederate Memorial Day, was held on a variety of dates—from early June in the 1870s to mid–May in the 1890s. In some states, Confederate Decoration Day was a state holiday; in Tennessee, it was a day designated for local observance.

Memorial Day orations in Knoxville National Cemetery, with few exceptions, emphasized two points: the bravery soldiers displayed in preserving the union and the desirability of veteran reconciliation. T.A.R. Nelson, a United States congressman who represented Knoxville as the war began and remained loyal to the Union, went farther. He praised his adversaries on Memorial Day, 1869, maintaining that their tenacious defense of the Confederacy elevated the stature of the Union soldiers who defeated them. "They were brave men who fought against us," he said, "and these soldiers around me here I think will agree that in honoring the Confederate dead we honor the living Union soldier. They were bone of our bone, and a victory over them was a victory indeed. We should honor their graves as well as those of our own dead."[15]

In May 1873, the commanding officer of the 79th New York Regiment wrote to William Rule during his first turn as mayor asking him to decorate the graves of comrades who had died in the defense of Fort Sanders. Rule reported in his 1900 history of Knoxville that this request "was handsomely complied with" during ceremonies following the grand Memorial Day parade to the national cemetery.[16]

More than flowers decorated graves in the national cemetery the next spring. According to a legend supported by related facts, Knoxville resident Laura Caitlin Richardson began the nationwide custom of placing American flags at each grave on Memorial Day. In charge of decorating the cemetery on June 2, 1874, Richardson apparently was disappointed by the flower selection. In a downtown Knoxville store, she found some bulk rolls of fabric printed with American flags, cut them

6. Memorializing the Dead (1868–1898)

Wood engraving depicts orphans decorating their fathers' graves with American flags in Philadelphia's Glenwood Cemetery on Decoration Day 1876. According to a Knoxville story, the flag custom began in 1874 in Knoxville National Cemetery (Library of Congress).

out, and attached them to 3,500 small sticks. Then she and other volunteers from the GAR's women's auxiliary planted a flag at each grave.[17]

Andrew Johnson spoke among those miniature flags on Memorial Day. The June 3 *Press and Messenger* reported that the former president's message was "pertinent" and "eloquent," but provided no specifics. Johnson, living in Greeneville and running for a seat in the U.S. Senate, had remained in Knoxville that evening to promote his candidacy. New York editors then in town wined and dined him. One editor enthusiastically endorsed Johnson, who would win that autumn's election but die the next summer. "Daniel Webster, the expounder of the Constitution," the editor proclaimed, "and Andrew Johnson, the defender of the Constitution." The president whom Republicans had impeached for defying Congress and who had opposed the Fourteenth Amendment to the Constitution and all civil rights for freed slaves must have gratefully received the accolade.

Knoxvillians remembered that Decoration Day for an incident that apparently caused a far greater sensation than Johnson's speech or the novelty flags. As had been the custom for several years, thirty-seven young girls, representing the nation's thirty-seven states, were packed into a vehicle and returning to town following the ceremonies. They began singing, with enthusiasm, the lyrics of "We'll hang Jeff Davis from a sour apple tree" to the tune of "The Battle Hymn of the Republic." This did not please Confederate veterans.

A writer who signed himself "Ex-Reb" told readers of the *Press and Herald* that it was "exceedingly unfortunate that the managers of the Decoration exercises could not have adopted a programme that would have been devoid of insult to the rebel element of this community." The writer concluded that such scenes might be avoided by moving the Confederate dead into the national cemetery and commemorating all soldiers in one place. "Union Soldier" then wrote a letter to agree that a common burial ground would result in "cultivation of a kindlier and better feeling among a people so essentially one in blood, interest and destiny." This was not a universal attitude, as a third writer, who signed himself only "Union," made clear in the *Knoxville Weekly Chronicle* several days later. "Union" suggested that harmony could not be achieved until "rebel music and rebel oratory be suppressed also."[18]

On Memorial Day, 1875, Xen. Wheeler, a U.S. district attorney from Chattanooga and a Union veteran, told a cemetery crowd that if the

Andrew Johnson served as wartime governor of Tennessee until he became vice president and then president of the United States upon Abraham Lincoln's assassination. Johnson, who lived in nearby Greeneville, spoke at Knoxville National Cemetery's Decoration Day service in 1874 (Brady-Handy Collection, Library of Congress).

6. Memorializing the Dead (1868–1898)

purpose of the annual memorial services in the national cemetery were to revive hatred of the former enemy, then they should be discontinued. "We have assembled to discuss none of the questions that divided our people from 1861 to 1865," he maintained. "Those questions have been forever settled, and have passed into history."[19] Most orators from the mid–1870s through the 1890s similarly proclaimed that old disagreements had all but disappeared and reconciliation was at hand. Veterans in East Tennessee and, to a lesser extent, throughout the nation marched between cemeteries, decorating both Union and Confederate graves.

On Memorial Day 1886, members of Knoxville's UCV post presented an "American Eagle" flower arrangement to representatives of the GAR gathered in the national cemetery. Speaking from a rostrum designed specifically for Memorial Day ceremonies, GAR member Washington Ledgerwood maintained that "the most kindly and patriotic feelings now exist" between former enemies. He predicted that "if an invader would insult that flag of the two united armies now, the boys of the gray and the boys of the blue would be found side by side defending that old flag and the proud bird of the mountain."[20]

Still, some Memorial Day speakers refused to embrace their former foes. In 1889, J.C. Burrows, a former Union officer and a congressional Republican then representing Kalamazoo, Michigan, discussed his role in capturing Knoxville in 1863. He commended the bravery of the soldiers and their officers who preserved the union. He acknowledged that the nation had been reunited since the war, but he said he still had no respect for secessionists. "I acknowledge allegiance to my State," he said, "but if Michigan should strike a blow at the Union I would rise to strike her as I would a foreign foe."[21]

Speakers more rarely mentioned the war's role in ending slavery. One of the few who did, Dr. Thomas C. Warner, pastor of First United Methodist Church and a Union veteran, presented an impassioned address to an estimated crowd of 10,000 people crammed into Knoxville National Cemetery in 1892. He praised the Union soldiers who died fighting to end the evils of slavery and secession. He also acknowledged that he respected ex-Confederates who had come to "rejoice that the confederacy proved a failure." But then he condemned "that blindness that will not see, that persistency in error which still maintains that the cause so surely lost was the cause of justice...."[22]

At the cemetery's Memorial Day observance in May 1896, GAR member Isaac Ziegler praised the suffering and heroism of Union soldiers buried in the graveyard. He reminded a large crowd that those soldiers had died to produce "the freedom day of a race, emancipated from bondage, and of a nation redeemed from iniquity." He said this, apparently without irony, less than two weeks after the U.S. Supreme Court upheld the constitutionality of racial segregation in *Plessy v. Ferguson*. In a speech more conciliatory to former Confederates, Tennessee congressman Allen S. Tate said that "these patriots died that this might be one country, that these men of the south might be our brothers, and that we might remain one people and one flag...." Tate also said he had no doubt that Southerners and Northerners alike would defend that flag against any enemy.[23]

Reports of Memorial Day activities in Knoxville in 1898 yielded their customary position on the front page of the *Knoxville Tribune*. The more important news was that eight regiments had been ordered to move from their training grounds at Chattanooga to Tampa, Florida, on their way to fight the Spanish in Cuba. Memorial Day services in Chattanooga itself were upstaged on that same front page by ceremonies attending the burial of two soldiers of the Fifth Illinois Regiment who had died in Chattanooga's training camp. "Ladies, who had come to decorate the graves of the heroes of 1861–'64 [*sic*]," reported the *Tribune*, "then fairly covered with flowers and evergreens the graves of these young heroes in a cause, which removes all sectionalism from the federal cemetery and makes it now a national cemetery indeed."[24]

The addition of soldiers from Illinois expanded burials in Chattanooga National Cemetery to American veterans from all sections of the country, but it did nothing to end isolation of the Confederate dead. The expansion of national cemeteries in the late nineteenth century from almost purely Union burial grounds to cemeteries that would take any U.S. soldier who died after the war, including indigent veterans, did not include Confederates. "This evolution bypassed Confederate soldiers," wrote John Neff. "Their sons, some of whom went off to fight in the Spanish-American War, were eligible for burial. But for at least thirty-five years, no Confederate soldier who died while under arms resisting Federal authority was ever buried in a national cemetery."[25]

Compared with the spirited commemorations of Memorial Day in Knoxville National Cemetery, Confederate mourners on their separate grounds in Bethel Cemetery held considerably more sedate services throughout the late nineteenth century. Confederate Decoration Days were always more lightly attended than Memorial Day ceremonies in the

6. Memorializing the Dead (1868–1898)

national cemetery. No one paraded out to Bethel Avenue. Musical presentations were muted. For Confederate veterans and their allies, Decoration Day remained primarily a day of mourning the dead by placing flowers on graves. Most speakers paid subdued respect to the men buried there.

Knoxville attorney and former Confederate Captain George Washington in May 1871 praised Confederate ideals and battle prowess and lamented the loss of so many young soldiers. But he also recommended that Confederate veterans honor the Union dead. He said, "Let us in the true spirit of Christian charity and loving kindness concede to our fallen brothers that they were animated by convictions as strong, if possible, as our own."[26]

Some speakers qualified their remarks. The Rev. E.E. Hoss, the young pastor of Knoxville's Church Street Methodist Episcopal Church, South, addressed an audience assembled in Bethel's grove on May 15, 1872. He explained that he would "say nothing of the justice of the cause in which [the dead soldiers] were engaged. Mayhap had I been of years, I would have differed from them." But he added that he awaited the day when "a whole nation, re-united in fraternal esteem, shall give honor alike to those who fell upholding the Bonnie Blue Flag, and to those whose lives were surrendered battling for the Star Spangled Banner."[27]

On May 25, 1886, five hundred people, including Confederate veterans and GAR representatives, gathered at Bethel to hear the Rev. David D. Sullins, president of Centenary Female College in Cleveland, Tennessee, and a former Confederate chaplain, say he did not want to stir up old embers. "We come not to commemorate strife," he explained, "but memories of those here in response to one of the noblest calls of humanity, never intending to detract from the honor of the boys who stood in our front."[28]

All the words in the world probably meant less to the veterans involved than a quiet incident that occurred on Confederate Decoration Day in 1893. The Rev. James Park, pastor of Knoxville's First Presbyterian Church, had presented a fairly typical Decoration Day address. He had said that peace had prevailed and "today 'the gray and the blue' soldiers of the south and soldiers of the north ... mingle in all the walks of social and business life."[29]

Veterans of both armies remained to talk in the cemetery following the service. Most focused their attention on Augustus G. Weissert, national commander of the GAR, who had traveled to Knoxville from his home in Milwaukee. Former Confederate Major J.W.S. Frierson, a Knoxville business leader and rising president of the Fred Ault Bivouac of the UCV, approached Weissert, removed his Confederate "badge," and presented it to the visitor. Smiling at his former foe, Frierson warned Weissert that he could not wear the badge, but he hoped he would keep it as a souvenir. Weissert accepted the gift and, in exchange, presented Frierson with the GAR button from the lapel of his coat. Concluded the *Knoxville Tribune*: "Surely the war is over."[30]

In May of 1898, the LMA spread wreaths and flowers throughout the cemetery, and the GAR contributed a floral wreath in the design of a U.S. flag. S.F. Wilson, a Tennessee Supreme Court justice who gave the Confederate Memorial Day address, had lost an arm in battle, so he spoke with authority of the sacrifices Southern soldiers had made. He maintained that the cause of the South was right and the principles for which Confederates had fought had been preserved. Much of the crowd no doubt approved. Then he spoke of soldiers of the North and South marching together against Spain and winning the first naval battle of the war. The assembly applauded with enthusiasm.[31] General John Wilder no doubt received a similar reception when, a few days later in the national cemetery, he commended the Northerners and Southerners "marching in a solid phalanx" against Spain. So did countless other speakers in Northern and Southern cemeteries on Memorial Day 1898, when they addressed a war that many expected would permanently reunite Americans.

7

Monuments to the Dead, Reunions for the Living (1868–1898)

As East Tennesseans reburied and memorialized their war dead, relations among the living began to stabilize. Violence related to wartime animosity was rare by the late 1860s. Most Knoxville businessmen who had fought on opposite sides decided, sometimes grudgingly, that the need to rebuild the region's economy should take precedence over old disputes. Commerce, manufacturing, and transportation did revive, and the town flourished. A visitor from Virginia was so impressed by the region in 1869 that he called Knoxville "perhaps the widest awake and livelist [sic] town of its population, not only in Tennessee, but in the Southern States."[1]

Veterans began to congregate, reminisce, and carouse in separate Union or Confederate groups. Both opened lodges on Knoxville's Market Square in the late 1860s. The city's GAR veterans and a Confederate group known as the Felix Zollicoffer brigade (after a brigadier general who had been killed commanding forces in East Tennessee early in the war) held meetings in second-floor halls within shouting (and shooting) distance. Members of these rival lodges must have engaged in some lively conversations as they passed on the street.[2]

Veterans gathered in partisan lodges throughout the reunited nation, but everyone did not join the reunion. Some veterans, trying to forget the most traumatic years of their lives, eagerly got on with business. There is no indication that Reuben Bernard or William McCorkle joined veterans' organizations. They were busy soldiering and doctoring.

As for fraternizing with the former enemy, results were mixed. Some friends who had opposed each other during the war renewed their ties. Some veterans remained bitter and despised the other side for the rest of their lives. Tension between these attitudes never fully dissipated, but it did relax somewhat as men adjusted to living in a re-United States. "What veterans felt about past enemies was indeed diverse," wrote M. Keith Harris, "but the plain fact of reunion impelled veterans to edge toward some kind of conciliatory message."[3]

In East Tennessee, a significant early impediment to reunion was the struggle for political control. During the latter decades of the nineteenth century, a number of ardent Unionists made East Tennessee the most Republican region in the South. These men included Tennessee governor and newspaper editor William Brownlow; former Ohioan and Union Brigadier General John T. Wilder; and Republican Party boss L.C. Houk, a former Union colonel from Blount County. The political imbalance fostered resentment among East Tennessee Democrats, many of whom had been Confederates.[4]

Although he eventually embraced some conservative Democrats and former Confederates, Brownlow was particularly polarizing. After complaining bitterly about the "rebels in our midst" at the end of the war, he supported driving "traitors" out of the state.[5] Then he enthusiastically promoted civil-rights legislation, which Democrats and some conservative Republicans just as enthusiastically opposed.

Brownlow left the governor's office to serve in the U.S. Senate. He returned to Knoxville a very sick man. Before he died in April 1877, Brownlow supported Republican Rutherford B. Hayes in the election of 1876 with his old, unyielding thunder. If Hayes were not elected, Brownlow said, all that had been accomplished by Reconstruction would be lost. Former Confederates, he complained, were "deaf to the lessons of the terrible past." They were "determined to carry out their purposes, and render their past treason respectable."[6]

Hayes' calculated decision to end Reconstruction and virtually abandon the Republican Party's support for civil rights discouraged the dying Brownlow. Five months after Brownlow died, the newly elected president visited Tennessee on his so-called Southern Reconciliation Tour. In a speech at Knoxville on September 21, 1877, Hayes urged sectional reunification. "As I demand respect from the man fighting against me, for my convictions," said the former Union brigadier, "I yield the same measure of respect to him who fought for his convictions."[7] By contrast, Brownlow rarely had yielded ground to the opposition.

On the other side, outspoken Knoxville physician and historian

7. Monuments to the Dead, Reunions for the Living (1868–1898)

J.G.M. Ramsey remained an unreconstructed Confederate and a Democrat until he died in 1884. Ramsey, who had served as a Confederate treasury agent and field surgeon, blamed Brownlow for hiring an arsonist to torch his home after Union soldiers occupied Knoxville in 1863. Writing to a correspondent in 1870, Ramsey explained, in irrational denial, that he had suffered losses "in a righteous cause though not a *lost cause*. Our rebellion was a success—is a success in that it has disintegrated the union forever and forever."[8]

Despite these opposing views by old warhorses, Oliver Temple in his 1899 regional history of the war placed primary blame for continuing partisan friction not on Brownlow and Ramsey but on younger men. "It was not the Confederate or Federal soldiers who kept alive the smouldering embers of the late unfortunate civil war," he wrote, "but ambitious politicians who had for the most part grown up since the war." The *New York Tribune* had said much the same thing about the entire country a quarter of a century earlier, observing that "the bulk of the people of this country North and South do not hate each other, and it is a wretched piece of dishonesty on the part of the politicians whose trade is loyalty to make them believe they do."[9] By the mid-1870s, as Reconstruction was nearing its end, many of the nation's leaders had begun emphasizing reunion, or at least a willingness to acknowledge the other side's point of view.

Civil War officers did the same while describing the war's battles in print. The *Century* magazine published articles by both Union and Confederate officers, turning their work into book form in 1887 as *Battles and Leaders of the Civil War*. The *National Tribune*, published monthly by the GAR, provided primarily Union veterans' commentary on the war. Meanwhile, *Century*, *McClure's*, and other popular magazines published fiction by Joel Chandler Harris, Thomas Nelson Page, and other writers that frequently emphasized the reunion of former enemies. These writings, along with personal memoirs and other publications, provided a basic set of facts, opinions, and emotions that helped to determine how veterans and Americans in general viewed the war. As time passed, the themes of mutual respect and reconciliation gained momentum with writers, veterans, and the public at large. Many veterans from Boston to Birmingham made peace with the past, even while those determined to defend their rightness and even righteousness never stopped advocating for their cause.

Almost all white veterans, South and North, eventually did agree

This illustration accompanied the final installment of Joel Chandler Harris's story, "Azalia." in the October 1887 issue of *Century* magazine. It shows Confederate and Union soldiers lying arm in arm on a battlefield. The Confederate died while providing water to the dying Union soldier. The enslaved man found his owner with canteen in hand. Such stories supported veteran reconciliation (author's collection).

on one point: while emphasizing shared white heroism, they excluded blacks from the reconciliation process. Individual Confederate veterans organizations, as well as the UCV after it formed in 1889, refused to accept black members. The GAR, founded nationally in 1866, accepted but did not always welcome blacks. Some GAR posts were integrated,

7. Monuments to the Dead, Reunions for the Living (1868–1898)

others segregated. In the northern counties of East Tennessee, both integrated and all-black posts operated in Knoxville, Sevierville, Maryville, and other communities.[10]

Veterans marched in step with the larger society's views on race. "In the half century after the war, as the sections reconciled, by and large, the races divided," explained David Blight. In the wake of Reconstruction, many Northerners tolerated or even approved of the South's renewed racial oppression, including widespread lynchings, mass murders, black codes, and later Jim Crow laws that legalized racial segregation and marginalized black Americans. By the end of the century, most writings about the war, as well as speeches at commemorative gatherings, virtually ignored discussion of slavery and continuing suppression of civil rights. Reconciliation among white veterans could not have proceeded without the North's concession on that issue.[11]

Meanwhile, many in the North began reconsidering the heritage of white Southerners. East Tennesseans were central to that process. As Nina Silber explained, "The 1890s cult of Anglo-Saxonism encouraged northerners to reevaluate all southern people in a more approving light.... In the eyes of many northern observers, the white mountaineers held the key to the North's reconciliation with the South." High among newly discovered virtues of a people once derided for backwardness, according to the emergent opinion, was the mountaineers' relative isolation from black Americans. "Like many northern whites, the mountaineers did not understand the workings of race relations or the features of slavery," Silber explained. "Their ignorance was viewed as a wholesome attribute which enhanced their patriotism as well as their racial purity."[12]

White veterans followed various paths to reunion. They met at dedications of monuments erected on battlefields, in town centers, and in cemeteries, and they held reunions all over the country. At first, these gatherings were entirely blue or entirely gray. All Confederate armies had not yet surrendered when Federal soldiers assembled to erect the first permanent war monuments on the two battlefields at Manassas, Virginia, in the late spring of 1865. Union officers, enlisted soldiers, and hundreds of civilians gathered to praise the valor of the men in blue who had fallen on those fields. Observed the *New York Times*, "In no better way can the deaths of the hundreds of nameless dead, who fell in defense of our liberties, be kept green in the memories of future generations."[13]

Union veterans turned out in force when the Gettysburg National Cemetery Association dedicated the nation's first major Civil War memorial on July 1, 1869, the sixth anniversary of the first day of the battle whose casualties filled the cemetery. The Soldiers' National Monument, designed as a memorial to the battle and the Union soldiers who fought it, remains the dominant structure in the cemetery. Indiana Governor Oliver P. Morton crafted his ardent dedicatory speech not only for veterans but for thousands in his audience whom he knew had supported the Union cause. He did not aim to heal Southern wounds. "Slavery lies buried in the tomb of the rebellion," he maintained. "The rebellion, the offspring of slavery, hath murdered its unnatural parent, and the perfect reign of liberty is at hand."[14]

With the exception of several battlefield markers erected by Union regiments at Gettysburg and on other fields of battle in the 1870s and 1880s, veterans created few war memorials until individual states erected major battlefield monuments at Chickamauga and Chattanooga, Gettysburg, and other national military parks in the 1890s. Meanwhile, scores of monuments, often created by choosing various style elements from suppliers' catalogs, appeared in town squares and on courthouse lawns throughout the North. Audiences at the unveiling of these monuments, almost solely Northerners, heard denunciations of the Confederacy, as well as calls for reunification.

While federal officials discouraged the building of Confederate battlefield monuments until the latter years of the nineteenth century, women led the way in erecting modest memorials in Southern cemeteries. Romney, West Virginia, claims to have erected the first Confederate cemetery monument in 1867. Hollywood Cemetery's monument in Richmond dates to 1869, and Raleigh, North Carolina, erected a cemetery obelisk in 1870. The Danville, Virginia, LMA unveiled its monument in September 1878 in the town's primary cemetery, Green Hill, adjacent to hundreds of Union graves in Danville National Cemetery. One side of the monument described its purpose as a "Memorial Tribute of Virginia's Daughters to the Fallen Brave." Another side emphasized the soldiers' dedication to the Confederate cause: "Know that these fell in the effort to establish just government and perpetuate constitutional liberty. Who thus die will live in lofty example."[15]

Almost all of these early Confederate monuments—from the late 1860s through the 1880s—were erected in cemeteries with the primary purpose of mourning and commending the bravery of the Confederate dead and commemorating the cause for which they fought. That cause

7. Monuments to the Dead, Reunions for the Living (1868–1898)

invariably was presented as an attempt to preserve states' rights under the Constitution.

Beginning about 1890, Confederate monuments more forthrightly presented themselves as more than memorials to the dead. With the huge bronze tribute to Robert E. Lee leading the way on Richmond's Monument Avenue, more elaborate monuments appeared outside cemeteries— along boulevards, in town squares, on courthouse lawns, and on college campuses. Speakers at the dedications of these monuments, often featuring over-sized sculptures of Confederate military leaders on horseback, focused on praising the Lost Cause and justifying the rebellion. Few Union veterans living in the South attended the dedication of Confederate monuments, in cemeteries or elsewhere. Many black Southerners viewed these more ostentatious displays as assertions of white supremacy.[16]

The situation in East Tennessee was entirely different from most places, South or North, or elsewhere in Tennessee. Memorials of any kind were late to arrive. Former Union and Confederate veterans often attended dedication services together.

The Confederate monument in Knoxville's Bethel Cemetery, dedicated on Confederate Memorial Day 1892, was the first major memorial in upper East Tennessee. A Confederate soldier, facing north, tops the 48-foot-tall marble monument (photograph by Paul James, Knoxville History Project).

Sons of East Tennessee

The first major cemetery memorial and the first significant monument of any kind in the northern counties of East Tennessee was dedicated on Confederate Memorial Day, May 19, 1892, in East Knoxville. Thousands of Knoxvillians, including Confederate and Union veterans, assembled in Bethel Cemetery to see the second largest Confederate memorial in the state, after the Mt. Olivet memorial in Nashville. The LMA of Knoxville had first proposed building a memorial to the Confederate dead in 1867, but it took a quarter of a century for the women to raise $5,000 to complete the work. Much of that money came from Union as well as Confederate veterans.[17]

The LMA proudly unveiled a forty-eight-foot-tall shaft of Tennessee gray marble topped by a statue of a stalwart Confederate soldier, firearm in hand, facing north. In what almost certainly was not an intentional gesture of reconciliation, a local soldier who had fought for the Union modeled for the sculpture. At the base of the shaft, a stone cutter engraved poetry commending the "heroic courage and the unshaken Constancy" of the dead. The names of the cemetery's sixteen hundred soldiers, most buried in unmarked graves, are engraved on separate stone slabs. Few individual gravestones dot the cemetery.[18]

Former Confederate General Edmund Kirby Smith, then a professor at the University of the South at Sewanee, Tennessee, led a parade through the city to the cemetery north of town. The crowd listened to speeches both combative and conciliatory. U.S. Senator William Bate, a former Confederate major general and Tennessee governor from Nashville, delivered the primary address—a rousing defense of the Confederacy. He defended the institution of slavery, and praised the patriotism and heroism of soldiers who had defended the right of seceding states to "preserve the Constitution and thereby save the Union." Bate's intransigence represented a departure from generally conciliatory Confederate Decoration Day addresses in Knoxville: on secession, in particular, it reflected thinking in the rest of the state more than in East Tennessee.[19]

In 1896, members of the GAR and their supporters paraded through town before laying the cornerstone of what five years later would become the sixty-foot-tall Union Soldiers Monument in Knoxville National Cemetery. The memorial was intentionally taller than the monument in Bethel Cemetery. Significantly, the Knoxville monument, fashioned to look like a segment of an ornate castle, was designated as Tennessee's state memorial to Union soldiers.

Again, both Union and Confederate veterans attended the

7. Monuments to the Dead, Reunions for the Living (1868–1898)

The Union Soldiers Monument dominates Knoxville National Cemetery. The cemetery began burying Union soldiers before the war ended, but the cornerstone for the sixty-foot-tall monument was not laid until 1896. It is Tennessee's state memorial to Union soldiers (photograph by Christine Brubaker).

ceremony. One of the speakers, former Union officer William Rule, discussed the difficulty many mountain men faced in deciding which side to support in 1861. Most, he said, "chose to remain in the Union ... and sealed their devotion to the cause they espoused, with their blood and their lives." He contended that if the Union Army had won the First

Sons of East Tennessee

Battle of Manassas, East Tennessee would have joined West Virginia as a separate state loyal to the union.[20] What were largely partisan events, even with Confederates in attendance, encouraged such speculation.

Just as the first battlefield and cemetery memorials honored the dead of one side or the other, the first veteran reunions were all for the blue or the gray. These initial reunions gathered comrades who had fought together in regiments, corps, or entire armies. Northern veterans gathered to congratulate themselves for preserving the union and, less often, for ending slavery. Confederates commemorated a crusade for the right of secession that had yielded only to what surrendering General Robert E. Lee had termed "overwhelming numbers and resources." But as the nation relaxed its most restrictive Reconstruction measures and passions cooled, white veterans of both sides, in limited numbers, began holding joint reunions. At least for a few days during these affairs, they tried to reconcile, or at least ignore, old differences. Southerners seeking to improve their economy with Northern aid and Northern veterans returning to Southern battlefields as tourists helped spur these joint gatherings.[21]

The first major reunions drawing substantial numbers of both Union and Confederate veterans were held during the nation's centennial celebration in 1875 and 1876. At the anniversary of the battle of Bunker Hill in April 1875, veterans from Northern and Southern states sang nostalgic songs, including "Dixie," which mingled with "shouts of a reunited and heartily reconciled people," according to the *New York Tribune*. In 1876, a Chattanooga newspaper said a bicentennial reunion of veterans from both sides proved that "Chattanooga knows no North, no South, no East, no West," but only "one indivisible country." The following year, veterans from both sides also attended Chattanooga's Union and Confederate Memorial Day services.[22]

Blue-gray reunions grew in popularity in the 1880s and by the 1890s had become the primary events where veterans could reminisce about and even celebrate their war experiences. As historian James Alan Marten has observed, most veterans by then thought of themselves as a special class of Americans who "recalled their service proudly and rarely expressed regrets at having followed the flag of either side into battle."[23]

Tennessee's GAR members began holding annual encampments in 1885. They invited Confederate veterans to the third encampment, at Knoxville, in the spring of 1887. Reconciliation was the theme. Knoxville attorney and former Confederate Captain H.H. Taylor maintained that

7. Monuments to the Dead, Reunions for the Living (1868–1898)

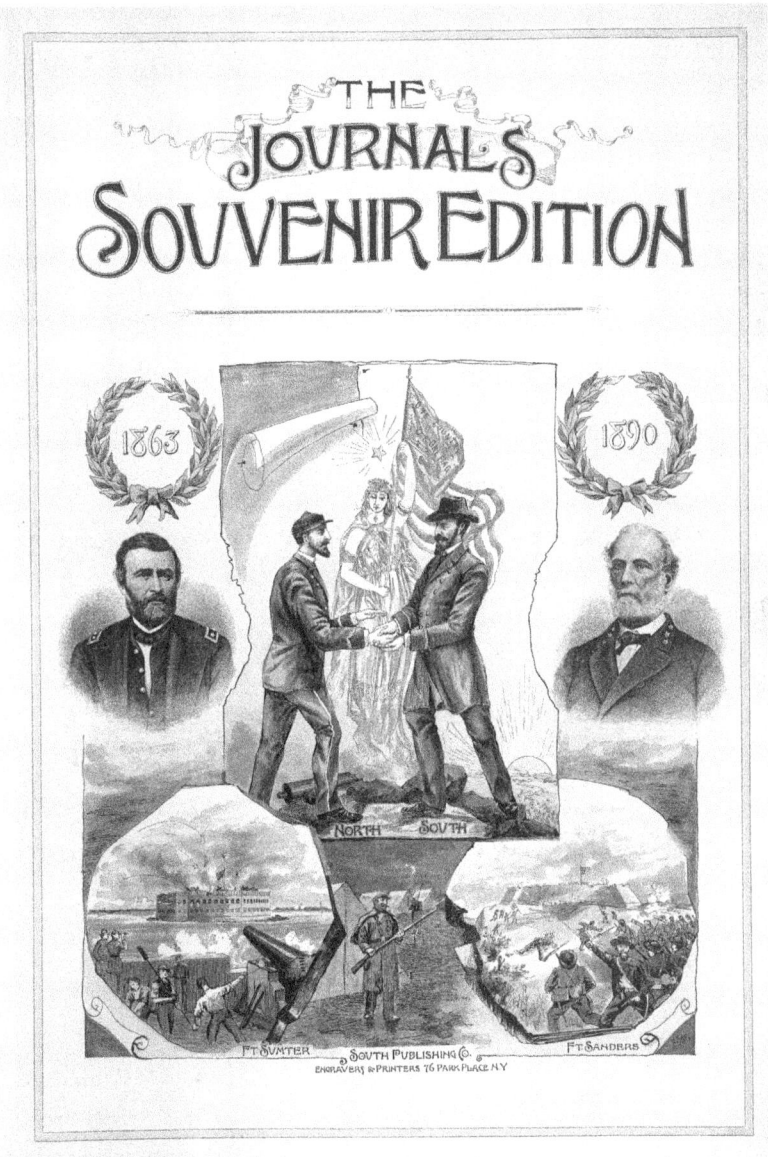

The *Knoxville Journal* published a souvenir edition on October 7, 1890, for that autumn's Blue-Gray Reunion. The cover's centerpiece depicts Union and Confederate soldiers warmly greeting each other (Thompson Photograph Collection, McClung Historical Collection, Knox County Public Library).

Sons of East Tennessee

"all the scars of sectional strife" had healed and that "we meet as friends and citizens of a common country." Former state GAR leader Edwin E. Winters responded in kind. The GAR's purpose, he said, was not to maintain "the prejudices and animosities of the war, but to heal the scars and promote the peace of the common country."[24]

Knoxville staged one of the nation's first and largest blue-gray reunions over three sunny days in early October 1890. Organizers invited all Union and Confederate veterans of the Knoxville siege and battle of Fort Sanders. Hundreds of veterans marched in a parade. Ten thousand citizens cheered. The veterans toured what was left of the fort, which had been altered substantially by development in an expanding city. Veterans of the Seventy-ninth New York Highlanders, who had defended the fort in 1863, visited the graves of their comrades in the

Thousands of residents lined the streets of downtown Knoxville on October 8, 1890. They waited for hundreds of Union and Confederate veterans to stage a parade during one of the first and largest blue-gray reunions in the country. Cars on the street railway system continued operating until the parade began (McClung Historical Collection, Knox County Public Library).

7. Monuments to the Dead, Reunions for the Living (1868–1898)

national cemetery. Then everyone enjoyed a huge fireworks display over the fort's remains.

Lieutenant General James Longstreet, whose Confederate troops had failed to breach Fort Sanders' walls in 1863, joined the reunionists. "No effort was made to keep him out this time," observed the *Knoxville Journal*. The Highlanders made the general an honorary member of the regiment.[25]

The *Knoxville Tribune* welcomed the reunionists to the city, noting that they "will talk and laugh over the scenes of the war, which ended twenty-five years ago with no more bitterness in their hearts than men who laugh over their school-boy fights and pranks. The ex-soldier of either side who carries bitterness in his heart today was a very poor soldier in 1863. The brave soldiers have already forgiven each other." Joshua Caldwell, a young Knoxville lawyer who had been a child during the war,

This expansive photograph was taken during the Blue-Gray Reunion of October 1890 from the University of Tennessee campus looking toward the old Fort Sanders battlefield. The so-called "Monster Tent," upper left, could seat fifteen thousand people (Thompson Photography Collection, McClung Historical Collection, Knox County Public Library).

expressed his opinion of the significance of the occasion in a speech at the fort. "We have met to remember and to forget," he said. "To remember the heroic deeds and the mighty works of the past, and that we are reunited, and to forget all else." He also said something that must have surprised those in his audience who believed a primary purpose of the war had been to kill as many soldiers as possible on the other side. "After all we were never enemies," he insisted. "We were of one race. We were one in history and in hope."[26]

Members of the Baker family of Hawkins County joined the reunionists. Of nine related men named Baker who attended, eight had served in the Union Army and one had been a Confederate soldier. The Bakers must have made an impression as they strode through the crowd: they reportedly averaged six feet in height and three hundred pounds in weight.[27]

Five years after the big reunion, in mid–September 1895, Knoxville staged an "encampment week" for veterans who came from a gathering in Louisville, Kentucky, and continued south to help dedicate the Chickamauga and Chattanooga Military Park on the Tennessee-Georgia border. The Sons of Union Veterans organized this reunion, which featured fireworks and decorated businesses on Knoxville's Gay Street. Union and Confederate veterans again paraded through the city they had struggled to control more than three decades earlier.

Two natives of Ireland rode together in a carriage. The *Knoxville Journal* reported that John Leahy had served with the Union and Michael Culliny with the Confederacy "on many a contested field. They stood up in the carriage with hands grasped and above them the flag of a united country. Woe would have been to the man who should have spat upon that flag."[28]

The veterans moved on to the Chickamauga battlefield where U.S. Brigadier General J.S. Fulerton, chairman of the Military Park Commission, explained that the dedication of the park "marks the beginning of a regenerated national life…. Now survivors of both sides harmoniously and lovingly come together to fix their battle lines and mark the places now and forever to remain famous as monuments to the valor of the American soldier."[29]

Of the many governors, North and South, who addressed the dedicatory audience, Tennessee's Peter Turney, a former Confederate colonel, was more conciliatory than most, perhaps because his state hosted the ceremonies. He concluded that the South's cause had been just but

7. Monuments to the Dead, Reunions for the Living (1868–1898)

added quickly that the two sides had met "not to shake hands over a bloody chasm, but to bury that chasm out of sight and march to the music of the Union."

Despite the overall tone of reconciliation, speakers disagreed over the issues of slavery and secession throughout the three-day dedication. Illinois Governor John P. Atgeld, too young to have served in the war, argued that Confederates wrongly fought for and failed to preserve "the perpetuation of human slavery." Alabama Governor and former Confederate Colonel William C. Oates countered by defending the constitutional legality of slavery. He said Confederates "fought for the right of our States to regulate and govern our own affairs, free from the dictates of others...."[30]

Nashville staged the next major event in the state to mark the one-hundredth anniversary of Tennessee statehood. The Tennessee Exposition—from May through October 1897—portrayed the old South in a nostalgic glow while boosting the state's industrial progress; but it also showed off contemporary military might. The program featured young soldiers and their weapons in mock battles and military encampments. They proudly carried American flags, which the American Flag Association promoted that year as the object of a new nationwide holiday—Flag Day.

On "Confederate Veterans' Day," June 24, the exposition focused on older warriors who wore gray uniforms. The event featured a massive parade, the singing of "Dixie," and the shouting of the "rebel yell." Thousands of former Confederates, including more than two dozen generals, gathered to honor the valor of those who had fought for the Confederacy. But the exposition's *Official History* emphasized that these Southern soldiers "cheered two flags" and "were ready now to fight under the stars and stripes with the same devotion and courage they displayed when fighting under the stars and bars."[31]

That reference was specific to the Spanish-American War. The *Official History* was not published until the spring of 1898, as the war began. So, although everyone did not agree on the sources of provocation or fully accept the outcome of the Civil War, the state exposition's official record was clear: Tennesseans were united in their determination to go to war—under one flag—once again.

8

Reuben Bernard and William McCorkle (1865–1898)

Unlike many men who fought in the Civil War, Reuben Bernard and William McCorkle were well past their teens and early twenties. Bernard was twenty-eight when hostilities began; McCorkle was nearly thirty-one. The war may not have changed more mature men as much as eighteen-year-old recruits, but their lives would not be the same. Bernard and McCorkle walked very different paths after 1865, but they forever shared the trauma of surviving four years of fierce combat. And they certainly would have had strong feelings about their sons fighting in a war with Spain in 1898, when the fathers were relatively old men.

In 1865, Reuben Bernard had avoided post-war friction in East Tennessee by returning to the frontier. There he soldiered alongside Union comrades and ex-Confederates in a "peacetime" army charged with subduing the remaining Plains Indians. Few Civil War veterans would have been inclined to fight old battles while waging new campaigns against a common foe. To the contrary, former opponents who fought and fraternized in the Indian wars helped foster reunification. "Without the enthusiasm of a popular imperialism first generated by the Indian wars and later dramatically consolidated during the Spanish-American War," wrote historian Cecilia O'Leary, "the impetus for cultural reunification would have been significantly delayed."[1] The historian Frederick Jackson Turner provided a context beyond the military for this commingling of Americans from different sections of the country in his 1893 essay on "The Significance of the Frontier in American History." In the West, Turner wrote, "North and South met and mingled into a nation."

8. Reuben Bernard and William McCorkle (1865–1898)

He added, "...nothing works for nationalism like intercourse within the nation."[2]

Before traveling West to help resolve the nation's remaining "Indian problem," however, Bernard made that trip home in September 1865 to a family and a region that had been divided by war. At the time, he was more concerned about his personal life than fighting or reconciliating. He was thinking about a girl. Bernard traveled from Hawkins County to Washington to ask Alice Virginia Frank to marry him. He had met the teenager while on twenty-days' sick leave in Washington during October 1864. He lost the opportunity to add the battle of Cedar Creek to his list of fights, but he found his future wife. Reuben and Alice Bernard were married three weeks before Christmas 1866. She was seventeen; he was thirty-four.[3]

Between the engagement and the wedding, Bernard (who reverted to first lieutenant from his temporary brevet rank as colonel during the war), returned to New Orleans and was quickly ordered to travel to California, where the First Cavalry reorganized. As second in command of Company I, Bernard led a contingent in a successful campaign against the Snake Indians at Rattlesnake Creek in the summer of 1866. He was promoted to captain.

Bernard returned East, married Alice, and spent several years in the recruiting service based at Carlisle Barracks, where he and his company had drilled in 1863. Alice no doubt was pleased to live for a short time in an area that had not been threatened by hostile Indians for more than a century. Bernard was at home when their first child, Henry, was born in December 1867. The couple would have six more children.

A year later, Bernard traveled with his family from Pennsylvania to Fort Lowell in Tucson. The captain took charge of Company G of the First Cavalry, a command he would hold for fourteen years. His enemy was familiar: Cochise and the Western Apaches and Chiricahuas had been fighting soldiers and civilians in Arizona for eight years. Bernard led assaults on two villages in March 1869, killing several Apaches and destroying their camps.

In his report on the March attacks, a pacifistic Bernard said he believed the Apaches would stop fighting if given an opportunity. "If a reservation were given these Indians sufficiently large for them to hunt, plant, and burn mescal in," he wrote, "they would remain at peace."[4] Few military leaders or Washington politicians were ever willing to consider such a plan; they generally preferred the certainty of eradication of the native population.

Bernard the blacksmith lobbied relentlessly to mount his soldiers on the best horses. He also paid attention to the personal needs of his troopers. They repaid him with loyalty. "They loved his reckless eagerness to get into any fight within reach," biographer Don Russell observed. "There is a theory that no man who is disliked ever earns a nickname. That he was most unkindly, most irreverently, and probably most affectionately called 'Itchy Whiskers' proves that he was not disliked."[5]

In May 1869, Bernard took command at Fort Bowie. The cavalrymen went on frequent patrols to familiarize themselves with Apache country.

Brigadier General Reuben Frank Bernard near the end of his career. Bernard fought Apaches, Modocs, Bannocks and other groups of Indians until 1881. Later he served as deputy governor of the Soldiers' Home in Washington, D.C. (courtesy Austin Dopman, Bernard's great-grandson).

In the autumn of 1869, they were ready to fight. Three times at the end of October, they encountered Apache warriors in the Chiricahua Mountains, Cochise's natural fortress.

Bernard wrote a lengthy report on the first and toughest of these fights, which took place in the Chiricahua Pass on October 20. The captain had sixty-one troopers, from his own Company G and from Company G of the Eighth Cavalry. They were following the Apaches when they suddenly lost the trail. Bernard himself rediscovered it. One of his soldiers later said that Bernard "knew Indians and could make excellent guess as to their location when he wished to find them."[6]

Eventually, Bernard's troops caught up with a force of Apaches that

8. Reuben Bernard and William McCorkle (1865–1898)

severely outnumbered his men. The soldiers dismounted and engaged the enemy in a furious firefight. Cochise's defensive position was advantageous—on a mesa well above the bottom of Chiricahua Pass. Bernard spent much of the day directing his men to test for weaknesses in the Apache line. The two sides continually traded fire. Bernard reported that two of his men died and several were wounded while killing eighteen Apaches. He withdrew his entire force and did not fight again for a week.

Bernard considered this a victory because his soldiers had inflicted heavier casualties than Cochise usually suffered. He recommended thirty-two of his men for medals of honor. His letter of recommendation described how his men labored as they advanced with him up the steep, rocky mesa under heavy fire: "These men advanced under this fire until within thirty steps from the Indians, when they came to a ledge of rocks where every man who showed his head was shot at by several Indians at once. Here the men remained, and did good shooting through the crevices of the rocks until ordered to fall back, which was done by running from rock to rock, where they would halt and return the fire of the Indians." Bernard's superiors accepted the recommendation and the War Department awarded the medals. At the same time, Bernard was recommended for a brevet of brigadier general. He received a commendation but not the brevet. Congress had suspended the awarding of brevets during the Indian wars, so Bernard had to wait twenty years to become a brigadier.[7]

Bernard soon followed the Apaches, pressing his attack so forcefully that they scattered throughout the mountains rather than face another concerted assault. The next January he again pursued Cochise, killing several Apaches and destroying their camp. That ended Bernard's engagement with Cochise. The Chiricahua warrior struggled on until the autumn of 1872 when Major General O.O. Howard traveled to Cochise's camp and persuaded him to agree to a permanent peace.

Bernard successfully fought other Apaches, the Pinals, as 1870 turned to 1871. Then he left Fort Bowie behind for Fort Bidwell, California. He remained there until the end of 1872 and during this time his fourth child was born. John Jay Bernard took his grandfather's name.

Private Charles Hardin (later promoted up the ranks to major) joined Captain Bernard's outfit at Fort Bidwell. He immediately admired, and feared, "this big, black-bearded captain." He further described the thirty-eight-year-old Bernard: "I soon came to the belief that he made no mistakes and whatever he saw fit to encounter was sure to turn out all right. He believed that his troop could not be defeated. Without this faith in my captain I fear that my rather keen appreciation of the dangers in our encounters with the Indians could not have been concealed."[8]

Bernard's quiet time ended in early 1873 with the uprising of the Modocs under their chief, Kintpuash, popularly known as Captain Jack. The Modocs had left their reservation in southwest Oregon and returned to their ancestral lands on the Oregon-California border. Troops sent to return them to the reservation met resistance and the

Reuben Bernard's cavalrymen fought Modoc Chief Kintpuash (Captain Jack) in the rugged Lava Beds of northern California during the first weeks of 1873. This contemporary wood engraving shows Modoc men, women, and children in a cave that is today part of Lava Beds National Monument (Library of Congress).

8. Reuben Bernard and William McCorkle (1865–1898)

Modocs also attacked nearby settlers. Captain Jack's men then moved into the Lava Beds, a geologically challenging area with numerous caves and volcanic craters.

Bernard's soldiers formed part of a force of four hundred troopers drawn from the First Cavalry and several infantry regiments. The plan was to send Bernard's dismounted troopers into the Lava Beds from the east and the other soldiers from the west, trap the Modocs, and force them to surrender.

Rough terrain and dense fog defeated these plans. Over a two-day period in mid–January, the soldiers rarely saw the enemy, while the Modocs proved to be excellent marksmen. No one knew whether even one Modoc had been shot, while the Indians killed sixteen enlisted soldiers and wounded nine officers and forty-four enlisted men. Although the soldiers were ordered to retreat, Bernard's biographer, in defiance of apparent facts, claimed that he "had not been defeated at any point and his loss had been small. He had withdrawn only when ordered to do so."[9]

The army decided that Captain Jack's position was impregnable and pulled back. Bernard was detached for other duties. He was not present that April when the Modocs, during presumed peace negotiations, ambushed and killed General Edward Canby, who had been Bernard's commanding officer in New Mexico, or when Captain Jack ultimately was captured and hanged.

In the mid–1870s, Reuben and Alice Bernard purchased February Hill, a Federal-style home on four acres in Jonesborough, Washington County, just over 20 miles from Reuben's birthplace at Van Hill. The home apparently was used by Alice and their young children (they had five by 1876) as an alternative to living in frontier forts. Periodically, Alice traveled west to visit her husband. In 1880, as the Indian Wars wound down, the Bernards sold the Jonesborough house and afterwards lived on or near military posts.[10]

Following his encounter with the Modocs, Bernard did not engage in another skirmish until 1878. His troops, ordered to Boise Barracks in Idaho, put down an uprising of Bannock Indians. Joined by the First Cavalry's Companies A, F, and L, Bernard arranged his soldiers in four lines and charged the Bannock camp at Silver Creek on June 23. The captain reported that his soldiers killed about fifty Bannocks while losing four men.

More companies of the First Cavalry and other army contingents joined the pursuit. On July 8, they located the enemy in a strong position

Sons of East Tennessee

on Birch Creek in the Blue Mountains. With Bernard in command, the troopers rode up the mountain, pushed the Bannocks to another crest and then forced them into nearby timber. Charging uphill into enemy fire was a hard thing to make mounted men do. Before one of the charges, the captain provided a harsh incentive for his soldiers. "I want you all to keep good order, and no running," he reportedly said. "If anyone runs I will have him shot, so he might as well die by the enemy as by friends." Bernard lost five wounded men and twenty dead horses.[11]

Sometime during this campaign, Bernard had ordered a sixty-mile night march. After the troop had settled into camp, a number of officers grumbled about the distance they had traveled. Bernard listened for a while, then announced that he, at 45, was the oldest man in the group. He rose to his feet, turned a handspring and landed "with the grace of a circus acrobat," according to W.C. Brown, a lieutenant at the time. The grumbling ended.[12]

Bernard's troops were ordered to Fort Walla Walla, Washington, to rest and refit. They left to chase Sheepeater Indians in Idaho. That 1879 campaign turned into a sixteen-hundred-mile journey through rugged terrain with little immediate result. Other army units finally forced the Sheepeaters to surrender, after Bernard's troops wore them out.

In the summer of 1881, Bernard again faced Chiricahua Apaches in Arizona. He and his troops left a temporary base in Nevada to help elements of the Sixth Cavalry put down an uprising led by Cochise's son,

After fighting Cochise and his Chiricahua Apaches in Arizona in 1869 and 1870, Reuben Bernard and his men skirmished in 1881 with Chiricahuas led by Cochise's son, Naiche, shown here wearing a military uniform with medals. Adolph F. Muhr, who spent much of his life photographing American Indians, took this picture about 1898 (Library of Congress).

8. Reuben Bernard and William McCorkle (1865–1898)

Naiche, and other Apache leaders. The troopers skirmished with the Apaches on October 2 and the enemy headed for the Dragoon Mountains to the south. Two days later Bernard took charge of six companies from the First, Sixth, and Ninth Cavalry. He commandeered a train. Men, horses, and pack mules rode rails until they spotted the fleeing Apaches near Dragoon Pass. The train stopped, the box cars opened, and the chase was on. The cavalry followed the enemy for twenty miles until mountains intruded and all had to dismount and fight on foot. The Apaches escaped overnight and fled to Mexico, forcing Bernard to abandon pursuit.

These October skirmishes against the Chiricahuas marked Bernard's last two fights. His twenty-seven years with the First Cavalry ended November 1, 1882, when he was promoted to major in the Eighth Cavalry. He had just turned fifty.

The rest of Bernard's career was largely administrative, with the exception of one unusual incident. He was serving as commander of Fort McIntosh, near Laredo, Texas, in the autumn of 1886 when an armed riot broke out between opposing political factions. Without waiting for official authority to interfere in a civil uprising, Bernard marched troops into town, demanded the surrender of all firearms, and declared martial law. That ended the confrontation, albeit in an entirely unorthodox manner.

Henry Bernard, the family's first-born son, died at age nineteen in 1887. He had left Knoxville for his father's Texas post before Christmas 1886 and died of typhoid fever at the end of the next month. The University of Tennessee released a statement noting that he had been "an excellent student with many noble traits of mind and heart."[13]

Bernard received his delayed brevet as brigadier on February 27, 1890, the year the United States officially declared the frontier closed. The brevet was presented "for gallant service in action against Indians" at Chiricahua Pass, Arizona, in 1869, and at Silver Creek and Birch Creek, Oregon, in 1878. Don Russell might have added to that commendation that Bernard's service as "a master of minor warfare" and "an almost legendary figure" had more than earned the higher rank.[14]

Alice Bernard died in January 1891. Early the next year, at age sixty, Bernard married Ruth Lavinia Simpson, fifty-three, from Baltimore. Ruth died ten months later—on Christmas Eve, 1873—in childbirth at Bernard's station at Fort Robinson, Nebraska. Recognizing that he could not raise his eighth child alone on the frontier, Bernard sent Robert Simpson Bernard by train to his Baltimore in-laws. He dispatched a letter with the baby. "The little fellow has comenced [*sic*] his life with quite a history," Bernard wrote. "First he comes into the world causing the death of his Mother and then before he is fifteen days old makes a journey of thousands of miles in the middle of winter and gets through all right."[15]

Not long after he married for the second time, Bernard had been promoted to lieutenant colonel of the Ninth Cavalry, one of the original regiments the army had set aside for black enlisted men after the Civil War. The regiment was stationed at Fort Robinson, Nebraska. In early January 1896, Bernard traveled from Nebraska to Knoxville to attend the funeral of his second son to die, also at age nineteen and also while a student at the University of Tennessee. George Bernard, known for his "quiet demeanor and studious habits" succumbed, as had his older brother, to typhoid.[16]

Bernard retired from the army on October 14, 1896, his sixty-fourth birthday, and more than forty-one years after he had enlisted as a private in Knoxville. President Grover Cleveland appointed him deputy governor of the Soldiers' Home at Washington, D.C., which seems to have been a largely honorary position. Upon retirement, he also began serving as first president of The Order of Indian Wars of the United States, a society of veteran officers dedicated to preserving the history of the western wars. The full-bearded Bernard, renowned for his career as a field officer, finally had a desk job.

※※※

Compared with Reuben Bernard's record as one of the army's leading Indian fighters, William McCorkle led an unremarkable but productive post-war life providing medical care to residents of the Mooresburg area. He and Susan McCorkle had five children, including Henry Leftwich McCorkle in 1867. The growing family lived in several houses, but no one knows precisely where any of these places is located today. At least two homes sank beneath the waters of Cherokee Lake when the Tennessee Valley Authority impounded the Holston River.[17]

The record of McCorkle's medical practice is thin. He stated on his pension application that he "practiced obstetrics near home." A later newspaper account claimed that local resident Johnny Poindexter was the first baby McCorkle delivered. He treated adult patients as well. Writing to one of McCorkle's grandsons, one of the doctor's former patients warmly observed that McCorkle "was not only

8. Reuben Bernard and William McCorkle (1865–1898)

a very close friend of my family, but was our physician throughout his lifetime."[18]

In the autumn of 1871, McCorkle was one of two doctors summoned to a double homicide just north of Mooresburg. Following an argument over a borrowed coat, a father and son named Patton stabbed to death a father and son named Simpson. The physicians "rendered all the assistance in their power," to no avail, according to a news account. As one of the only doctors in the region, McCorkle would have been called in any emergency.[19]

He probably had no shortage of patients in most seasons. Malnutrition, poverty, and disease overran the South following the war. The causes, let alone cures, of many diseases were not known, so epidemics occurred with regularity. Respiratory diseases were the primary killers. The tragic experience of the family of Richard and Eliza Fain, the militantly Confederate family who lived east of Rogersville, was not atypical. Of the couple's twelve children who reached adulthood, five died of tuberculosis between the ages of 21 and 35. "Death from disease was quite common," wrote a Knoxville historian. "Tuberculosis, diphtheria, smallpox and a hundred other maladies carried off people of all ages. There were terrible plagues to be dreaded. The cholera epidemic of 1873 was especially severe in Tennessee." Towns not far from Mooresburg, particularly Jonesborough and Greeneville, suffered high mortality.[20]

Tennessee created county boards of health in 1885, but county health officers were primarily charged with reporting on general health conditions, especially problems in county jails and among residents of county "poor farms." As for dealing with the medical concerns of other groups, including epidemic outbreaks, individual doctors were on their own.[21]

McCorkle practiced within three miles of Galbraith Springs, a popular summer health resort owned by the Galbraith family, which included Joseph Galbraith, the husband of the McCorkles' second child, Jennie. The Galbraiths had made a fortune quarrying marble before they went into the resort business. When it opened in the 1850s, Galbraith Springs included a 30-room hotel with a restaurant serving locally grown food and spring water with a high iron content, a dance pavilion, a bowling alley, and a swimming pool. Tennesseans, Virginians, and an increasing number of Northern tourists visited the place. McCorkle enthusiastically commended the springs to cure "dyspepsia, diseases of the liver, diseases of the bladder, female distresses, sick headaches, scrofula, rheumatism, cutaneous diseases, sore eyes, erysipelas, and other diseases requiring a tonic."[22] The doctor may have based his opinion of the water's worth on both medicinal and familial considerations.

During his later years, as he delivered babies and treated older patients for communicable diseases, McCorkle himself suffered from debilitating illnesses, including chronic bronchitis and a recurring cancerous growth on his back.[23] He may have been forced to reduce his patient load; but, as a doctor who regularly made house calls, he would have remained a substantial presence in the community.

9

Henry McCorkle (1867–1898) and John Jay Bernard (1872–1898)

Henry McCorkle and Jack Bernard seem to have been inclined from an early age to follow their fathers into military service. Practical experience followed inclination. Given a strict military regimen at the University of Tennessee and extended duty at western army posts, they were well prepared for war.

William and Susan McCorkle were in their mid-thirties when Henry Leftwich McCorkle was born on the family farm at Mooresburg on April 20, 1867. It would have been natural for the obstetrician to assist in delivering his first son, the third of the couple's five children. The boy took his mother's family name as his middle name.

McCorkle enjoyed favored status in the family from early childhood. Dr. McCorkle would later say that his son "was always a great favorite of mine, and went fishing and hunting with me." He added that the young McCorkle recalled the place where he had killed "the first rabbit I ever shot running." Henry McCorkle was still fishing in 1896 when he told his father that angling near his army base in Missoula, Montana, was improving, but "won't be first-class until July."[1]

McCorkle attended the newly created public schools of Hawkins County and then the private Academy of Rogersville. He joined Mooresburg's Presbyterian Church when he was sixteen and soon was elected a deacon. His religious activities while attending the University of Tennessee included the presidency of the Knoxville YMCA.[2] University records do not indicate his church preference, but he more than likely continued his Presbyterian affiliation at one of Knoxville's churches after he enrolled at the university with 209 other students in September 1885.

Lieutenant Henry Leftwich McCorkle's photograph as it appeared in the 1899 University of Tennessee yearbook, the *Volunteer*. McCorkle attended public and private schools before entering the university (Betsey B. Creekmore Special Collections and University Archives, University of Tennessee, Knoxville Libraries).

Nearly a century old, the university had survived significant early challenges only to close during the Civil War as forces from both sides alternately occupied the campus on a hill just west of downtown Knoxville and near the site of Fort Sanders. When Union troops permanently occupied the campus in 1863, they demolished one building and damaged the rest. The university applied for and finally, in 1873, received federal financial support. A congressional committee reported that it supported funding because the school was "the only educational institution of known loyalty, in management and influence, in any of the seceding States during the war" and was "surrounded by a population known for their loyalty and sacrifice to the cause of the Union."[3]

Coupling this money with earlier federal aid as a land-grant institution, the university began to flourish in the 1870s, but then foundered again, beset by financial and political turmoil. Its fortunes improved once more in 1887 when university trustees appointed thirty-two-year-old Charles W. Dabney, Jr. to lead the school into the twentieth century. Dabney had directed the North Carolina agricultural experiment station and served as official state chemist. He brought the educational philosophy he had developed in North Carolina to Tennessee and virtually imposed it on the university. Dabney required all

9. Henry McCorkle (1867–1898) and John Jay Bernard (1872–1898)

The University of Tennessee campus as it appeared in 1879, six years before Henry McCorkle began his freshman year with 209 other students (Betsey B. Creekmore Special Collections and University Archives, University of Tennessee, Knoxville Libraries).

students to take courses in mechanics and what was often called "New South scientific agriculture." He also added courses in science. This revised curriculum, defined as "practical" and viewed as progressive, replaced much of the old classical structure.[4]

Military training had been and would remain for several years an integral part of the academic schedule. "The 174 [undergraduate] students who matriculated in 1887 were cadets in an all-male military school, subject to military discipline for infractions of rules and procedures," according to a university history. The school apparently made an effort to appeal to students and families with both Union and Confederate associations by combining the colors of blue and gray in cadet uniforms. Watching cadets drill, a state senator who had participated in the Confederate assault on Fort Sanders told the young men that he appreciated the uniforms' dual colors.[5]

The university's transformation must have pleased McCorkle, who took multiple classes in mathematics and the sciences and excelled at military drill. He rose through the cadet ranks to become captain of a company his senior year. He played sports and was especially fond of baseball. He was a member of Pi Kappa Alpha fraternity and the Philomathesian Literary Society.[6]

McCorkle practiced his Christianity at church, at the YMCA, and in his dormitory. A memorial tribute noted that when a fellow student laughed at him one night as he prayed in his room, McCorkle "forcibly put him out and told him with an earnestness of both speech and blows that his mother had taught him to say his prayers when he was a baby, and he proposed to continue to do so as long as he lived...." His primary attributes included "his vigorous manliness, his admirable common sense, and his sterling moral character." He also was praised for his wit, sense of humor, and love of music.[7]

In June 1889, McCorkle graduated with a bachelor's degree in science. Although Dabney by then had begun moderating the university's military program, the graduating class wore uniforms, and their "manly forms [were] resplendent in gilt buttons and epaulettes," according to a newspaper report. Commencement exercises began with a stirring rendition of "Preist's War March." The graduating cadets, their families, and prominent citizens of Knoxville enthusiastically cheered the military tune.[8]

At twenty-two, McCorkle was well over six feet tall and fair-skinned and light-haired like his father. Unlike his father, he was not sure, at first, what to do with the rest of his life. He taught school in Hawkins County for a year, then moved to Knoxville to work in a clothing store. In the spring of 1891, he decided to take advantage of his experience as a leader of university cadets and applied for an officer's position in the army. After taking a highly competitive, week-long test, and with the recommendation of then U.S. Senator Isham Harris, he was commissioned a second lieutenant and assigned to Company G of the Twenty-fifth Infantry Regiment.[9]

An incident occurred that September, on the night before McCorkle left Knoxville for the army, that illustrates his popularity and good humor. A guest at a going-away party of McCorkle's business and social acquaintances presented him with what the *Knoxville Journal* described as "an elegant gold headed silk umbrella, the finest to be had in town." McCorkle accepted this umbrella, apparently viewed as a silly and somewhat embarrassing gift for a soldier, "like a man," and he and his friends parted company.[10]

The regiment McCorkle joined was one of two infantry and two cavalry regiments of black men. All of the enlisted men in the

9. Henry McCorkle (1867–1898) and John Jay Bernard (1872–1898)

Buffalo Soldiers of the Twenty-Fifth Infantry Regiment, some wearing buffalo robes, pose in the snow at Fort Keogh, Montana, in 1890. Henry McCorkle joined the regiment as a second lieutenant the next year. All of the regiment's enlisted men were black. Most officers were white (Library of Congress).

Twenty-fourth and Twenty-fifth Infantry and the Ninth and Tenth Cavalry were black; all officers, with the exception of several lieutenants, were white. Comanches referred to the enlisted men as "Buffalo Soldiers" for uncertain reasons; Spanish soldiers would later call them "Smoked Yankees" for obvious reasons. Coincidentally, the Ninth Cavalry was Reuben Bernard's regiment from 1892 until he retired, so he was one of McCorkle's fellow officers of Buffalo Soldiers.

The Twenty-fifth was stationed in Montana, with headquarters at Missoula, from 1888 until the beginning of the Spanish-American War. Elements of the regiment played a minor role in the Pine Ridge Campaign, which climaxed with the slaughter of Lakota Sioux at Wounded Knee Creek in December 1890. It was the last major campaign of the Indian wars.

McCorkle arrived in Missoula the better part of a year following Wounded Knee. His first few months in service were quiet, but in the spring of 1892, labor unions working in the Coeur D'Alene mining district of Idaho declared war on mine owners. The unions blew up several mines and men died in the blasts. McCorkle's company and two others traveled to Idaho that July to assist in guarding mine trains, scouting, and making arrests.[11]

In September 1892, McCorkle, then twenty-five, married Mildred Ritzius, the eighteen-year-old daughter of Henry and Amelia Ritzius. During the Civil War, Captain Ritzius had served with the Fifty-second New York Regiment. Following the war, he joined the Twenty-fifth Regiment and served at various western forts before settling at the Missoula post. In July 1893, Henry and Mildred McCorkle produced a grandchild. They christened him Guy Alexander McCorkle.

The next spring, Company G left Fort Missoula for Montana to assist U.S. marshals in controlling members of "Coxey's Army." Hundreds of unemployed workers angered by an ongoing depression had marched on Washington, D.C. They were led by Ohio businessman Jacob Coxey and his teenage son, Jesse, who wore a military uniform that, in a colorful appeal for unity, blended blue and gray. Auxiliary Coxey "armies" formed in western states. The U.S. Army assisted in putting down these smaller rebellions.

That summer the regiment patrolled from Billings back to Fort Missoula, guarding Northern Pacific Railroad personnel, trains, bridges, and tunnels from striking railroad workers. Missoula's *Anaconda Standard* later praised the regiment, noting that "the prejudice against the colored soldiers seems to be without foundation for if the Twenty-fifth Infantry is an example of the colored regiments there is no exaggeration in the statement that there are no better troops in the service."[12]

The next few years were relatively uneventful. To maintain their skills, the soldiers participated in regular marching and small arms drills. Tapping into a rising national craze for sporting activities, Second Lieutenant James A. Moss, an 1894 West Point graduate who joined Company G and quickly befriended McCorkle, established the Twenty-fifth Infantry Bicycle Corps. The small group of riders served as scouts and couriers. But the Rocky Mountain terrain, the poor state of roads, and a sufficiency of more versatile horses eventually undermined the project. Meanwhile, McCorkle was appointed to the relatively sedentary job of post treasurer.[13]

There was plenty of time for recreation. McCorkle wrote to his older sister, Jennie, in the winter of 1895: "We are having a gay time here now, something nearly every night, card parties, sleigh rides & weddings and hops. Mill [his wife, Mildred] is doing first rate in the baby line." McCorkle described his eighteen-month-old as "the prettiest little

9. Henry McCorkle (1867–1898) and John Jay Bernard (1872–1898)

fellow with blue eyes, rosy cheeks & light hair, but his hair is going to be darker than mine I believe. He is very tall & big too, for his age, and is into everything."[14]

McCorkle maintained a garden. He wrote to his father in the spring of 1896 that he had planted peas, lettuce, radishes, onions, salsify, and celery. Then, speaking to his father's profession, he explained that a soldier in the regiment who had been shot in the lung had died of blood poisoning because doctors could not find the bullet. An autopsy discovered the lead lodged against a rib near the spine. "I guess it would have been a big operation to have found & cut out the ball wouldn't it?" he asked.[15]

This settled period ended when the army designated the Twenty-fifth as the first unit to move east in preparation for war. T.G. Steward, an African Methodist Episcopal Church minister and, in later life, a Wilberforce University professor, served sixteen years as chaplain of the Twenty-fifth Regiment. In one of his several books, he observed, "What could be more significant, or more fitting, than that these black soldiers, drilled up to the highest standard of modern warfare, cool, brave and confident, themselves a proof of American liberty, should be called first to the front in a war against oppression?"[16]

On April 10, 1898—Easter Sunday—the soldiers left Missoula and traveled by train to Chickamauga National Park. Chickamauga was one of seven major "concentration camps" established throughout the country to train seven army corps to fight in a hot, wet climate. All four black regiments eventually traveled to Chickamauga. Thousands of white soldiers also camped on the old Civil War battlefield.

Steward wrote that he was pleased by "the fraternity that prevailed among black and white regulars" as they trained together. He could not say the same for the racist reception extended to the black regiments by the press. Their stay in the camps was short, he wrote, "but it was long enough for certain newspapers of Chattanooga to give expression to their dislike to negro troops in general and to those in their proximity especially."[17]

In late April, not long after the regiment's arrival in Tennessee, Henry, Mildred, and five-year-old Guy traveled from the training camp to Mooresburg on a week-long furlough. William McCorkle later remarked that Guy told "some big tale" during that week and that Henry chastised him. "I am afraid you are going to learn to tell stories—you must not do that," he told the child. "I never told my father a story in my life." The doctor observed that Guy looked much like Henry when he was a boy. He also said that Henry took out an $8,000 life insurance policy for Mildred and Guy "for fear something would happen to him." According to a later newspaper account, "a presentiment existed in his father's mind" that Henry McCorkle "would be killed in Cuba when he started for that place."[18]

Henry visited friends in Knoxville and then left his wife and son with his parents. It was the last time he would see them. It also was the last time he would celebrate his birthday: he turned thirty-one on April 20 and returned to his military camp five days later. The next day, he was recommended for promotion to first lieutenant. Shortly thereafter, he was appointed commander of Company G.

In early May, the army dispatched Henry McCorkle and his regiment to Tampa, Florida, the staging point for an anticipated assault on Spanish forces in Cuba.

※※※

The fourth of Reuben and Alice Bernard's seven children was born at his father's military post at Fort Bidwell, California, on April 1, 1872. John Jay Bernard spent his boyhood hunting, fishing, and engaging in such sports and other activities as were available on an army post and at the family's Tennessee residence at Jonesborough. Like his father, he loved horses. As a young boy, he rode with Reuben Bernard and his company of cavalry from Brownsville, Texas, almost directly north to Fort Meade near Deadwood, South Dakota—a distance approaching two thousand miles.[19]

He attended army post

John Jay "Jack" Bernard, in civilian clothes, from the 1899 University of Tennessee yearbook, the *Volunteer*. Bernard attended army post schools and a preparatory school in East Tennessee before entering the university as a sophomore in 1890 (Betsey B. Creekmore Special Collections and University Archives, University of Tennessee, Knoxville Libraries).

9. Henry McCorkle (1867–1898) and John Jay Bernard (1872–1898)

schools and a preparatory school in Jonesborough. In the autumn of 1890, he began his studies as a sophomore at the University of Tennessee. There were 215 undergraduate and graduate students that year; the school was still small enough so that President Dabney could get to know each student. Bernard entered the university just over a year after Henry McCorkle graduated. Although they never sat in a classroom together, the two apparently became acquainted while McCorkle was working in Knoxville after graduating and teaching school. According to Dabney, the men developed a friendship that was suspended until they met again on the way to war.[20]

Bernard concentrated on chemistry and geology. He no doubt was pleased when the expansive Science Hall opened in 1892. Bernard's memorial tribute in the *University of Tennessee Record* said he was noted "on the one side for his love of athletics and military drill, and on the other for his conscientious and accurate work." He played baseball and football. Like McCorkle, he joined the Philomathesian Literary Society. A fellow student said Bernard had been converted to Christianity during a week of prayer at a new YMCA building completed on the campus in his junior year. While in Knoxville, he attended First Presbyterian Church.[21] He may have encountered fellow Presbyterian Henry McCorkle there.

Bernard excelled as a cadet and served as lieutenant and adjutant of his company during his senior year. While he received military instruction similar to McCorkle's, not all students did. Under Dabney's continuing leadership, the university made military drill voluntary for juniors and seniors and ended military discipline outside the cadet corps.[22]

The school admitted its first female students in the autumn of 1893, a semester after Bernard graduated. The young man may have regretted that young women had not arrived earlier. He was an active member of Kappa Sigma fraternity and, while it was said that the blue-eyed, brown-haired student was "as popular among non-fraternity men as among the Greeks," it also was said that "in the society of ladies he was always a favorite." For several years, he was president of the University Cotillion Club. "Within the circle of his intimate friends, he was fairly idolized," a friend recalled. "There was a simplicity and directness about him that appealed peculiarly to college men. His quiet dignity and manly bearing commanded universal respect."[23]

When he ventured away from the small campus, Bernard

encountered a thriving town known for its carousing element. In the early 1890s, Knoxville hosted some one hundred saloons and an informal red-light district. Knoxvillians enjoyed vaudeville shows nearly every night and opera festivals each spring. Bicycling and horse racing were popular. The town had a competitive pro-baseball team, which must have attracted interest from baseball-playing Bernard and McCorkle.[24]

Bernard received his Bachelor of Science degree in mining engineering in June 1893. He seemed to be embarking on a promising career in the sciences, and the faculty appointed him an instructor in chemistry for the 1893–94 academic year. His friends urged him to continue at the university. After consulting with Dabney and others, however, Bernard decided to follow his father into the army.

In the summer of 1894, after failing to obtain an officer's commission by direct appointment, Bernard enlisted in the First Cavalry. He joined Troop I, one of his father's early units, then located at Fort Bayard, New Mexico. Later the troop moved to Fort Huachuca, Arizona, where Bernard was appointed corporal, then sergeant. His assignments included scouting rebellious Apache Indians in New Mexico and Arizona.[25]

Bernard spent nearly three years in the cavalry before once again applying to the War Department for a commission. This time he succeeded. The army appointed him second lieutenant and shifted him to the Fourth Infantry in the spring of 1897. He joined Company B at Fort Sheridan, Illinois.

A sensational incident occurred at that post in October 1897. While serving as officer of the guard, Bernard ordered a prisoner, Private Charles Hammond, to appear before a summary court on charges of insubordination. Hammond refused to leave the guardhouse and walk to the court, so Bernard referred the matter to Captain Leonard Lovering, commander of Company C. Lovering reportedly kicked and prodded Hammond with his sword and ordered other soldiers to drag the prisoner to the court, where he arrived bleeding and crying.

That November Lovering pleaded not guilty to a charge of ignoring "good order and discipline" before a general court-martial. Bernard and other witnesses testified to the abuse Hammond had suffered. Lovering was found guilty and reprimanded. Soldiers under his command carried their resentment with them to Cuba.[26]

Bernard celebrated his twenty-sixth birthday April 1. Eighteen

9. Henry McCorkle (1867–1898) and John Jay Bernard (1872–1898)

days later the second lieutenant and his regiment left Fort Sheridan on their way to war. The Fourth Infantry, bypassing Chickamauga, traveled directly to Tampa, arriving April 22, two weeks before McCorkle's regiment. Robert Travis, a soldier in Bernard's company, kept a record of the journey. He reported that the soldiers rode in sleeping and baggage cars while officers enjoyed a Pullman sleeping car.

The regiment passed enthusiastic crowds all along the route. At a small rail station in Georgia, a young girl gave the soldiers an American flag she had made herself. She asked them to carry it to Cuba and return it to her when they came home. "The flag at once became a sacred emblem to all the members of our company and was carried through the campaign from Daiquiri to Santiago," Travis reported. "It would have been the last thing to be given up and there was not a man in the company who would not have fought to the bitter end to retain this small emblem."[27]

The soldiers eventually would return the flag to the little girl, but first they had to carry it through the sweltering jungles and across the deadly battlefields of Cuba.

10

Preparing for War (Winter 1898)

On the morning of April 22, 1898, the American gunboat USS *Nashville* fired on a Spanish freighter transporting lumber from New Orleans to Rotterdam. The *Nashville* was part of an American fleet on its way from Key West to block Spanish ships from entering Havana harbor. Nineteen miles out of port, the *Nashville's* commander had noticed smoke in the distance, chased it, and encountered the *Buena Ventura*. After signaling the unsuspecting freighter to stop, without result, the *Nashville* fired two warning shots. The second, closer blast abruptly halted the lumber boat, whose captain told a *New York Sun* reporter that "we did not know there was any war on."[1]

The *Nashville* accompanied the *Buena Ventura* and its subdued crew back to Key West. The whole town turned out to examine the war's first prize. "Thousands stood on the docks, climbed up the trees and took to the rowboats, all yelling and cheering like mad," reported the *New York Sun*. They were applauding the first shots fired in what the Spanish would term the "Disaster of 1898," but many Americans would view as "a splendid little war" that abruptly extended the nation's reach in the world.[2]

Commander T. Washburn Maynard, a Knoxville native and career naval officer, commanded the *Nashville*. Tennessee newspapers celebrated the association. The *Knoxville Sentinel* ran a banner headline—"Knoxville Man Fires First Shot of the War"—across the top of its front page. "To East Tennessee belongs the honor of making the first capture," proclaimed the *Maryville Times*.[3] At fifty-three, the fledgling conflict's hometown hero was nearing the end of a distinguished naval career. After capturing the *Buena Ventura*, Maynard took three more ships and cut Spanish underwater cables connecting Cuba with Spain.

10. Preparing for War (Winter 1898)

During the Civil War, the captain's father, Horace Maynard, had represented Knox County in the U.S. Congress as a Republican and early ally of Abraham Lincoln. He was one of many Civil War–era fathers whose sons now would wage their own war. Some of those sons would die or be terribly maimed; others would be exhilarated by their combat experience and recall it as the highlight of their lives. All who survived the Cuban campaign would develop respect for the initially fierce Spanish resistance and the relentlessly hostile island climate.

Americans had been monitoring events in Cuba since insurgents had fought unsuccessfully for independence in the 1870s. In 1895, revolutionaries again began rebelling against brutal Spanish rule. As the conflict continued, American newspaper

Knoxville native T. Washburn Maynard commanded the American gunboat *Nashville* that fired the first shot of the Spanish-American War. Captain Washburn was wounded in subsequent action. He continued in the service following the war and retired as a rear admiral (Betsey B. Creekmore Special Collections and University Archives, University of Tennessee, Knoxville Libraries).

correspondents regularly reported Spanish atrocities. In January 1898, the United States sent the USS Battleship *Maine* to monitor the rebellion and to protect American citizens on the island. In mid–February—two months before the *Nashville's* encounter with the *Buena Ventura*—the *Maine* exploded and sank in Havana harbor. American saber rattlers immediately blamed the Spanish for blowing up the ship and killing 266 sailors and marines; they lobbied for war. Others thought the explosion might have been accidental and reserved judgment until the incident could be investigated.

Journalist and historian Stephen Kinzer has argued that the debate

The U.S.S. *Nashville*, commissioned in August 1897, was the first of three navy ships to be named for Tennessee's capital city. In the spring of 1898, the gunboat's crew captured four Spanish ships between Florida and Cuba before cutting the undersea cable between Cuba and Spain (Library of Congress).

that ensued was the most significant in American history. "It was arguably even more momentous than the debate over slavery because its outcome affected many countries, not just one," he wrote. "Never has the question of intervention—how the United States should face the world—been so trenchantly argued." The debate essentially pitted those who believed America was destined to expand its power in the world (and, in the process, free the Cuban people) with those who thought the country should mind its own business.[4]

Civil War veterans had strong opinions. Many worried that combat in Cuba would kill thousands and create a new generation of crippled soldiers. But other aging veterans offered to fight again. Virginian R.B. Foster wrote to the Secretary of War, "I know what war means, and as I once fought against the grand old U.S. flag I now desire to offer my services to you with the hope that you may give me a chance to have the honor of protecting ... the flag against which I fought."[5]

President William McKinley, who had enlisted in the Union Army

10. Preparing for War (Winter 1898)

Kurz & Allison created this dramatic depiction of the February 15, 1898, explosion of the U.S. battleship *Maine* in Havana Harbor shortly after the incident. Dramatic illustrations and descriptions of the *Maine*'s sinking and the death of 266 sailors and marines helped persuade Americans to go to war with Spain (Library of Congress).

at eighteen and finished the war as a brevetted infantry major, initially rejected conflict. He told Colonel Leonard Wood, who later would lead the First United States Volunteer Cavalry, better known as the Rough Riders, "I have been through one war, I have seen the dead piled up; and I do not want to see another."[6]

Other leaders, including U.S. Senator Henry Cabot Lodge and Assistant Secretary of the Navy Theodore Roosevelt, argued persistently for war, eventually overwhelming House Speaker Thomas Reed, leader of the opposition. When New York Governor Levi Morton urged Reed to do more to dissuade House members from launching a war, the frustrated Speaker replied, "Dissuade them! The Governor ... might as well ask me to stand out in the middle of a Kansas waste and dissuade a cyclone!"[7]

Many newspapers quickly predicted and even welcomed war. They included New York City's sensationalist papers, William Randolph

Sons of East Tennessee

Hearst's *Journal* and Joseph Pulitzer's *World*. Both raised the price of their papers from fifty cents to sixty cents while boosting conflict with exaggerated or fabricated stories. Many Southern newspapers beat a similar drum while providing more accurate reports. On February 18, three days after the explosion in Havana, the *Nashville American* suggested that, if war came, Tennessee would readily renew its reputation as the Volunteer State. The *Knoxville Sentinel* said that if it was found that the Spanish government or a Spanish "miscreant" had destroyed the Maine, Spain should immediately pay reparations. If the country balked, the paper suggested, American ships should assemble at Havana and bombard "the hoary fortifications where thousands of [Cuban] political prisoners have perished."[8]

As time passed, the *Sentinel* became increasingly distressed by the lack of action in Washington. "The only thing worse than war is national dishonor," the paper said in mid–March. The *Maryville Times* already had adopted the drumbeat: If the Spanish were guilty of the Maine disaster, the editor said, the newspaper would follow "the language of Capt. Gibson:

> Polish up my rusty saber;
> Dig up my blunderbuss,
> I'll forsake my field of labor
> And will fight the Spanish Cuss."[9]

On March 21, a U.S. Naval Board of Inquiry officially reported that the *Maine* had been mined. Within days, a Spanish investigation contradicted that verdict, favoring a ship-board accident. Most Americans accepted the mine theory and war talk blossomed. Some politicians took the opportunity to express a blatantly masculine attraction to war or to promote imperial ambitions.

McKinley remained reluctant to start shooting. On April 11, he called for congressional authorization to intervene in Cuba. The *Sentinel* ran two columns of man-on-the-street interviews the next day. Most respondents commended the president's caution. "The most commonly expressed sentiment seems to be, to go ahead, even before we are sure we are right," Knoxville Judge H.H. Ingersoll told a reporter. "But the country can surely better endure a just suspense than an unjust war."[10]

Congress spent two weeks debating the issue before formally declaring war on April 25, two days after Spain had done the same and

10. Preparing for War (Winter 1898)

three days after Washburn Maynard had fired the first shots. In his history of Knoxville, William Rule said the declaration of war resolved an impasse, "by which the public mind was greatly relieved and satisfied that something was to be done that would redound to the honor of the country."[11] From then on, sentiment for the war accelerated, along with movement of military units to Southern states.

"In April, everywhere over this good, fair land, flags were flying," observed Kansas journalist William Allen White. "Trains carrying soldiers were hurrying from the North, from the East, from the West, to the Southland.... Everywhere it was flags; tattered, smoke-grimed flags in engine cabs; flags in buttonholes; flags on proud poles; flags fluttering everywhere."[12]

Leonard Wood, on his way to Tampa in early June, watched similar crowds smiling and waving flags as the Rough Riders passed. "All the cost of this war is amply repaid by seeing the old flag as one sees it today in the South," he wrote his wife. "We are indeed once more a united country." Wood's second in command, Lieutenant Colonel Theodore Roosevelt, who had left the naval department to go to war, said "grizzled ex-Confederates" told him "they had never dreamed in the bygone days of bitterness to greet the old flag as they now were greeting it, and to send their sons, as now they were sending them, to fight and die under it."[13]

Neither the United States nor Spain was prepared for this fight. The U.S. Navy had not maintained an adequate fleet of warships, but the Spanish navy was utterly inept. Admiral Samson's ships, including the *Nashville*, quickly blockaded Havana. After Commodore George Dewey destroyed a small Spanish naval force in Manila Bay in the Philippines in early May, Samson moved his ships to pin down the remaining Spanish fleet in Santiago at the end of the month. When the Spanish ships emerged from the harbor's narrow mouth in early July, Samson shattered them. The war at sea was over.

The ground war got off to a much slower start. Spain maintained 160,000 soldiers spread throughout Cuba. Many of these troops were in the Havana area and others were concentrated in large, but disconnected, garrisons designed to repress the Cuban resistance throughout the country. The U.S. Army numbered only twenty-eight thousand regular troops. Most of them, including Henry McCorkle and Jack Bernard, were stationed in the West. McKinley called for 125,000 volunteers on April 23 and another 75,000 a month later.

Sons of East Tennessee

Astute observers realized that many of the first soldiers on the battlefield would come from former Confederate states. "Their proximity to Cuba would necessitate this," the *Knoxville Sentinel* observed in late February. A month later, the *Sentinel* informed its readers that assault troops appropriately would include the Twenty-fourth and Twenty-fifth Infantry and the Ninth and Tenth Cavalry because "the sons of American slaves will go to Cuba to set the Cubans free." The black troops, also known as the "Immune" regiments, would be better able to handle the heat and disease of the climate, the paper reported: "They can go with impunity, where white men would die as by a pestilence."[14]

Soon after the black regiments and other army regulars assembled at Chickamauga in early May, in preparation for leaving for staging camps at Tampa, an odd juxtaposition of active soldiers and Civil War veterans occurred on the Chickamauga battlefield. As army regiments trained nearby, Union and Confederate veterans mingled and exchanged war stories on "Tennessee Day," May 12. Tennessee, which had erected four monuments and forty-seven regimental markers, composed largely of Tennessee marble, transferred them to the federal government that spring. In a speech in which he recalled at length the Confederacy's struggle for independence, former Confederate Lieutenant General Alexander P. Stewart, a representative of the National Chickamauga Park Commission and a native of Rogersville, lauded the "righteous" Lost Cause. But he also assured his audience that Americans "rejoice as one people" following early victories at sea.[15]

After the regular troops left Chickamauga, volunteer regiments from all over the country moved in. They were trained by regular army officers, some of whom had fought in the Civil War. John Rutter Brooke, a Union brigadier general in the Civil War, had been elevated to major general by 1898 and took command of the training camp. Thomas Lafayette Rosser, a former Confederate major general of cavalry, took charge of training cavalry recruits.

Tennessee had authorized four volunteer regiments. Altogether, these regiments enlisted more than four thousand men. Some of the recruits trained at Chickamauga, others in Knoxville. Only the First Tennessee Infantry engaged in combat and that was during the early stages of the Philippine Insurrection. None of the regiments fought in Cuba and only one—the Fourth Volunteer Infantry, raised in East Tennessee—traveled to that island for post-war duties.

The Fourth Tennessee was the first regiment mustered in under

10. Preparing for War (Winter 1898)

Knoxville residents lined Gay Street on July 13, 1898, to watch the Fourth Tennessee Regiment march off to serve in the Spanish-American War. The volunteers had trained at Camp Poland, just outside the city. They arrived in Cuba for police duty well after fighting ended (Thompson Photograph Collection, McClung Historical Collection, Knox County Public Library).

McKinley's second call for volunteers. Its companies assembled July 13, four days before Spain surrendered. The forty-seven officers and 1,247 enlisted men trained at Camp Poland, a wooded area on the outskirts of Knoxville. George Leroy Brown, a regular army officer who had served as commandant of cadets at the University of Tennessee, served as regimental colonel. The first elements of the Fourth Infantry arrived in Cuba in December 1898, and policed Santa Clara Province until returning to the United States in April 1899. The regiment lost more than one hundred men, primarily to disease and desertion, before being mustered out of service in early May.[16]

Although Tennessee volunteers never faced combat in Cuba, Tennesseans in the regular army would play major roles, as they had in the Civil War. Charles Cantrell, a Tenth Infantry private from Smithville, DeKalb County, received a medal of honor for rescuing wounded men

Sons of East Tennessee

from in front of the Spanish lines on San Juan Hill. Alfred Ray, a Tenth Cavalry sergeant from Jonesborough who had been enslaved before the Civil War, received a battlefield promotion for planting the first American flag on San Juan Hill. Seventeen men from Tennessee fought with the Rough Riders.[17]

At least eighty-two University of Tennessee students and graduates served in regular and volunteer army regiments or in the navy. Forty-nine, including Henry McCorkle and Jack Bernard, were commissioned army officers. Eight, including Washburn Maynard, were commissioned naval officers. Enthusiasm for the war infected the Knoxville campus. "The spirit of patriotism on University Hill is at high tide," reported the *Knoxville Sentinel* in early June. University President Dabney wrote to a friend a month later, "Our boys are so deeply interested in the war that I think they have forgotten everything else."[18]

McCorkle, Bernard, and other regular army soldiers who concentrated at southern training camps in Chattanooga, New Orleans, Mobile, and Tampa must have been especially eager to see action. McCorkle had obtained his commission as second lieutenant in 1891. Bernard had enlisted three years later. Both had joined the army after most American Indians had succumbed to the relentless advance of European settlement. The prospect of war with a foreign nation certainly would have appealed to young soldiers bored by routine peacetime service.

But beyond that yearning for combat, some soldiers from Southern states had something to prove that their Northern counterparts did not. *Harper's Weekly* editor George William Curtis expressed his doubts: "Whatever view we may take of that [lost] cause," he wrote to a correspondent in the South, "...and whatever titles of honor may be justly due to its official leader, I cannot admit that patriot is one of them, except in some sense as yet unknown to me." Some GAR members also expressed concerns about Southern patriotism and loyalty to a union that the Confederate States of America had attempted to destroy.[19]

Acknowledging this criticism, a veteran of a Confederate brigade from Texas wrote to Secretary of War Russell Alger, offering to raise a regiment of former Confederates. "All we ask is an opportunity to let our actions speak for our loyalty," he said. Another writer told President McKinley that as "a true Southerner and Mississippian," he would "support the *Union now* and *forever.*"[20]

Many Southern politicians and newspaper editors assured their

10. Preparing for War (Winter 1898)

Northern counterparts that they would do their share of fighting. Tennessee's U.S. Senator Benton McMillin told fellow congressmen that his state would furnish a soldier for each volunteer sent by Massachusetts, "to keep step with him and go shoulder to shoulder to the conflict." The *Nashville American* maintained that the South would be "as quick to espouse the nation's quarrel as any other portion of the country."[21]

Some Southerners remained aloof. Especially in the deep South, newspaper editors did not rush to embrace war. Some Florida papers opposed armed conflict because the state's ports would be exposed to attack from the sea. Editors elsewhere argued that the situation could be resolved short of war.[22]

S.A. Cunningham, editor of the *Confederate Veteran*, supported a united front against Spain but had other concerns. He thought it would have been better if the army had switched from uniforms of blue to brown, a color more suitable for tropical warfare and less provocative to Southern veterans. But Cunningham had concerns about reuniting North and South that went well beyond the choice of uniform colors. "By and by, the fraternity may be complete between the North and the South," he wrote, "but it will not occur through anything that is humiliating to the people of the latter section. Personal honor is above country.... The Southern people should be diligent to maintain the truth of history and to induce cooperation to maintain the government of the fathers. They believe still in a white man's government."[23]

McKinley was no white supremacist, but he understood the need for the South to maintain sectional pride while proving its loyalty to the union. The president appointed two former Confederate cavalry generals to significant military positions. Sixty-one-year-old Joseph Wheeler was a longtime Democratic congressman from Alabama. Sixty-three-year-old Fitzhugh Lee, General Robert E. Lee's nephew and a former governor of Virginia, was serving as consul-general in Havana. McKinley made both men major generals of volunteers. McKinley's initiative persuaded many advocates of reconciliation that, as the *Birmingham News* declared, the president thus "wipes out the last vestige of sectional lines with one stroke of his pen."[24]

But they were the only former Confederates named to top command posts. Secretary of War Alger had served as a Union colonel. Major General William Shafter, commander of the Cuban invasion force, had been a brevet brigadier in the Union army. Major General Nelson Miles, Brigadier General Henry Lawton, and other high-ranking army personnel were Union veterans. All of the naval leaders—Admiral George Dewey, Rear Admiral William Sampson, and Commodore Winfield Scott Schley—had served in the Union navy.

The death of twenty-four-year-old Ensign Worth Bagley assuaged many concerns about Southern loyalty. On May 12, Spanish batteries opened fire on the torpedo boat *Winslow* off the coast of Cuba. As the *Winslow* backed away, shrapnel from a Spanish shell tore into Bagley and several sailors. The first and only American naval officer killed in the war, Bagley was a son of a former Confederate major from North Carolina. To many observers, Bagley represented not only the South's loyalty to the union, but also reunification of North and South. "The South furnishes the first sacrifice of this war," observed the *New York Tribune*. "There is no north and no south after that, we are all Worth Bagley's countrymen." The *Atlanta Constitution* said much the same: "the blood of this martyr freely spilled upon his country's altar seals effectively the covenant of brotherhood between the north and south and completes the reconciliation which commenced at Appomattox."[25]

By mid–May, the theme of reconciliation had become an essential element of the nation's war rhetoric. Congress had set the tone April 25 when a band played both "The Battle Hymn of the Republic" and "Dixie" to accompany the declaration of war. Robert L. Taylor, Tennessee's popular governor and an accomplished orator, telegraphed a stirring message to McKinley: "Tennessee awaits your call to volunteers; the blue and the gray will march together under Old Glory keeping time to 'Yankee Doodle' and 'Dixie' and the fur will fly and the earth will tremble."[26]

The *Nashville American* predicted that the war would erase sectional friction "and give us a closer union than has existed since 1860." Editorialized the *Knoxville Sentinel*, "War is a unifier. The last vestige of sectionalism will have to go." In a poem designed to be sung to the tune of "Dixie," the *Florida Times Union* declared, "We are all Yankees now." Writing in the *New York Journal*, Henry Watterson said the prospect of war had united the nation, "emancipating both sections of the union from the mistaken impression that we ever were, or ever could be, anything else but one people."[27]

Henry McCorkle, Jack Bernard, and most other young soldiers heading for Tampa were not so concerned about reconciling sectional differences lingering from a war waged long before they were born as they were about serving with honor in Cuba. "This was a generation of men both inspired and burdened by the glory their fathers had won in

10. Preparing for War (Winter 1898)

the Civil War," observed historian David Traxel, adding, "Young men wanted a real, if romantic, whiff of gun smoke, blood, and steel. They wanted a chance to be their own heroes."[28] Burdened, inspired, realistic or romantic, these men were on their way to war under one flag, cheered by Americans north and south.

11

Sailing from Tampa to Cuba (Spring, 1898)

The navy assembled its North Atlantic Squadron at Key West because it is the closest port to Cuba. The army gathered its regiments at Tampa—not an obvious choice—because Henry B. Plant successfully promoted his hometown and his transportation enterprise. One of Florida's first major entrepreneurs, Plant persuaded the War Department that his network of trains and steamboats, the Plant System, could carry thousands of combatants from their training camps through Florida to Tampa. Officers could stay in his opulent Tampa Bay Hotel. Soldiers could camp and drill in open areas near town. Then they all could ride Plant's railroad out to Tampa Bay, board transport ships, and steam into the Gulf of Mexico.

Nearly thirty thousand men in regular and volunteer regiments—double the number of the town's residents—set up camps in the greater Tampa area in the spring of 1898. Jack Bernard's Fourth Regiment, numbering about 460 officers and men, camped at Tampa Heights in the northeastern section of town. Henry McCorkle's Twenty-fifth Regiment, at similar strength, camped nearby at Ybor City, Tampa's cigar-making center. The two regiments, along with the First Regiment, combined as the Second Brigade of the Second Division of the Fifth Army Corps, the primary invasion force.[1]

McCorkle, Bernard, and other officers immediately began directing their troops through monotonous maneuvers in the sand. While there is no record of an encounter between the two lieutenants, it seems probable that, among a relatively small number of junior officers, they would have renewed their Tennessee ties in Tampa or on the transport boat they shared crossing to Cuba.

11. Sailing from Tampa to Cuba (Spring, 1898)

Soldiers wearing standard-issue blue flannel shirts, blue or brown wool trousers, and felt hats entirely inappropriate for the climate drilled every day but Sunday amid pines and palmettos on the sand flats. They persevered through heat and humidity that approximated the sweltering conditions they would endure on the island. Many overdressed soldiers had difficulty adjusting to Florida's Gulf Coast and its pestiferous inhabitants. "Tampa is, collectively speaking, a BUM place," Henry A. Dobson, a first sergeant in the 1st District of Columbia Infantry, wrote to his parents in Washington. Dobson complained about the food and water, his health, the recruits he supervised, and the climate in general. "Well, this is the strangest birthday I've ever had," he wrote on June 7, his 20th birthday, "sand, heat, fleas, flies, gnats, hunger, dirt, and an intense desire to walk up our front steps." Kathleen Blake Watkins, writing for the *Toronto Mail*, provided an even more colorful account of army life in Tampa. She said a New York recruit, on his first day in camp, was "bitten by mosquitoes, stung by a tarantula, had a touch of malaria, ran his bayonet into his hand, sat down on a giant ants' nest, trod on an alligator, found a snake in his boot, and said he felt like a dirty deuce in a new deck."[2]

Soldiers spent large amounts of time test-firing the weapons they would carry to Cuba. Regular troops used Model 1896 Krag-Jorgensen rifles. Under controlled conditions, the Danish-designed Krag's accuracy was comparable to the Model 1893 Spanish Mauser rifle, but Mausers would prove to be more accurate (and deadly) and easier to use on the battlefield. Both Krags and Mausers used smokeless-powder cartridges and fired a five-round clip. Most hastily-armed American volunteers carried older, single-shot Springfield rifles with black powder cartridges; the substantial cloud of smoke they emitted when discharged betrayed a shooter's position.[3]

The man in charge of all this firepower, Major General William Shafter, had risen through the ranks in the Civil War and then had fought Indians on the frontier, earning a Medal of Honor. But in 1898, he was sixty-three years old, weighed three hundred pounds, and suffered from varicose veins and gout. Critics worried that these debilitating conditions would affect his capacity to coordinate an army corps during a major campaign.

While junior officers camped near their troops, Shafter and other high-ranking officers and their aides lodged in Plant's 511-room, 900-foot-long, five-stories-high, red-brick, Moorish hotel. The general and his brigadiers spent hours discussing strategy on the hotel's enormous front porch. Richard Harding Davis, the widely known journalist temporarily corresponding for Hearst's *New York Journal*, described these planning sessions as "the rocking-chair period of the war."[4]

On weekends, officers attended military balls and concerts in the hotel's ornate ballroom or fraternized at other locations. Enlisted men visited restaurants, bars, and bordellos, or simply walked the sandy streets. Most establishments did not welcome black troops—a situation the Buffalo Soldiers had endured throughout the journey south.

On their final excursion into Tampa on June 6, soldiers of the Twenty-fourth and Twenty-fifth Infantry encountered a challenging situation well beyond the segregation of facilities. Intoxicated white volunteers from Ohio decided to use a two-year-old black child for target practice. A soldier grabbed the boy from his mother and held him upside down while his comrades took turns aiming to hit a sleeve of the child's loose-fitting pajamas. A trooper finally put a bullet through the boy's garment and the volunteers returned him to his hysterical mother. When they heard about this atrocity, Buffalo Soldiers, already angered by their general reception in Tampa, began firing their weapons, wrecking saloons and cafes that had refused to serve them, and breaking into white brothels. The Second Georgia Volunteer Infantry intervened to stop the "Tampa riot," with the result that twenty-seven black soldiers and several white volunteers received serious wounds and did not travel to Cuba.[5]

On the evening of June 7, Shafter and Brigadier General Evan Miles, commander of McCorkle's and Bernard's brigade, talked at length by telegraph with President McKinley in Washington. Following that conference, Shafter told his officers to prepare to move out of Tampa. All that night and well into the next day, Plant's trains ran back and forth on a single set of tracks, moving troops over the nine miles between town and port.

Chaos reigned at the wharves as thousands of men boarded transport ships. Artillery, horses, and tons of food, water, and other supplies (including stacks of recently varnished coffins) accompanied them. The ships had insufficient space to hold twenty-five thousand troops, so thousands of men would be left behind. Just over eight hundred officers, more than fifteen thousand enlisted men, and nearly a hundred war correspondents would go to sea. Only officers and artillery batteries were permitted to take horses, so most of the cavalry left without mounts.

11. Sailing from Tampa to Cuba (Spring, 1898)

Photographic print from one-half of a stereograph card shows a busy scene on the dock at Port Tampa, Florida, in early June 1898. Soldiers in the foreground are loading cargo bound for Cuba aboard transport ships docked in Tampa Bay (Library of Congress).

Henry McCorkle's father-in-law, Captain Henry Ritzius, was one of the Twenty-fifth Infantry's officers who remained in Tampa. "Your father wont [sic] be apt to go to Cuba," Henry informed Mildred in the first of half a dozen letters he wrote to her in June 1898. "They seem to be leaving the old fellows behind."[6] The captain was fifty-nine.

The Fourth and Twenty-fifth regiments, minus Ritzius and the injured Buffalo Soldiers, boarded the transport ship *Concho*, which had been refitted with bunks for troops and stalls for horses. For a few days— until officers decided the ship was overcrowded—a battalion of the Second Massachusetts Volunteers joined them. Then, along with everyone else, the regiments remained in port, enduring the heat in close quarters while the anchored boats washed about in the bay for the better part of six days. Rumors that Spanish Admiral Pascual Cervera y Topete's fleet in Santiago Harbor had steamed out and was waiting in ambush stalled the invasion. In fact, the U.S. fleet, commanded by Admiral William Sampson, had trapped Cervera in the city's harbor on Cuba's southeast coast.

McCorkle criticized the continued delay in a letter to his wife, noting that "things have been balled up a lot so far, an order will come and in a little while another will come revoking the first etc. but I guess we can fight when the time comes." A witty newspaper correspondent also critiqued the lengthy wait by rephrasing Hamlet's ambivalent lament: "Cu-be, or not Cu-be; that is the Key Westion."[7]

The next day, when Shafter verified that there was no flotilla outside Tampa Bay, the army at last began to move toward Key West. Thirty-two transport ships and five barges carried the troops. The battleship *Indiana*, torpedo boats, and cruisers traveled in advance and alongside to

Soldiers pace the deck or look out to sea on the transport ship *Rio Grande No. 2*. Thirty-two transport ships and five barges carried twenty-three hundred soldiers and their supplies to Cuba (Philip S. Hench Walter Reed Yellow Fever Collection, Albert and Shirley Small Special Collections Library, University of Virginia).

11. Sailing from Tampa to Cuba (Spring, 1898)

protect the transports. This assemblage formed the largest military force ever to leave the United States up to that time.

Riding on the lead transport ship, the *Seguranca*, Shafter still had not revealed his destination. He feared that if the Spanish learned where he was headed, they would have time to concentrate forces at the point of attack. Even on June 15, after a week at sea, McCorkle did not know the army's destination. He described the slow journey across an indigo sea: "There are about thirty-seven vessels in all besides the war vessels.... It is a grand sight to see all of them steaming along.... I hope the next time I write I will have some news to write about. I guess you will see it in the papers though before you get my letter. You neednt [sic] expect anything brilliant of me but I hope I will do my duty."[8]

Conditions on the transports were odious. Fresh water and rations were insufficient. Soldiers insisted that the canned meat issued to them in Florida and on the transport ships was left over from the Civil War. Civil War soldiers often had called their canned meat "embalmed beef" and the term seemed appropriate again in 1898. Wearing flannel and wool uniforms caused continual distress. Adding to the misery, the threat of contracting malaria, typhoid and other tropical diseases was ever present in close quarters. Boredom made everything seem worse.

Commanders segregated soldiers. Black troops always slept on the lowest deck, so the enlisted soldiers of the Twenty-fifth stayed in cramped quarters below the troops of the Fourth Regiment and, temporarily, the Massachusetts volunteers. "We were huddled together below two other regiments and under the water line, in the dirtiest, closest, most sickening place imaginable," wrote regimental chaplain T.G. Steward. "For about fifteen days we were on the water in this dirty hole, but being soldiers we were compelled to accept this without a murmur." During the day, on the upper deck, white troops remained on the port side and blacks on the starboard.[9]

The open air made the journey more tolerable. "The weather on our trip out was fine," reported the Fourth Regiment's Robert Travis, "the sun shining bright and warm during the day, with a nice cool breeze, that was a real treat to us after having suffered so much from heat during our camp at Tampa." Bands played "The Star Spangled Banner" and "Yankee Doodle." Soldiers periodically burst into song with "Bill Bailey" or "I Don't Like No Cheap Man" or the ever-popular "Hot Time in the Old Town Tonight." The Rough Riders, traveling on a nearby vessel, changed the words of the song to "There'll be a hot time in Cuba next week."[10]

Sons of East Tennessee

On June 19, Jack Bernard wrote "a long and cheerful letter to a young lady friend," a fragment of which a Knoxville newspaper later printed. Bernard's relationship with this woman must have been close: he acknowledged that she had asked him to come to her Knoxville home to recuperate if he were wounded in battle. "It seems to me I love the old state more and more; for it is more like home to me than any other place I have ever been," Bernard wrote. "Really it is the only home I have ever known. And I am coming home just as soon as this war is over."[11]

The precise destination of the transports finally became clear the next morning. The flotilla rounded the eastern tip of Cuba and headed west along the southern shore toward Santiago, Cuba's second largest city after Havana. Fortifications manned by more than ten thousand Spanish soldiers surrounded the town's thirty thousand residents. Admiral Sampson had requested that General Shafter's flotilla enter the heavily fortified bay so that the army could make a frontal assault on the forts. Shafter had decided otherwise: he planned to land east of Santiago, march inland, and attack the city from the rear.

"We are going to try to land tomorrow morning probably about daylight," McCorkle wrote on June 21. "We don't anticipate much opposition but of course we can't tell. We have seen lots of battleships and things, saw them firing at the fortifications yesterday...." McCorkle said the men were ready for a fight and "we dont [sic] fear them much on account of their poor shooting."[12]

Caspar Whitney, correspondent for *Harper's Weekly*, described the emotions that soldiers felt on approaching the coast of Cuba as ranging from the "thrill of alert expectancy" to a "hot desire" to see a foreign country. He said everyone felt "a sensation of relief—the grateful satisfaction of the hunter who suddenly views his quarry after long hours of weary chase and worrying delay."[13]

The first troops landed June 22 at Daiquiri, about sixteen miles east of Santiago. Shafter had his men ready to go well before sunrise. First, five warships bombarded the beach. Then soldiers began dropping from the transports into small landing boats, floated through rough waves, and jumped onto a dilapidated pier. Some men missed the pier and had to swim ashore. Burr McIntosh, a correspondent for *Leslie's Illustrated Newspaper* who swam to the beach, said the undertow was the strongest he had ever encountered. Dozens of horses drowned in the surf. Two men of the Tenth Cavalry fell between boat and pier and drowned when

11. Sailing from Tampa to Cuba (Spring, 1898)

The first American troops march into the Cuban jungle at Daiquiri, east of Santiago, on June 22, 1898. They had dropped from landing boats into a rough surf and made their way to shore. Two men and dozens of horses drowned (Library of Congress).

their equipage dragged them beneath the sea. Corporal Henry Williams of McCorkle's company nearly died after his boat capsized.[14]

The landing would have been far worse if the enemy had remained to oppose it. Under pressure from a force of several hundred Cubans, Spanish soldiers had abandoned Daiquiri for inland fortifications.

McCorkle and Bernard were among about six thousand soldiers who landed safely amid a multitude of mosquitoes and land crabs at Daiquiri. James Moss, Company G's second lieutenant, provided subsequent details. The Fourth and Twenty-Fifth Infantry and the rest of the Second Brigade marched three miles inland, then back three miles, then forward three miles, and camped. The next day they marched another six miles "through a wild, picturesque, jungle-like section of tropical luxuriance." The soldiers had moved, haltingly, toward Siboney, a coastal town several miles west of Daiquiri. Meanwhile, over the next two days, the rest of the army came ashore at Siboney and moved inland.[15]

Sons of East Tennessee

Aside from trails between villages and an occasional clearing, the exotic tangle of palm trees, bamboo, tropical bushes, ground vines, and varied tall grasses made much of the island nearly impenetrable. This density alarmed some men. "The jungle had a kind of hot, sullen beauty," noted a young soldier. "We had the feeling that it resented our intrusion—that, if we penetrated too far, it would rise up in anger and smother us."[16]

The Spanish chose to make their initial stand at the village of Las Guasimas and lost the field. Major General Wheeler, who had not commanded soldiers since the Civil War—among other exploits, he had staged a cavalry raid during Longstreet's siege of Knoxville—led the attack. After climbing a tree and training his magnifying glasses on retreating Spanish, Wheeler temporarily forgot where he was. "I see them," he shouted. "They are running, the damn Yankees—no, no, I mean the Spaniards—are running away!"[17] Advancing on a different section of the field, the dismounted Rough Riders marched into an ambush. They recovered after taking significant casualties and eventually forced the rest of the Spanish defenders to withdraw.

McCorkle mentioned this skirmish in a June 26 letter: "Haven't had much resistance, so just the Rough Riders and 10th Cav had a brush two days since [.] our side lost in killed & wounded about 40 or 50, they found 67 dead Spaniards [.] they say they carried lots of wounded away, we are slowly approaching the town & can see her from near here." McCorkle said he wished he "could be in Tenn., just a few minutes."[18]

The Second Brigade belatedly had marched to the battle site over mountainous terrain, Lieutenant Moss explained in his memoir that a stop-and-go approach irritated the men who "endured great suffering, and a number of men were overcome by the heat." The troops had taken a wrong trail and marched for thirteen hours in a loop back to their camp. Soldiers in other units for a brief time referred to them as "The Lost Brigade."[19]

The troops spent the next few days moving short distances and camping without encountering the enemy. The entire army was concentrating around Sevilla, an inland town near Las Guasimas and nearly halfway between Daiquiri and Santiago. Supplies, including food and clean water, were insufficient for thousands of soldiers. McCorkle explained to his wife that he made his own meals—mostly hard tack, bacon, coffee, and island coconuts. He improvised his bedding, using part of a rubber boat and a rubber blanket. He said he expected "severe

11. Sailing from Tampa to Cuba (Spring, 1898)

fighting" in a short time but looked optimistically to the future. "If we have to stay here long after the war you can come over [.] it is a fine country," he wrote.[20]

The weather abruptly turned damp—a depressing departure from the sunny journey to the island. A heavy rain on June 28 rendered the Twenty-fifth Regiment's camp "wet and slushy," Moss reported. On that day and the next, a soldier in the Fourth Infantry said the regiment "laid in camp all day."[21] The soggy soldiers marked time in anxious anticipation of the attack on Santiago.

McCorkle wrote from "Near Santiago, Cuba, June 29, 1898," to "my dearest Mildred" and with "love to Ma and Pa." It is evident that drops of rain fell on the paper as he penciled the note. "We are still here and haven't fit [sic] any more but expect to today or tomorrow," he explained. He said he had dreamed of being home. "The Spanish seem to have lost their grip," he concluded, "but they may have some surprise for us. We have marched through their country right to their den...."[22]

On June 30, Bernard wrote from Cuba for the first time since his June 19 letter to his "lady friend" in Knoxville. "We left the boat without knowing that we were off for good and consequently we have nothing," he told his father, then living at the Soldiers' Home in Washington. "As it rains a couple of times each day, I have been wet ever since I landed. I sleep in the mud and cover with my coat." He said his regiment had marched through dense jungle until reaching the outskirts of Santiago. "We can see the city from the first line and probably a movement will be commenced tomorrow or may be tonight," he wrote. "The town is beautifully situated for defense and we expect a hard fight." After describing the Cubans as "a lot of savages, worse than our Indians," he concluded, "You can be sure that I am o.k., until you hear officially that I am not."[23]

As Bernard wrote to his father, General Shafter and his aides rode to a hill known as El Pozo to get a closer look at the outer Spanish lines defending Santiago. With the aid of field glasses, Shafter could see forts, blockhouses, deep trenches, and long lines of barbed wire protecting San Juan Hill and Kettle Hill and, four miles away, El Caney. These defenses looked formidable but not impregnable. Shafter believed that the faster an assault could be made—before Spanish reinforcements arrived and yellow fever season erupted—the better his chances of taking Santiago. He scheduled the attack for early the next morning. Half the army—the Second Division—would overwhelm the Spanish forces guarding El Caney. Then those troops would join the First Division and

Sons of East Tennessee

Wheeler's Cavalry in an assault on San Juan Hill. Having taken command of all of the heights, the Americans would bombard Santiago.[24]

Shafter made his battle plan and then, feeling ill from the day's exertions and extreme heat, the gouty general lumbered into his tent and put his division commanders in charge of the war.

12

The Battle at El Caney (July 1, 1898)

Standing on a brushy hillock rising above the jungle, Captain Allyn Capron, Sr. trained his field glasses on El Viso, a small but substantial stone fort a mile away. El Viso commanded a ridge just south of El Caney, a small village on a rise about four miles northeast of Santiago. The fort blocked approaches to El Caney from the south and east—the approaches, because of the topography, that the American army would be forced to take.

The fifty-one-year-old artillery captain shifted his glasses slightly to the village itself. Spanish soldiers defended four wood blockhouses, smaller than the fort, that framed El Caney's palm-thatched houses. The village's church had loopholes and towers from which sharpshooters could pick off attacking troops. Capron saw that the Spanish had an abundance of secure locations from which they could defend the town.

The captain moved his field glasses to the southwest, toward Kettle and San Juan hills near Santiago. Similar defensive features were in place there, but they were not Capron's concern and he spent little time examining them. He prepared his four cannons to loft shells at El Viso. He told the gunners of Light Battery E, First Artillery, to fire quickly and accurately. Capron planned to destroy El Caney. He wanted to make the Spanish pay in blood for killing his son.

Allyn Capron, Jr., a twenty-seven-year-old Seventh Cavalry captain who had joined the Rough Riders on their way to Cuba, had been leading dismounted troopers at Las Guasimas on June 24 when Spanish bullets tore through his body. He died on the field. Two days later, Burr McIntosh, the war correspondent for *Leslie's*, watched as the senior Capron wiped away tears on approaching his son's raw grave. Capron paused to reflect. He asked how his son had died. But when officers offered Capron

Sons of East Tennessee

his son's effects, the captain rejected them. He wanted no reminders of his loss.[1]

Following General Shafter's orders, Capron directed his men to begin firing at 6:15 a.m. on July 1. He would keep the guns in action all morning and much of the afternoon. According to a news account, Capron would remain "standing close up to the guns and taking chances with his men." He would fire on the fort, then blast the blockhouses and entrenchments, then return to the fort.[2]

The infantry assault on El Caney would begin shortly after Capron opened fire. The attacking soldiers would have a tougher task than anyone anticipated. The Spanish lines were protected not only by the fort, blockhouses, and church, but also by entrenchments carved into solid rock and lines of barbed wire. Sharpshooters climbed to the tops

This dramatic photograph shows three of Captain Allyn Capron, Sr.'s cannons firing on El Viso, a stone fort at El Caney, Cuba. Capron continued firing his artillery throughout the battle. The picture was taken by William Dinwiddie, correspondent and photographer for the *New York Herald* (Library of Congress).

12. The Battle at El Caney (July 1, 1898)

of palm trees and into the church belfry so they could fire at attacking infantrymen. The defensive lines were formidable, but a modest force of just over five hundred Spanish troops had assembled to repel more than 6,600 Americans. William Shafter's generals told him the overwhelmingly superior American force could take El Caney in two hours. They had miscalculated badly: the operation consumed nine.[3]

The troops had begun marching from Sevilla toward El Pozo on the afternoon of June 30. There was only one substantial path between the villages and all of the troops used it, in single file. The *New York Herald*'s Richard Harding Davis said the procession "was as though fifteen regiments were encamped along the sidewalks of Fifth Avenue and were all ordered at the same moment to move into it and march downtown. If Fifth Avenue were ten feet wide, one can imagine the confusion." The narrow file marched from daylight into darkness to reach the army's staging area. Frank Norris, a correspondent for *McClure's* and *Century* magazines and a popular novelist, traveled with Brigadier General William Ludlow's First Brigade of Major General Henry Lawton's Second Division. Norris reported that no one talked as the soldiers began trudging through the rain at 5 p.m. But the jungle was not quiet: "There was the monotonous squash of many boots churning up the mud of the road, the click of swinging cups against bayonet scabbards, the indefinable murmur of a moving army that recalls the noise of the sea or of forests."[4]

Henry McCorkle's and Jack Bernard's regiments tried to march one behind the other near the middle of the line. They slogged toward their first major battle through ankle-deep black mud that sucked at their boots.

Cuban guides led the procession as intelligence officers scanned the terrain from a balloon, which, counter-productively, alerted the Spanish to the line of attack. At El Pozo, as darkness fell, the regiments divided. McCorkle, Bernard, and the rest of the Second Division moved along one fork of a trail north toward El Caney and bivouacked in the jungle about 10 p.m. The bulk of the Fifth Corps—the First Division and Wheeler's cavalry—traveled on another fork a short distance southwest. That path led to the base of San Juan and Kettle hills.

Lawton's four brigades had separated as they approached El Caney. Brigadier General Adna Chaffee's three regiments of the Third Brigade swung around to the north and east. Ludlow's three regiments of the First Brigade moved in south and west of the village, where they were able to support Captain Capron with rifle fire. Colonel Evan Miles' three regiments of the Second Brigade, including McCorkle's and Bernard's units, marched behind the others. Eventually they would move between Chaffee and Ludlow to form a continuous line of assault. Lawton's independent brigade—two regiments commanded by Brigadier General John Bates—brought up the rear.

Meanwhile, Spanish scouts kept Lieutenant General Arsenio Linares y Pombo, commander of all Spanish troops in the vicinity of Santiago, informed of the American movement. A seasoned veteran of the campaign against Cuban insurgents, the general believed that the Americans might attack from the sea or from any direction on land. So he adopted a cautious plan of defense, positioning most of his troops and artillery in Santiago's inner fortifications, facing in all directions. Only a fraction of his artillery and infantry—most of the soldiers representing three companies of the first battalion of the Twenty-ninth Constitutional Regiment—manned the formidable outer defenses running from El Caney to San Juan. These men were dressed appropriately for the climate in thin blue and white pinstriped cotton "pajama" uniforms and straw sombreros. They were well armed with Mauser rifles. Many had been seasoned by fighting Cuban forces. But it is doubtful that they understood the size of the force that was about to hit them. Even when he knew a concentrated attack was imminent, Linares made no attempt to reinforce the forward lines because he feared simultaneous assaults from other sectors.

The front lines of the American army were poised to move forward when Capron fired the first of his 3.2-inch cannons. Frank Norris had joined a cluster of correspondents on the hill with Capron. He watched as the artillery blasted stone from the front of the fort. Then he turned his attention to the infantry fire: "It began as corn begins to pop, irregularly and with pauses. Then it gathered volume and rippled and rolled and spread till it awoke a great echo somewhere up in a little gully in the hills."[5]

Advance elements of Ludlow's regiments moved within a few hundred yards of El Caney. The Spanish maintained a steady fire against any movement. A Spanish soldier shot Ludlow's horse from under him. Another wounded Lieutenant Colonel John Patterson as he led the Twenty-second Infantry. The troops of the Second Massachusetts, the only volunteer regiment in Lawton's division, made especially easy targets. Their black-smoke-spewing Springfields marked them for

12. The Battle at El Caney (July 1, 1898)

sharpshooters. Ludlow eventually pulled them from the front line and moved them to his left flank.

Meanwhile, on the right, Chaffee's men edged closer to Spanish positions. Standing behind trees, taking advantage of a sunken road, and digging in where possible, the soldiers attempted to avoid a continuous barrage of Mauser bullets. "One proceeded after the manner of the Biblical serpent, and if one didn't actually 'eat grass,' one kept remarkably close to it," explained Captain Arthur H. Lee, a British military attaché accompanying Chaffee's troops.[6] From their elevated positions, Spanish sharpshooters fired whenever a target appeared. Three shots incapacitated Lieutenant Colonel Joseph T. Haskell, commanding the Seventeenth Regiment. Lieutenant Walter Dickinson, also of the Seventeenth, was shot four times and died the next day. The Seventh Regiment suffered more casualties than any other American unit in the battle.

Caspar Whitney, covering the war for *Harper's Weekly*, also braved the Spanish fire with Chaffee's regiment. He described the fighting during the early morning as sounding like an incessant explosion of firecrackers. He added, "It was easy to distinguish the sharp metallic crack of the Mauser from the crash of the Krag-Jorgensen volleys, which assailed the ears like continuous quick ripping of linen."[7]

And then, from about 10 a.m. until 1 p.m., the lethal racket virtually stopped. Ludlow halted the attack so that his men, who had marched and fought for several hours, could rest. Reserves replenished ammunition on the front lines. Spanish and American sharpshooters continued to fire at anyone who moved. But few moved. As the temperature rose into the nineties and high humidity made breathing difficult, many American soldiers removed their heavy flannel shirts.

Meanwhile, after resting in a mango grove for several hours, Colonel Miles' regiments filled the gap between Ludlow and Chaffee. With the exception of the independent brigade, all of Lawton's division—nearly six thousand men—were now in position.

About 1 p.m., Lawton ordered Ludlow to direct a steady fire against the fort while Miles' and Chaffee's advance units—more than fifteen hundred troops—prepared to renew the attack on the few hundred Spanish defenders of El Caney. The Fourth and Twenty-fifth regiments of Miles' brigade formed battle lines, with Chaffee's Twelfth Regiment to their right. For all of these troops, the obstacles were a steady climb through two rows of trees, a barbed-wire fence they had to cut, an open

Sons of East Tennessee

El Viso, a stone fort atop a rise, guarded the town of El Caney. As line officers in Major General Henry Lawton's Second Division, Henry McCorkle and John Jay Bernard led their companies in attacking Spanish soldiers who defended the fort and village on July 1, 1898 (Library of Congress).

field of pineapples, scrub bushes that offered some cover, and then four hundred yards of open sawgrass leading to the fort and the village.

As the fresh troops of the Twenty-fifth moved into position, soldiers carried the dead and wounded from previous fighting to the rear. As he watched the procession of mangled men, Second Lieutenant James Moss thought to himself, "It all seems like a dream—a terrible dream!" A wounded soldier of the Second Massachusetts warned Moss

12. The Battle at El Caney (July 1, 1898)

that, "the buggers are hidden behind rocks, in weeds and in underbrush, and we just simply can't locate them; they are shooting our men all to pieces."[8]

McCorkle's and Moss's Company G, along with Bernard's Company H, formed the first firing line of the Twenty-fifth Regiment, with companies C and D in support. The soldiers crouched in the jungle eight hundred yards from what was left of El Viso. The Fourth Regiment deployed to the immediate left of the Twenty-fifth, with Company H linking with the advance companies of the Twenty-Fifth. Bernard must have been within a few hundred yards of McCorkle and Moss.

"Ye gods! it is raining lead!" observed Moss. "The line recoils like a mighty serpent, and then, in confusion, advances again! The Spaniards now see them and are pouring a murderous fire into their ranks! Men are dropping everywhere! ... The bullets are cutting the pineapples under our very feet—the slaughter is awful!"[9]

As soldiers sloshed through ruined, prickly pineapples and cut their way through even pricklier barbed wire, Spanish sharpshooters steadily picked them off. Desperately, soldiers formed small groups and tried to hold their positions. Just after 2 p.m., Capron began moving his battery to a new rise. He reduced the distance between his cannons and El Viso to within one thousand yards and concentrated his fire on the fort and the blockhouses. Destructive artillery shells tore into the fortifications, but they stood on the highest ground and their defenders continued to blunt the attack.

As Spanish sharpshooters and limited artillery hit more targets, the psychological damage also increased. Officers at the front recognized that this situation could not continue. All along the line, field commanders decided it would be better to charge uphill into withering fire rather than be targeted individually in place. Almost simultaneously, they urged their troops to attack.

Standing up or crouching only slightly, as line officers were expected to do, McCorkle and Bernard led their men through steady sniper fire. McCorkle told the guide on the left of his company to stay close to the Fourth Infantry. "Forward, march! Guide left. Don't fire until you see somebody; then fire to hit!" McCorkle ordered as his men haltingly moved toward the fort and the village. "Balls flew like bees, humming as they went," recalled the guide. As the charging soldiers encountered barbed wire and other obstacles, "the only thing left was to go ahead or die; or else retreat like cowards. We preferred to go ahead."[10]

Sons of East Tennessee

The Twenty-fifth's Companies G and H supported each other. First one company would rush forward, fire weapons, lie down, and reload; then the other would do the same. McCorkle's men were lying down, reloading, and the lieutenant was kneeling on one knee beneath a cherry tree when a sharpshooter shot him through his right arm and lungs. First Lieutenant Henry Kinnison, of Company E, was standing near McCorkle when he was hit. He reported that McCorkle simply murmured, "I'm done for," and died.[11]

Lieutenant Moss also was close to McCorkle when the bullet struck. Immediately taking command of the company, Moss cried out, "Come ahead! Let's get at these Spaniards!" and continued leading the charge. Lieutenant J.S. Murdock, commanding Company C, also fell with a wound; Moss took charge of his company as well. Almost simultaneously, Spanish fire hit other soldiers. "A man on [McCorkle's] right exclaims, 'ugh,' and dropping his rifle, falls dead!" Moss recalled. "Another just in front cries out, 'I'm shot!' Bullets are dropping like hail.' Spanish fire twice repelled an officer and two privates attempting to carry McCorkle's body to a sheltered area. A third effort succeeded."[12]

Bernard's company began moving forward, slightly behind McCorkle's, at about the same time. Bernard also stood or knelt as he advanced, continually exposing himself. A Spanish soldier, also probably a sharpshooter, shot him through the neck. He lingered, unconscious, for two hours before dying.[13]

H. W. French, a first lieutenant in the Fourth Regiment who had attended the University of Tennessee with Bernard, said he was not far away when the second lieutenant fell. "I simply know he died fighting like the brave fellow he was," he reported. "His company was deployed as advance to the regiment, and while making a rush across an open space he was picked out by a sharpshooter." John Maxwell, covering the Fourth Regiment's action for the *Chicago Tribune*, reported that Bernard was "absolutely fearless on the field. He refused to lie down when he might have saved his life." Robert Travis, with Company B in the advance battalion with Bernard, said the lieutenant's death was "deeply regretted by all, as he was a general favorite with the men of the company."[14]

Captain Leonard Lovering, who had been reprimanded at Fort Sheridan the previous autumn after Bernard and others testified that he had abused a private, again commanded the Fourth Regiment's Company C during this fight. Maxwell reported that Lovering "thought nothing of his own danger and took little heed of the shrapnel that sung over

12. The Battle at El Caney (July 1, 1898)

his head." Lovering dug small trenches for individual soldiers and carried wounded men to safety while under fire. Thereby, he "did much to redeem himself in the eyes of his men."[15]

The Fourth Regiment did not continue all of the way to the fort, instead staying in place and firing on the village, thereby facilitating the Twenty-fifth Regiment's advance. While covering the Twenty-fifth, however, the lead companies of the Fourth remained exposed to Spanish fire. Commending the regiment in his report, Colonel Miles said, "its steady front and accurate volleys greatly assisted the advance of the remainder of the brigade upon the stone fort."[16] Near the end or the fight, Bates' independent brigade also joined the attack.

Frank Pullen, a sergeant-major in the rear ranks of the Twenty-fifth, described the final charge: "Some one gave a yell and the 25th Infantry was off, alone to the charge. The 4th U.S. Infantry, fighting on the left, halted when those dusky heroes made the dash with a yell which would have done credit to a Comanche Indian." Pullen further reported that the "dash" was actually "a tough, hard climb, over sharp, rising ground, which were a man in perfect physical strength, he would climb slowly."[17]

Moss recalled various other officers urging their men to the top of the hill: "A young officer is running up and down, back of the firing line, and waving his hat above his head, is exclaiming to the men in the rear: 'Come on, come on, men—we've got 'em on the run!' 'Remember the *Maine*!' shouts a sergeant. 'Give them hell, men!' cries out an officer. 'There's another!' shouts a soldier—bang! bang! bang! and another Spaniard drops. Four are shot down in the door of the fort."[18]

The Twelfth Regiment arrived at El Viso at about the same time as the Twenty-fifth. In contributions to Lawton's official report on El Caney, Third Brigade commander Adna Chaffee and Twenty-fifth Regiment commander A.S. Daggett fought another battle over who actually captured the fort.

Lawton supported the position of Chaffee and other observers that the Twelfth got to the fort first, took the Spanish flag, and "practically closed the battle." Lawton's Report did not name the individual who captured the flag, but other sources did. Captain Arthur Lee said William Randolph Hearst's star reporter, James Creelman, who accompanied Chaffee's troops, entered the fort first and was "shot through the shoulder in a successful attempt to recover the Spanish flag that was lying on the glacis." Hearst himself had watched the battle from the vantage point of Capron's battery. When he discovered that Creelman had been

William Glackens drew this sketch of the Twelfth and Twenty-Fifth Infantry about to capture El Viso for the October 1898 issue of *McCall's* magazine. The two regiments disagreed about which arrived at the fort first. Glackens became a realist painter and one of the founders of the Ashcan School of American art (author's collection).

injured, the publisher hurried to the field hospital to interview him. Hearst's July 4 story in the *New York Journal* quoted Creelman as saying he entered the fort first.[19]

Daggett was equally adamant that because of the bold advance of his regiment beyond the rest of the brigade "the Twenty-fifth Infantry

12. The Battle at El Caney (July 1, 1898)

caused the surrender of the fort." Moss and Pullen supported Daggett in their memoirs. Moss said the Spanish presented a white flag of surrender to the Twenty-Fifth Regiment. Pullen said Private T.C. Butler of Company H "was the first man to enter the blockhouse at El Caney, and took possession of the Spanish flag for his regiment" before an officer of the Twelfth Regiment ordered him to give it to him. Pullen further clarified and amplified the role of the Twenty-fifth: "The Negro played a most important part in the Spanish-American War. He was the first to move from the west; first at Camp Thomas, Chickamauga Park, Ga.; first in the jungle of Cuba; among the first killed in battle; first in the block-house at El Caney, and nearest to the enemy when he surrendered."[20]

After taking El Viso, the Americans still had to fight their way through the village's defenses. Moss described the last stage of the battle, as his two companies entered El Caney. The soldiers moved steadily up the hillside, with men falling periodically from continuing Spanish fire. Some troops paused to shoot at Spanish soldiers who remained in the town. Others reached an area slightly above one of the blockhouses and began shooting through its roof until, as Lieutenant Moss reported, "the Spaniards are falling over one another to get out!"[21]

Overwhelmed, the survivors fled the town late in the afternoon. General Joaquin Vara del Rey y Rubio, commander of El Caney's forces, and his two sons died in the closing moments of the battle. American soldiers and newspaper correspondents found dozens of bodies in the fort, blockhouses, and trenches. "After the surrender of the Spanish works, I went up to examine them," Robert Travis wrote in his diary. "The trenches were filled with the dead and wounded, the latter being cared for by our men. I saw one Spanish officer, sitting up in one of the trenches, with a small Poodle dog in his arms. He was stone dead, having been shot through the head, the dog was alive and growled at us as we passed."[22]

Several journalists and soldiers commented on the bravery of the outnumbered Spanish soldiers. "The trench-fighting of the Spaniards with their Mausers was in very fact the heart and centre of that day's work," reported the journalist Joseph Edgar Chamberlin. Chamberlin, who accompanied the Seventeenth Regiment of Chaffee's brigade, thought that "the heroism of our men appears none the less in the light of the heroism of their antagonists."[23]

Of the more than five hundred Spanish soldiers guarding the fort and town, an estimated thirty-eight were killed, 138 wounded, and 160 captured. Most of the rest fled during the last moments of the battle to the inner trenches at Santiago.[24]

The attacking army's losses were more substantial, as is commonly the case when an army attacks an entrenched force. Eighty-one Americans died. Of the 360 who were wounded, dozens subsequently died. Compared with the massive casualties on Civil War battlefields, these were relatively minor losses. As a percentage of soldiers actually engaged in combat, however, they were significant. Speaking at the dedication of a battle monument at El Caney several years later, Lieutenant Colonel Alfred C. Sharpe, who served with the forces that attacked San Juan Hill, said the troops in the Cuban battles sustained more casualties, without halting their advance and waiting for supporting troops, than anyone previously had thought possible. He particularly mentioned the Seventh Regiment at El Caney and several regiments at San Juan. He commended the American army as a whole, claiming it had established "a new world record," with some regiments suffering casualty rates greater than thirty percent.[25]

The Fourth and Twenty-fifth regiments also sustained heavy losses. The Spanish killed Bernard and First Lieutenant William C. Neary, of the Fourth Regiment. They also killed eight other soldiers and wounded an officer and thirty enlisted men in that unit. McCorkle and eight enlisted men died in the Twenty-fifth Regiment. Three officers and twenty enlisted men were wounded.[26]

The only other soldier in McCorkle's company who died on July 1 was Aaron Leftwich, a black private, also from Hawkins County. The fact that Aaron's surname is the same as McCorkle's middle name, which Henry took from his mother, Susan Leftwich McCorkle, may be more than coincidental. According to a McCorkle family descendant, the Leftwich family at one time owned slaves in Virginia. Slaves often took their owners' surnames. Leftwich is not a common name, so it seems possible that Aaron Leftwich was descended from Africans who had been enslaved by the Leftwich family.[27]

McCorkle and Bernard received personalized posthumous commendations from their commanding officers. Daggett said in a General Order to his regiment that "the genial, generous-hearted McCorkle fell at his post of duty, bravely directing his men in the advance on the stone fort. He died as the soldier dies, and received a soldier's burial. He was beloved by all who knew him, and his name will always be fondly remembered by his regiment—especially by those who participated in

12. The Battle at El Caney (July 1, 1898)

the Santiago campaign." Daggett instructed the officers of the regiment to wear a badge of mourning for McCorkle for thirty days. In his contribution to Lawton's report on the battle, Major Stephen Baker, commander of the Fourth Regiment, said, "The conduct of the troops was simply perfect. First Lieut. W.C. Neary and Second Lieut. J.J. Bernard, Fourth Regiment, proved their distinguished bravery by laying down their lives on the field."[28]

Meanwhile, Teddy Roosevelt was making himself famous. Well before Henry Lawton's troops had killed or captured the last Spanish troops remaining at El Caney, Roosevelt, the Rough Riders, and other lead elements of the First Division had struggled up Kettle and San Juan hills, overwhelming their severely outnumbered defenders. By early evening, the American army held all the heights near Santiago. The United States had won the ground war in Cuba, essentially, in one day.

13

Burial and Memorial (July 1898–Winter 1899)

On the night of July 1, the soldiers of Lawton's Division faced solemn obligations before they could leave El Caney, retrieve the blanket rolls and haversacks they had shed before the assault, and join the rest of the Fifth Corps on the heights above Santiago. They had to bury eighty-one comrades. While most of the exhausted soldiers rested and ate pineapples, mangoes, and limited rations, soldiers of the Pioneer Corps dug graves. They rushed to bury the dead before dusk.

As the gravediggers worked, friends of the deceased searched corpses for personal effects to return to grieving families. In a pocket of Jack Bernard's uniform jacket, a soldier found the letter the lieutenant had written to his father the night before the battle describing his activities up to June 30, concluding, "you can be sure that I am o.k., until you hear officially that I am not." In an accompanying note, Bernard had requested that, in the event of his death, the letter be mailed to General Reuben Bernard at the Soldiers' Home in Washington.[1]

Charles Hodges, captain of the Twenty-fifth Regiment, located Henry McCorkle's body, stripped it of everything of value, and gave the materials to Elmer Scherrer, the regiment's assistant surgeon. Scherrer sent the materials to Mildred McCorkle, his sister-in-law. These items, which remain within the McCorkle family, included McCorkle's wedding ring, an elaborately engraved military-issue sword, a Bible embossed with his name, and his battle wallet. Inside the wallet were three coins, including an 1898 "Indian Head" penny. The wallet also contained the business card of a Tampa dentist and a $150 promissory note written in June to Milton B. Ochs, a former Knoxvillian who was serving as a funeral agent at the Bank of Chattanooga. Obviously, McCorkle had made funeral arrangements before leaving Tennessee.

13. Burial and Memorial (July 1898–Winter 1899)

Henry McCorkle was carrying this battle wallet when he was shot at El Caney. Items found in the wallet included a $150 promissory note written to a funeral agent at the Bank of Chattanooga to cover McCorkle's potential funeral arrangements (courtesy Maynard McCorkle, a great-grandson of H. L. McCorkle).

The wallet also contained a tiny lock of hair taken from Guy McCorkle at birth. Hodges clipped a lock of Henry McCorkle's hair to add to the mementos.[2]

In addition, S.C. Staunton, who identified himself as an acting assistant surgeon, sent Mildred McCorkle a "sleeve-link" marked "McC" on the advice of Mildred's father, Captain Henry Ritzius. Staunton said a soldier of the Twenty-fourth Infantry had found this cuff link following the battle of San Juan Hill.[3]

After the Pioneer Corps buried the dead men, soldiers from their regiments erected crude wood or stone memorials on top of or near the graves. In keeping with longstanding military tradition, the army buried officers separately and with more elaborate markers.

A headboard with name and regiment, supported by a pile of boulders, marked McCorkle's grave. Smaller stones formed a cross on the grave itself. Seven of the Twenty-fifth Infantry's eight fatalities,

Sons of East Tennessee

In addition to crude wood or stone memorials used temporarily to mark graves of Americans killed in Cuba, a common practice was to peel the bark from trees and carve names of the dead on bare trunks. This photograph, taken in late July 1898, shows the names of Lieutenant H. L. McCorkle on the left and seven privates of McCorkle's Twenty-fifth Regiment on the right. It appeared in newspapers nationwide beneath the heading "Trees as Monuments" (from *The Martial Graves of Our Fallen Heroes* by Henry C. McCook, 1899, U.S. Army Heritage and Education Center, Carlisle, Pennsylvania).

13. Burial and Memorial (July 1898–Winter 1899)

including Aaron Leftwich, were buried in a common grave beside McCorkle. Their names were inscribed on two headboards. And then soldiers scraped bark from two young trees growing just behind the headboards and again inscribed the names—McCorkle's on one tree, and Leftwich's and the other privates' on the other.[4]

The Pioneer Corps buried soldiers of the Fourth Regiment and the Second Massachusetts Volunteers several hundred yards southwest, at the edge of a mango grove. They buried Jack Bernard and First Lieutenant Charles Field, of the Second Massachusetts, side-by-side. Soldiers surrounded both graves with oblong arrays of stones. Additionally, they marked Bernard's grave with a square box cover, inscribed with his name and regiment, and Field's grave with a small wood cross. Nearby, two large graves contained enlisted men. Most of these men were unnamed. Many men had thrown away parts of their clothing and other belongings in the heat of the jungle battle. Bodies mutilated by head wounds were especially hard to recognize. Soldiers did not begin

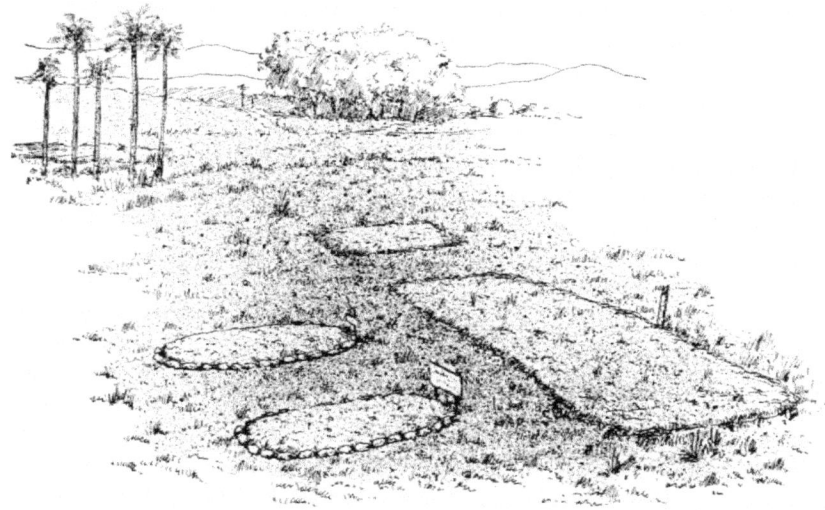

John Jay Bernard's Cuban grave site, sketched at front center, was adjacent to the graves of other officers and enlisted men. According to Henry McCook, who made the sketch, the mound of earth was "surrounded with stones, and a square bit of box cover supported upon two sticks bears the inscription" (from *The Martial Graves of Our Fallen Heroes* by Henry C. McCook, 1899, U.S. Army Heritage and Education Center, Carlisle, Pennsylvania).

wearing identifying "dog tags" until two decades later in World War I, so identifying the dead was often difficult.[5]

After graves were made and marked, companies assembled at the sites. Lieutenant Moss reported that trumpeters blew "Taps" as soldiers "paid a last, silent tribute of respect to our comrades...." Then the regiments marched back to the grove of mangoes where they had left their possessions. They rested there that night. Robert Travis wrote in his diary, "We were very tired and worn out from hunger, which had been hardly felt, until the excitement of the battle was over."[6]

Despite a hard-fought victory and the prospect of quickly winning the war, the magazine correspondent Frank Norris observed no sense of triumph in the army as it moved away from the battlefield. Rather, he wrote, "a feeling of depression lay upon us, and upon the soldiers with whom we were marching. There was no great talk. It was a sorrowful army marching through the twilight after victory."[7]

The army buried another 124 soldiers on the slopes and peaks of San Juan Hill and Kettle Hill that evening as soldiers in the remainder of the corps lamented the loss and felt thankful they had survived. Their sorrow took some time to travel home. The first American newspaper accounts of the battles at El Caney and San Juan emphasized military success. "Victory Sure" read a July 1 *Knoxville Sentinel* headline. A July 4 banner headline in the *Knoxville Journal and Tribune* blared: "Most Thrilling Record for a Fourth of July Since the Bells of Independence Hall Rang." Then came the bad news. The July 4 *Sentinel* published a preliminary casualty list and the *New York Times* followed the next day.

Henry McCorkle's name was on that first list. Jack Bernard's was not. But the *Knoxville Journal*, published on the morning of July 6, did not list either man. This prompted University of Tennessee President Charles Dabney to write to Dr. William McCorkle. He said he was glad to see that a revised casualty list "inferred" that Henry, "a noble fellow and very dear to all his old friends here," had escaped the battle unscathed.[8]

It is not known if the army had informed McCorkle of his son's death by July 6, but it seems probable. The army apparently told Reuben Bernard that his son had died shortly after the news was telegraphed to Washington on the day of the battle. The general had gone to the War Department that day to ask that Jack Bernard be moved to a cavalry unit as soon as an opening occurred. He succeeded in his mission,

13. Burial and Memorial (July 1898–Winter 1899)

only to receive a telegram announcing his son's death before he left the department.[9]

The *Sentinel* finally confirmed McCorkle's death July 11. Along with a facial sketch apparently made from a photograph, the paper printed a lengthy obituary. It concentrated on McCorkle's record at the university and concluded with remarks about visits with friends in Knoxville during the lieutenant's leave in May: "Whenever reference was made to his going to war in his presence he became at once serious and refrained from talking about it. The many friends of Lieut. McCorkle are grieved at the sudden cutting off of what appeared to be a brilliant career for him."

Bernard's obituary appeared in the next day's paper, also with a sketch made from a photo. Misspelling his name "Barnard," the *Sentinel* said he was "one of the most popular young men who ever lived in this city." This obituary also focused on Bernard's achievements during his college years. It especially praised his service as captain of a student military company, noting that "he was one of the best disciplinarians who ever left the hill."

The *Sentinel* acknowledged the deaths of the lieutenants and others in a July 15 editorial: "Yea, ever through the pomp and circumstances of war there pulses that undercurrent which has its origin in the saddest words we know—He will not come home again." A friend of Henry McCorkle wrote a tribute to his memory that appeared in the same paper. "He was brave and unflinching in his duty," the anonymous writer said. "His friends are not surprised that he should have been found at the very front, risking and losing his life, while charging a fort under the deadliest and most concentrated fire of the enemy."

The university recognized the exclusive status of the lieutenants. Of the university's fifty-seven commissioned officers who had served in regular and volunteer army units and in the navy as of July 20, McCorkle and Bernard were the only two who had been killed. Perhaps President Dabney first noticed this association, but friends of the two men quickly spread the news.[10]

The Alumni Association adopted resolutions recognizing the lieutenants' service and sacrifice. McCorkle's brief, formal resolution capsulized his life, noting that "it is because he was a man among men, a gentleman, a soldier and a friend, that we are moved to tears of regret and emotions of sympathy for those who stand nearest and dearest to this dead soldier." Someone who apparently knew Bernard well wrote his resolution. "It is not rare to find the name of John among men," it read, "but there is something almost unerring in the general instinct which converts that name to 'Jack' when its bearer combines in his character all the rich and genial elements which make for popularity." The resolution lamented that the news that Bernard should die in "the serrocco-breath [sic] of bullet and shell that blew from the Spanish works at Santiago seems a far-off thing. To know that it was our own Jack Bernard thrills it with reality and drives it home to our hearts. Jack Bernard is dead. He represented for us the finest type of the American: bold, happy, genial, dauntless."[11]

On the afternoon of Sunday, November 13, the university held a memorial service in the large auditorium of Science Hall. The university's cadet corps and a delegation from the Fourth Tennessee Volunteer Regiment led a procession to the ceremony. President Dabney presented the main address to hundreds of friends of the lieutenants and the university. He outlined the soldiers' lives as students and military officers and provided those details of their deaths that he had been able to obtain. Dabney described a close relationship between the men. "The two were friends since becoming acquainted at the university," he said, "and though separated for a long time they were brought close to each other when death approached and died at the same time."[12]

Dabney introduced his comments by linking "The Soldier's Faith" (unquestioning devotion to a cause) to the university's mission: "Our object here is to train young men to war a good warfare, and we are thus taught to honor those who have fought a good fight, and especially those who have 'kept the faith.'" The November 14 *Knoxville Journal and Tribune* approved of this message. The newspaper commended the university's "aggressive patriotism" and the Science Hall service as a lesson to young men that "noble deeds are remembered when noble lives are ended."

Following the service, Mildred McCorkle, who had moved with Guy to her parents' home in West Point, New York, wrote on black-bordered stationery to her sister-in-law, Jennie McCorkle, in Mooresburg. She commented on the many soldiers of the Twenty-fifth Regiment who had written to her about Henry. "Oh, every thing seems like a dream," she concluded. "I seem to be in some thick haize. [sic]"[13]

Captain Hodges wrote one of those consolation letters. As he removed personal effects from Henry McCorkle's body, he told Mildred, he noticed that "he lay with a half smile upon his face. What *you*

13. Burial and Memorial (July 1898–Winter 1899)

will remember so well." Writing with "my eyes full of tears—I loved him, too—as did all of us," Hodges conveyed the essential assessment that McCorkle "died 'doing his duty'—like the gentleman he was...."[14]

During the summer and autumn of 1898, a legion of other soldiers, friends, and relatives of the families expressed their condolences and shared their remembrances of the lieutenants. Only a few of these letters remain in the McCorkle family. For example, one of Henry's childhood friends and a patient of Dr. McCorkle said Henry's death "called to mind all of our early associations when we were school boy & girl at the little log schoolhouse & [I] felt indeed as if it were a *personal* loss."[15]

William McCorkle wrote to his sister, Margaret, that he and his wife had received letters from several officers and hundreds of friends. The doctor said he was sad that his son "should be taken away, so young, when everything looked so promising for the future but such is life. He had never seen any trouble or sorrow, never had lost any of his near kin, brothers or sisters, died an almost painless death, and I hope he has received a high [sic] promotion than he could get here on earth."[16]

Letters of condolence, memorial services, and other special occasions periodically blunted or exacerbated the pain that the McCorkles and Bernards felt through the rest of that year. "Well, Xmas is nearly here and such a sad one as it will be," Mildred McCorkle wrote to her father at his western post on December 19. "I cannot help but think how happy we all were a year ago and how many changes there have been since then. Henry, Guy & I went to the Col's for Xmas dinner and Henry went out for a hunting trip the next day. How he loved to hunt. But now all is changed and always will be in this world."[17]

Life changed for survivors of the Fourth and Twenty-fifth regiments as well. They returned to New York in mid–August to reorganize before returning west—the Fourth to Fort Sheridan and the Twenty-fifth to several forts in Arizona. Both regiments would be dispatched early the following year to fight an insurrection against the American takeover of the Philippines, an elongated struggle that would prove to be far more challenging, and controversial, than the brief but deadly battles in Cuba.

✤ ✤ ✤

Following the surrender at Santiago, Spain signed a peace protocol halting all hostilities in mid–August. The Treaty of Paris formally ended the war December 10. Spaniards took down the flag that had flown over Santiago for nearly four centuries and Cuba became an independent nation. Spain also ceded Puerto Rico (following a brief struggle with American troops that summer), the West Indies, and the Philippine Islands to the United States for $20 million. The Spanish empire abruptly expired, and the United States became a world power.

The price in blood was shocking for a short war. Nearly 3,300 American soldiers and sailors died from war wounds or disease, almost ten times more from the latter than the former.

Some units had been devastated by disease. Robert Travis reported that his Fourth Regiment had left Fort Sheridan on April 19 with 450 soldiers. When the regiment returned to the fort on September 16, it mustered only 250 men "The few, who were fortunate to get back with the company, were only shadows of their former selves," he wrote in his diary. "Several have died, since we arrived, from the effects of our campaign and a great many are suffering from the effects of hardships endured in Cuba."[18]

Americans had mourned particularly the losses of July 1, the anniversary of the first day of the battle of Gettysburg and the deadliest single day for American soldiers since the Civil War. The extent of the damage done to other men would not be known for weeks or months. For example, Lieutenant Colonel Joseph Haskell, wounded three times while commanding the Seventeenth Regiment at El Caney, returned to his home in Columbus, Ohio, that August. On September 7, he was promoted to brigadier general for bravery on the battlefield. On the afternoon of September 16, he died of apoplexy. He was fifty-five.[19]

Life for thousands of American families would be burdened forever because of "the splendid little war," but patriotic fervor for the most popular conflict in U.S. history softened the nation's sorrow. Civil War veterans were especially energized by the outcome of the war. Beyond celebrating a decisive victory over Spain, leaders of veterans organizations emphasized that a significant consequence of the war was an acceleration of the reunion of North and South through shared experiences on the battlefield. "We only needed a common danger to arouse our people," commented a GAR commander. "No section of our country responded to arms more readily or more enthusiastically than the young men from Dixie."[20]

A singular event occurred in a Washington theater in mid–July, as reported in Knoxville and other newspapers. When an orchestra played "The Star Spangled Banner," only half the audience stood in recognition. This disturbed a former Union army officer and Indian fighter, one

13. Burial and Memorial (July 1898–Winter 1899)

Fitz Guerin staged this romantic tableau, entitled "Cuba Libre," following the war with Spain. It depicts aging Confederate and Union officers breaking the shackles that the Spanish used to restrain a young child wearing a crown inscribed "Cuba." Guerin had won a Medal of Honor as a Union soldier. He became famous as a society and celebrity photographer in St. Louis (Library of Congress).

"Captain Wilkinson," who wore his campaign uniform to the concert. But when Wilkinson cried out, "Three cheers for a reunited country!" according to the story, "every one, men and women, were on their feet, and there were some old men there whose eyes were full of tears...."[21]

Colonel S.S. Fordyce, of St. Louis, a former Union colonel who married the daughter of a former Confederate colonel, was one of many who articulated the position for total reunification: "This war with Spain is worth all it will cost in blood and treasure for the love it brings each for the other and the confidence it begets between the ex-soldiers of both armies, as well as the fraternal feeling it will create between the people of all states."[22]

Former Confederate Major General John Gordon, a white supremacist who for years had defended the politics of the antebellum South, had begun taking a more conciliatory position after becoming the first commander of the UCV in 1890. Gordon told the organization's annual convention in Atlanta in late July 1898 that he believed the cooperative effort in the war would lead "to the complete and permanent obliteration of all sectional distrusts, and to the establishment of the too long delayed brotherhood and unity of the American people, which shall never be broken nor called into question no more forever."[23]

Everyone did not agree with this sentiment. The acerbic Ambrose Bierce, who had begun collecting entries for *The Devil's Dictionary*, had learned to despise war as a Union soldier and was one of the few journalists who opposed war with Spain. He wrote a *San Francisco Examiner* column that August with a sarcastic pen, "Well, well, well!—Jo. Wheeler assisting at the hoisting of the American flag! Is it not all a dream—all these thirty-odd years of peace and reconciliation, ending in a fantastic Federal-Confederate war with Spain?"[24]

But this was a minority view and President McKinley knew it. In May 1899, early in his tour of the South to honor returning Spanish-American War veterans, McKinley visited the graves of some friends killed during fighting in Virginia's Shenandoah Valley. After leaving the national cemetery in Winchester, he crossed the street to view the graves of Confederates in their separate cemetery. The *Philadelphia Inquirer* approved of such goodwill gestures: "War has its evils which everybody can perceive, but it has indirect compensations often of the greatest magnitude, which the wisest cannot foresee. The war with Spain has been worth to the United States a thousand times its cost."[25]

In December, McKinley visited the Atlanta Peace Jubilee celebrating the end of the war. He told the Georgia legislature that the federal government "in the spirit of fraternity" should begin caring for Confederate as well as Union graves in national cemeteries. "The cordial feeling now happily existing between the North and South prompts this gracious act," he explained, "and if it needed further justification, it is found

13. Burial and Memorial (July 1898–Winter 1899)

in the gallant loyalty to the Union and the flag so conspicuously shown in the year just past by the sons and grandsons of these heroic dead."[26]

Some Southerners rejected this offer. They felt that their reasons for waging civil war were in no way respected by it. McKinley's initiative covered only those Confederates who had died in Union hospitals or prisoner-of-war camps and were buried in separate sections of national cemeteries. Confederates who died while bearing arms and Confederate veterans who died following the war still were not eligible for burial in national cemeteries. Some men indicated they would not welcome federal care for their graves in any case. One former Confederate wrote to the *Confederate Veteran* in complaint: "I wish you would file away in your papers that I don't think a Yankee tombstone would fit my grave."[27]

But many other veterans warmly greeted McKinley's declaration as a significant act of reconciliation. The Georgia legislature itself had cheered the president's announcement. One legislator, a Confederate veteran, reportedly "buried his head in his arms, and, while cheers rang out, cried like a little child." R.M. Barton, Jr., a Nashville judge, wrote the president as soon as he received the news: "As a son of an Ex Confederate, as a kinsman of Confederate dead, as the father of two boys who proudly wore the blue under your call, I want to add my personal thanks for the noble, wide and generous sentiments uttered by you at Atlanta." A Georgia woman wrote, "We are all McKinleyites now. So often have I been in the national cemetery at Chattanooga and wished that our Confederate dead could have their graves so well kept by the government, and in my heart felt rebellious that it was not so." Within one hour after reading the president's speech, she raised the American flag over her house.[28]

McKinley had settled the issue of who should maintain the grave sites of all Civil War soldiers buried in national cemeteries. Meanwhile, lush jungle growth was overrunning the graves of the Spanish-American War dead in Cuba.

14

Reburial and Reconciliation (April 2, 1899)

No one had anticipated so many graves.

Battle deaths in Cuba had been relatively light and field surgeons using sanitation techniques unknown to Dr. William McCorkle in the 1860s had reduced the fatality rate from wounds. But virulent yellow fever caught the army before it could escape the stifling climate in mid-August. Hundreds of soldiers would die of the disease on the island and dozens more after returning to the mainland.

Recognizing the danger of the impending epidemic, especially to soldiers who had never been exposed to tropical diseases in the deep Southern states, the War Department dispatched a committee from the National Relief Commission to Santiago. The committee arrived July 25 with medical supplies for soldiers suffering from yellow fever as well as battle wounds.

Henry Christopher McCook, the sixty-one-year-old pastor of the Tabernacle Presbyterian Church of Philadelphia, was a member of the committee. McCook had served as a Union regimental chaplain during the Civil War and now was chaplain of the Second Regiment of Pennsylvania Volunteers. He had written books on church history and several detailed studies of the behavior of ants and spiders. He was a close observer of nature. As he moved through multiple hospital camps, McCook noticed disruptions to foliage created by the hastily prepared graves of those who had fallen during the assault on Santiago.

After only three weeks, McCook later wrote, "it was evident that the rapid growth of tropical plants would soon hide the places of burial, and that the torrential rains would efface the writings hastily made upon the rudely constructed markers...." Moreover, McCook explained, the Fifth Corps soon would leave the island and "strangers indifferent or

14. Reburial and Reconciliation (April 2, 1899)

hostile to our cause and name would occupy the fields honored by the valor and consecrated by the death and burial of our heroes."[1]

The chaplain carefully examined and described the grave sites he found, including those of Henry McCorkle and Jack Bernard. He made preliminary notes on the position and condition of graves and returned to Washington in early August to confer with President McKinley. As a result of that meeting, McKinley ordered that more durable markers be erected at the graves. The president appointed David H. Rhodes, a longtime landscape gardener employed by the Quartermaster General's Office at Arlington National Cemetery, to lead a Burial and Disinterment Corps to Cuba. Rhodes took with him eight hundred sturdy wood headboards. They would not be enough. More than one thousand American soldiers eventually died in Cuba.

Rhodes and McCook arrived in Santiago in mid–August. Rhodes placed the headboards at the graves McCook had found and at additional sites he discovered. McCook helped treat the last of the sick soldiers preparing to leave the island before again concentrating on the graves, photographing and sketching many of them. He reported all of these activities in an exceptional book, *The Martial Graves of Our Fallen Heroes*. He dedicated the book "to the Memory of the Heroic Dead in a Conflict for Humanity" and sent copies to the families of every dead soldier and sailor. He described all graves in meticulous detail, including changes to the grave sites since he had first seen them. For example, he photographed an elaborate iron railing that had been arranged around Henry McCorkle's grave while McCook was in Washington. "It is almost certain that no foughten fields have ever been so promptly and thoroughly studied...," he wrote.[2]

Beyond noting the obvious value the comrades of fallen soldiers accorded these graves by clearly, and often creatively, marking them, McCook provided an anecdote to illustrate how important it was to the dead themselves that their burial spots be designated. He said former Union Colonel Caleb Churchman, of Delaware, told him that his son and only child, Second Lieutenant Clarke Churchman, had been killed while leading a company of the Twelfth Regiment at El Caney. On the day before he died, the lieutenant scribbled these words on a piece of paper: "If buried here I desire grave *plainly marked*." McCook included a photo of the note in his book.[3]

As the first Americans to fight on a foreign island, soldiers in Cuba understood not only that they might die far from home, but also that their remains might stay there. They may have inherited this concern from the previous generation. Thousands of Civil War soldiers died and were buried, at least initially, at significant distances from their homes, often adding to the grief of their families. It was "much more painful," a South Carolina woman explained in 1863, to lose a "loved one [who] is a stranger in a strange land."[4]

Many families, at their own expense, had disinterred bodies and removed them to the United States, but hundreds remained in the jungle. In late summer, Rhodes organized the Quartermaster Burial Corps, a group of civilian morticians and assistants. They were prepared, at public expense, to disinter all bodies of American soldiers and sailors remaining in Cuba and Puerto Rico for return to the United States. When he heard about these plans, Reuben Bernard resolved to rebury his son in Knoxville National Cemetery. When University of Tennessee President Dabney learned of Bernard's decision, he wrote to William McCorkle, urging him also to bury his son "here in the National Cemetery in his own South land, near to the University, where he had so many friends and which he loved so well." Shortly afterwards, Mildred McCorkle told her father that she also had asked Dr. McCorkle to have her husband's remains buried in Knoxville. "I will be so glad when he is laid to rest over here," she wrote.[5]

As McCook's book was going to press in March 1899, the author inserted a note that the government transport *Crook* finally had sailed from Cuba to return many of the exhumed bodies to the United States. The friends of these soldiers would be grateful, McCook wrote, even though "only the bony systems of our fallen heroes will rest in home graves. The soil of Cuba retains the sacred remainder, and this fact must continue to give the battlefield of Santiago a peculiar interest and honor, not only to Americans, but all friends of Free Cuba."[6]

The *Crook* docked at Brooklyn on March 29. It carried the remains of nearly seven hundred soldiers and sailors. Most had died of battle wounds or disease in Cuba and several dozen had died in Puerto Rico. On the afternoon of April 6, nearly half of these men were reburied in a new section of Arlington National Cemetery. President McKinley, other dignitaries, military officers, and a crowd estimated at fifteen thousand attended funeral services on the crest of the cemetery's southern slope overlooking the Potomac River. Flags draped wooden caskets placed next to open graves. Parents placed flowers on their sons' coffins. A band played "Nearer My God to Thee," Episcopal and Catholic ministers

14. Reburial and Reconciliation (April 2, 1899)

On April 6, 1899, the bodies of 336 soldiers and sailors who died in Cuba and Puerto Rico were re-interred in a new section of Arlington National Cemetery. The burial detail stood by the flag-draped caskets before lowering them into the ground (Philip S. Hench Walter Reed Yellow Fever Collection, Albert and Shirley Small Special Collections Library, University of Virginia).

committed the bodies to the earth, soldiers fired three volleys, and a bugler played "Taps."[7] The nation's solemn salute to the fallen soldiers — in the primary national cemetery — made front-page news everywhere.

Several days earlier, McKinley had issued an executive order honoring all of the Spanish-American War dead. He had commended "those who were sent to other shores to do battle for the country's honor, under their country's flag, [who] went freely from every quarter of our beloved land...." He had arranged for the services at Arlington, but also noted that the remains of many other soldiers and sailors already had been delivered to their families for burial elsewhere.[8] Among those others were the bodies of McCorkle and Bernard, which had been reburied April 2 in Knoxville.

April 2 was Easter Sunday. Being buried on Resurrection Day — the day on which churchgoers throughout the North had grieved for the assassinated Abraham Lincoln thirty-four years earlier — carried a special meaning for thousands of mourners from Knoxville and nearby communities.

Knoxvillians learned about the funeral services—to be held for a limited group at the university and for the general public at the grave site—shortly before they occurred. On March 29, the day the bodies reached Brooklyn, the *Knoxville Sentinel* reported that officers and enlisted men of the Sixth U.S. Volunteer Infantry and the Third Tennessee Volunteer Regiment would attend the services, the timing of which depended on the arrival of the coffins. Unstated was the fact that the soldiers closest to Bernard and McCorkle—the men of the Fourth and Twenty-fifth regiments—could not attend because they were fighting in the Philippines.

The city where these ceremonies would be held differed markedly from the small town young Reuben Bernard encountered in 1854 and the divided town that endured the Civil War. "In many ways Knoxville just after the war was not much changed from the village of 1800," observed a local historian. "Knoxville grew from a town to a city between 1870 and 1900." During those decades, Knoxville's population nearly quadrupled—from 8,682 to 32,673—as white farm families from rural areas surrounding the city moved to town to work in its varied industries. Commercial and manufacturing output grew with the population. But these changes came at a price. Coal used in factories and homes produced dirty air and adverse health conditions. Cows and hogs roaming unpaved streets created mud and muck in wet weather. Insufficient sewers contributed to constant foul odors. Those with means moved to the fringes of the city and built large homes, leaving white and black laborers in declining factory districts.[9]

Knoxville survived the national economic crisis of the mid–1890s and a fire that destroyed two blocks of buildings in the city's Gay Street business district in the spring of 1897. But the "million dollar fire" was only a temporary setback. Knoxville quickly rebuilt Gay Street. A huge new Market House replaced the smaller building Reuben Bernard had encountered when he arrived in 1854. The brick Victorian building became the centerpiece of Market Square and commercial Knoxville.[10]

The university also had grown. Nearly seven hundred students enrolled in 1899. President Dabney had continued to expand the curriculum. New structures had sprung up on College Hill, including an expansive mechanical engineering building—Estabrook Hall, named for a former president—that opened in 1898.[11] In a building erected earlier

14. Reburial and Reconciliation (April 2, 1899)

in the decade, the same Science Hall where the lieutenants' November 1898 memorial service had been held, the college community now would gather to pay its last respects to the university's heroes of the war with Spain.

The bodies came to Knoxville's Southern Railway Depot on separate trains. McCorkle's remains arrived early Sunday morning. William McCorkle, his daughter-in-law, Mildred, and her son, Guy, stayed with friends in Knoxville for nearly a week before the funeral and met the train. Bernard's body, accompanied by Reuben Bernard but evidently not by his third wife, Elsie May Camp Bernard, arrived just in time for the 3 o'clock service.[12]

A small and select army accompanied the caskets on their journey to the campus. The cortege included the university's uniformed Cadet Corps and all officers and enlisted men of the Third Tennessee and Sixth U.S. Volunteers. Representatives of the Sons of Confederate Veterans, Women's Relief Corps (the GAR's auxiliary), Daughters of the Confederacy, Daughters of the Revolution, Sons of the Revolution, and members of university organizations to which the lieutenants had belonged also marched solemnly to Science Hall.[13]

As an organist played a dirge, uniformed pallbearers conveyed the caskets, which had been covered with white cloths and draped with flags and flowers, into Science Hall. The auditorium was jammed with family, friends, Knoxville residents, university faculty and students, soldiers, and veterans. The crowd filled the auditorium's seven hundred seats; other mourners stood where they could. Hundreds of soldiers and Knoxville citizens remained outside the hall.

Elijah Embree Hoss, Sr., the forty-nine-year-old minister and editor of the *Nashville Christian Advocate*, the weekly newspaper of the Methodist Episcopal Church, South, presented the main address. A native of Jonesborough, Hoss had been president of two colleges and eventually would be elevated to bishop of his branch of the Methodist Church. His address was part sermon and part eulogy, with a nod toward reconciliation.

Following a lengthy theological introduction, Hoss commended the state's military history, emphasizing the courage of Tennesseans, Union and Confederate, during the Civil War. Then he spoke directly about the veterans in his audience: "What matters it to us now whether they were on the one side or the other? They were all Tennesseans, and all devoted to the right as God gave them to see the right. Traitors! Who dares to apply to any of them that opprobrious epithet? They were men of principles and undying courage." Further, he maintained, "the issues which drove them into opposing camps are settled" and "we can honor their memories without a trace of rancor or bitterness."

Hoss then turned to Tennessee's role in the Spanish-American War and especially the fate of McCorkle and Bernard. He said that the lieutenants' commendable records at the university were a "prophecy" of the way that they died. "The students who have been most exemplary in the recitation room and on the parade ground," he said, "are also the ones

LIEUT. HENRY L. McCORKLE
Twenty-fifth U. S. Infantry, Killed Near Santiago.

FIRST LIEUT "JACK" BARNARD
Who Was Among the Killed in the Fighting Before Santiago.

Left: On April 2, 1899, thousands of Knoxville-area residents gathered at the grave sites of Henry McCorkle and John Jay Bernard. If the mourners had images of the lieutenants in mind, McCorkle's would have been this block-print sketch published with his newspaper death notice (*Knoxville Sentinel*, July 11, 1898, Courtesy of the McClung Historical Collection, Knox County Public Library). *Right*: This sketch of John Jay Bernard was published with his death announcement a day after the notice of Henry McCorkle's death. A secondary headline noted that Bernard was "One of the Most Popular Young Men Who Ever Lived in This City" (*Knoxville Sentinel*, July 12, 1898, Courtesy of the McClung Historical Collection, Knox County Public Library).

14. Reburial and Reconciliation (April 2, 1899)

who have stood to their posts with the most signal fidelity in the open world." He quoted from their final letters—McCorkle telling his wife not to "expect anything brilliant of me, but I hope I will do my duty" and Bernard telling a "lady friend" in Knoxville that he loved Tennessee and would be "coming home just as soon as this war is over." Instead, Hoss said, Bernard "went home to that house of many mansions, where all true spirits are at last to find rest and peace. And now we have brought him home to the land of his brothers."

Following Hoss's speech, by which "the audience was moved to tears," according to the *Sentinel*, the cortege reassembled to convey the bodies two miles north to Knoxville National Cemetery. Members of the Ed Maynard Post, GAR, and the Fred Ault Bivouac, UCV, joined the funeral procession as it cut to the east and passed their headquarters on Gay Street. Hundreds of residents fell in behind.[14]

The lieutenants' funeral had become the central event of a sacred day. The joint service seems to have made an uplifting, yet melancholic, impact on its participants and observers. The *Journal and Tribune* noted that "never in the history of this city was a funeral more largely attended, there being a large number at the university and fully four thousand people at the cemetery." The day's temperature reached only fifty-three degrees, with a cool breeze, so some of those four thousand mourners left their Easter gowns and hats at home, or wore winter coats over them, awaiting more suitable weather to display spring finery.[15]

Hundreds of the mourners who entered the ten-acre cemetery by what was then the main gate off the Jacksboro Pike (now Cooper Street) had been there before and would go there again. Several Spanish-American War volunteers already had been buried, victims of typhoid as they trained in Knoxville during the summer of 1898. On April 4, another victim of disease, twenty-five-year-old Corporal Joseph C. Griffin, of the Eighth U.S. Infantry, would join them. Griffin, a stone cutter by trade, had died of yellow fever in Santiago that August. His father, J.M. Griffin, of Riverdale, just east of Knoxville, would purchase an unusually tall marble column to mark his son's grave.[16]

Most of the modest, identical gravestones of white Vermont marble that the mourners saw as they entered the cemetery were considerably older. They marked the three thousand Union graves dug after General Ambrose Burnside established the cemetery in September 1863. Those Federal soldiers remained the only burials until Secretary of War Alger opened all national cemeteries to the Spanish-American War dead in 1899.[17]

The crowd distributed itself amid the older gravestones arranged in concentric circles around the flagpole. The spectators looked slightly downhill through spare landscaping toward two adjacent rectangular holes with small heaps of earth beside them. Flowers covered the mounds. Pallbearers slowly carried the caskets to the burial place, where the lieutenants' families had assembled. Both men had been born in April; now they would be buried in April in bright spring grass along the narrow road that circles through the cemetery.

Most other Spanish-American War soldiers who died in 1898, many of them from disease, had been buried in a cluster. McCorkle's and Bernard's graves lay apart from the others, in the cemetery's section C, just outside the Civil War section and some distance from the unfinished Union monument. Today, even to someone who does not know their story, it is obvious that McCorkle and Bernard, who lie near one of the cemetery's sturdy black maple trees, are linked in a special way.

It is not likely that Reuben Bernard and William McCorkle, strangers to each other, determined the location of their sons' graves. It is more probable that Charles Dabney, in conjunction with cemetery officials, suggested the positioning. Dabney had known both students during their time at the university, had followed their later careers, and had characterized them as friends and eulogized them at length in the November 1898 memorial service. He had urged William McCorkle to follow Reuben Bernard's decision to bury his son in the national cemetery, and McCorkle quickly had made such arrangements with Bernard.[18] For Dabney to suggest that the lieutenants be buried together seems a natural extension of his previous actions. He also may have calculated that a combined burial would accentuate the contribution of the university's alumni to the war.

The Rev. Samuel Ringgold, rector of Knoxville's St. John's Episcopal Church, conducted the grave side service. Pallbearers lowered the caskets into the holes. The university's cadet battalion fired three volleys. The battalion bugler played "Taps."[19]

Reuben Bernard and William McCorkle, both in their late sixties, stood to the side of the caskets. Bernard, distinguished by the unusually long white beard he maintained late in life, probably wore his blue officer's uniform—the clothing he had worn throughout his lengthy military career. The taller, thinner, older McCorkle, thirty-four years after

14. Reburial and Reconciliation (April 2, 1899)

his surrender at Appomattox on another April day, most likely would have worn his Sunday suit.

If the fathers' minds wandered during the service, they might have encountered bittersweet memories. Perhaps Bernard recalled a cross-country horse ride with his cavalrymen and young Jack. And perhaps he thought about two younger sons who had died while attending the university. Perhaps McCorkle remembered summer days hunting and fishing with Henry. And perhaps, as the obstetrician watched his son's body disappear into the ground, he thought about the day he had welcomed him into the world.

If they turned to darker thoughts, both men may have wondered how the legacy of their military lives had affected their sons. The Rev. Henry Ward Beecher had defined that potential burden in a prayer to the crowd gathered for the Soldiers' Monument dedication in the National Cemetery at Gettysburg on July 1, 1869: "May the soldiers' children never prove unworthy of their fathers' name.... Let them be willing to shed their blood, to lay down their lives, for the sake of their country."[20] While it is unlikely that many Civil War veterans directly pressed the weight of those words onto their children, the rising generation must have felt it. Both Henry McCorkle and Jack Bernard had, indeed, followed their fathers' willingness "to lay down their lives for the sake of their country."

Both Knoxville newspapers commented on the aging fathers. The *Sentinel* said, "Two gray haired veterans of the civil war, on opposing sides, stood side by side at the graves yesterday and saw their sons, who wore the blue, buried together." The *Journal and Tribune* observed: "Another beautiful illustration, this, of the completeness of our reunion—the son of the old confederate soldier and the son of the old union soldier, die side by side fighting the battles of their united country."[21]

No one reported on what the central figures in this reunion tableau talked about as they spent the day following their sons' bodies from railroad car to university hall to cemetery plot. But we do know this: Before these fathers met for the first time on that Easter Day, before they shed and shared tears over fresh graves, they had to agree to bury their first-born sons side-by-side. Given the deliberate separation of Union and Confederate soldiers in Knoxville cemeteries, as elsewhere, their agreement to bury these two soldiers of another war together must have seemed a revelation.

Epilogue
Knoxville, Tennessee
(Memorial Day, 1899)

Nearly two months passed. The McCorkle-Bernard funeral became old news. Another crowd assembled in Knoxville National Cemetery to spread flowers on graves. Women who had set aside their Easter best because of cool temperatures on April 2 put on holiday dresses and bonnets on a warm but rainy Memorial Day. Their husbands wore dark suits and held umbrellas. Veterans retrieved uniforms to visit the graves of fellow soldiers.

"In two important respects, Decoration Day of 1899 differs from its predecessors," the *Knoxville Sentinel* observed two days before the holiday. "For the last time, perhaps, the heroes of the civil war will be seen processioning on the streets, and for the first time the heroes of that later war decorate the graves of the victims of the Spanish bullet and jungle fever."

The local chapter of the Women's Relief Corps had decorated each grave with flowers and flags. The *Sentinel* noted that the women honored not only Civil War veterans, but also "over the graves of Spanish-American heroes, some of them sons of federals and some of confederates, flowers and tears were mingled, on the one as on the other, showing that these heroes, although born under different flags perhaps, had died for the now one flag of a people reunited."[1]

The women of the Relief Corps discovered that other flowers had preceded theirs. On May 18, Confederate Memorial Day, representatives of the Knoxville LMA had decorated Confederate graves in Bethel and Old Gray cemeteries. Then they had walked up to the national cemetery and placed garlands on the graves of McCorkle and Bernard.[2]

These two graves were now designated by stones considerably

Knoxville, Tennessee (Memorial Day, 1899)

First Lieutenant Henry Leftwich McCorkle's gravestone stands beside the stone of John Jay Bernard in Knoxville National Cemetery. Both men were born in April and buried in April (photograph by Shawn Poynter/Poynter Photo Company).

larger than the standard marble markers on the mass of Civil War graves. The side-by-side stones were alike in size but distinctive in detail. With the exception of a smooth face for its inscription, Henry McCorkle's gravestone was rough-cut gray granite, simply executed. Jack Bernard's was smooth white marble, most likely from an East Tennessee quarry. A sculpted spray of marble military equipage topped the stone. Both inscriptions provided name, rank, military unit, birth and death dates, and place of death at El Caney, Cuba. Bernard's inscription also noted that he was General R.F. Bernard's son.

Epilogue

Second Lieutenant John Jay Bernard's gravestone complements the stone of H. L. McCorkle that stands several feet away in Knoxville National Cemetery (photograph by Shawn Poynter/Poynter Photo Company).

On May 30, an estimated three thousand spectators settled among the Union gravestones circled on the hillside just above the lieutenants' beflowered graves. GAR representatives introduced the Memorial Day program with a reading of the Gettysburg Address. Confederate veterans presented an American flag composed of red, white, and blue flowers. Knoxville attorney George Winstead provided the main address. He spoke at about the same time that William Rule was telling another large crowd at Nashville National Cemetery about the conciliatory graveside meeting of William McCorkle and Reuben Bernard and the

Knoxville, Tennessee (Memorial Day, 1899)

reunification of Americans "even though they may have radically differed in the past." Near the end of his patriotic remarks, Winstead said something similar.

"The Spanish war demonstrated that we are now in fact one people having a common country, a common interest and one flag. In that war the cause of the United States was espoused by the ex-federal and the ex-confederate alike," he said. "We had going out from our own state university two young men, Bernard and McCorkle, one the son of an ex-federal soldier, the other the son of an ex-confederate soldier." Both men, Winstead observed, "offered up their lives as a sacrifice on the altar of their country...."[3]

The *Knoxville Journal*, Rule's newspaper, had run an editorial that morning expressing the same sentiment. The newspaper said that a few weeks earlier two lieutenants had been buried, "one the son of a confederate soldier, the other a son of a union veteran; both fell in the bloody fighting around Santiago, where deeds of bravery and gallantry added new lustre to American arms."[4]

Other newspapers republished this story, usually in severely abbreviated form, but occasionally with some length and drama. The *Cincinnati Post*, as an extreme example, employed a multi-banked heading: "OVER A GRAVE / White Haired Veterans Clasped Hands / ONCE THEY FOUGHT ON DIFFERENT SIDES / SPAIN KILLED THEIR SONS / A Common Sorrow Made Them One." The *Post* story said the joint burial "was typical of a reunited country. Bernard's father, a Federal in the Civil War, and McCorkle's father, a Confederate, met at the double tomb and clasped hands of sorrow, when, over a third of a century ago, they drew swords of anger."[5]

Clearly, on Memorial Day 1899, many American newspaper readers viewed Henry McCorkle and Jack Bernard as heroes of the war with Spain and their fathers as exemplars of national reconciliation, or at least reunification. That opinion surely prevailed among mourners attending the Knoxville ceremony, which ended with a volley fired by Spanish-American War veterans and the playing of "Taps" at the flagstaff.

Memorials to the lieutenants continued for several years. Students dedicated the University of Tennessee's 1899 yearbook to them. Full-page biographies followed a dedicatory note: "Their lives were of no less honor than their deaths." In June 1900, the university honored McCorkle and Bernard with a memorial tablet in the chapel of Science

Epilogue

Hall. University of Tennessee law professor C.W. Turner noted that the tablet and a similar marker for naval Lieutenant Valentine S. Nelson were the first memorials to former students ever erected on the campus. He said he hoped the tablets would "keep their memory green in the spot where once they worked and studied and furnish a perpetual inspiration to the cadet companies they once commanded."[6]

In 1901 and subsequent years, the university recognized the lieutenants and other Spanish-American War veteran alumni for military service that "would not be discreditable, we feel, to any institution." In a baccalaureate address delivered in June 1904, University President Charles Dabney emphasized the importance of teachers fulfilling their responsibilities to children and their schools. Paraphrasing, he said they should heed Henry McCorkle's pledge in his last letter home to "expect nothing brilliant of me; but I will do my duty."[7]

Fellow soldiers also memorialized the lieutenants by designating the McCorkle-Bernard Camp of Spanish-American War Veterans in the spring of 1900. Eventually, the camp split into two Knoxville posts: Jack Bernard Camp No. 1 and Lieutenant H.L. McCorkle Camp No. 2. Through the 1940s, and perhaps later, the McCorkle Camp draped its namesake's portrait in black every July 1. Battery McCorkle, named for the lieutenant, defended the minefield of Fort Moultrie, South Carolina, from potential mine sweepers between 1901 and 1920. Bernard Avenue, running adjacent to Knoxville National Cemetery, was renamed for Jack Bernard. The Bernard Camp dedicated a statue of a "Hiker"—what rank-and-file Spanish-American War soldiers called themselves—in front of Knox County's Old Courthouse in 1940. The statue memorializes fallen soldiers, sailors, and marines who served in Cuba, Puerto Rico, the Philippines, and China from 1898 to 1902.

But remembrance of the lieutenants has gone the way of the first-of-its-kind Science Hall memorial tablet, which the university now cannot locate.[8] Recognition of the one-time-only meeting of their fathers is equally obscure. Mildred McCorkle, who remarried in 1908 and died in 1961, may have been the last person to associate the McCorkle and Bernard families with the nineteenth-century process of veteran reunification and reconciliation. A story that made headlines briefly but emphatically in 1899 has virtually disappeared from historical memory.

✥✥✥

Knoxville, Tennessee (Memorial Day, 1899)

The Jack Bernard Camp No. 1, United Spanish War Veterans, placed a statue of a "Hiker" on the lawn in front of Knox County's third courthouse in 1940. Enlisted men who went to war at that time called themselves "Hikers." At least fifty similar statues, designed by Theo Alice Ruggles Kitson, a well-known Massachusetts sculptress, stand throughout the United States (photograph by the author).

Epilogue

By the time Reuben Bernard died in 1903 and William McCorkle in 1910, many Civil War veterans were already gone. Many had reconciled with their former enemies; at least they had professed reconciliation when they gathered at reunions and during the nationwide celebration following the defeat of the Spanish. Paul Buck commended this achievement in 1937. "How different it would have been had the generation of the war died unreconciled and bequeathed to children the antipathies of their lives!" the historian wrote. "Then would the task of reunion have been complicated beyond the hope of solution, for nothing is more ineradicable than hatreds that are inherited."[9]

This sentimental perception of reconciliation continued through the twentieth century, even as political and cultural divisions between North and South persisted and it became obvious that residents of both sections had never fully reconciled their opinions on why the war was fought or how it should be viewed in retrospect. In recent years, the Confederate flag and monuments to the Confederacy and its leaders increasingly have become flash points for controversy and violence. The Confederate flag has been removed from most Southern state houses and county courthouses, banned from NASCAR races, and denigrated by many Americans as a symbol of white supremacy. Still, its display persists on private property, along major highways, and on t-shirts and knick-knacks. Dozens of Confederate monuments have been vandalized, destroyed, or moved to less visible locations. Some observers cheer these changes as necessary correctives to a distorted interpretation of history that has exacerbated racial tension; others lament a loss of Southern heritage and sectional identity. Addressing divergent opinions about the war and its legacy, M. Keith Harris commented in 2014, "Civil War veterans have long passed, but their memories compete for dominance still."[10]

East Tennessee's memorialization of its Civil War past has diverged from the rest of Tennessee and the South as a whole. The region contains relatively few overt reminders of the war. Unlike most Southern cities, Knoxville has no significant streets, buildings, or schools named for Confederate leaders. The most common manifestations of Confederate pride—replicas of the battle flag and marble, bronze, or granite memorials to the Lost Cause—are not so evident as they are elsewhere. Young men who decorate their vehicles with "rebel flags," an East Tennessee author has noted, may not know or care that their ancestors might have been Union soldiers determined to defeat the armies that marched beneath those flags.[11]

Knoxville, Tennessee (Memorial Day, 1899)

In a section once fractured by conflict, the building of war memorials by both sides has been spare. The counties of East Tennessee have far fewer Civil War monuments, Union or Confederate, than counties in Middle or West Tennessee. For his book on Tennessee Civil War monuments, Timothy S. Sedore counted "at least twenty-five" monuments in East Tennessee among about four hundred statewide. In a Knoxville newspaper interview, Maryville College history professor Aaron Astor explained this dearth of monuments: "A lot of people decided they just weren't going to build anything. It was a miserable memory, too. The community was so divided that people were not eager to remember it."[12]

In Middle and West Tennessee, almost all monuments (outside the military parks, which contain primarily Union monuments) were dedicated to the Confederacy. Contrarily, East Tennessee towns contain a fair number of Union monuments. In Greeneville, both Union and Confederate memorials stand on the Greene County Courthouse lawn: a bronze and granite statue of a "loyal and true" Union soldier offsets a stark stone slab honoring Confederate cavalry General John Hunt Morgan. Another small monument in Greene County memorializes the five Union men hanged for burning the railway bridge across Lick Creek in 1861. Eight of East Tennessee's Confederate monuments were erected between 1921 and 1931, a period of increased awareness among UDC members of the importance of representing a Confederate view of the past through memorials.[13]

Within the City of Knoxville, except for the monumental tributes to the dead in National and Bethel cemeteries, there are only two significant Civil War monuments. They stand about two blocks apart, near the site of Fort Sanders before development overran it. Considering that they mark a short but fierce battle that cemented Union control of Knoxville and East Tennessee, they are modest memorials. Thousands of Knoxville residents and University of Tennessee students probably have passed the old marble monuments without taking much notice.

The UDC erected the first of the two in 1914 on top of the hill near Laurel Avenue and the present Seventeenth Street, where the Confederates attacked the fort. At that time, many members of the UDC, founded twenty years earlier in Nashville, actually were daughters of Confederate soldiers. Some of their fathers had died in the assault and the daughters were raised by widows. Nothing suggests that the UDC had an agenda beyond marking a battlefield before it was overrun by development and memorializing the 129 Confederate soldiers who died there.[14]

Epilogue

The United Daughters of the Confederacy in 1914 erected a modest memorial to the 129 Confederate soldiers who died attacking Knoxville's Fort Sanders in November 1863. Speakers at the memorial's dedication emphasized the bravery of the Confederates and also acknowledged the fort's defenders (courtesy Alan Sims, InsideofKnoxville.com).

Several veterans—mostly Confederate, but also including William Brownlow's son, former Union Lieutenant Colonel John Bell Brownlow—attended the unveiling of the seven-foot-tall monument of pink Knox County marble. This was not a celebratory event: many men had died in a futile attempt to assault a reinforced fort. One veteran brought

Knoxville, Tennessee (Memorial Day, 1899)

a "blood-spattered, bullet-torn battle flag" that had survived the attack. He draped the old flag over the monument, on the top of which a battle flag had been carved in marble.[15]

Beneath the flag and an engraved Southern Cross of Honor, the UDC inscribed four lines of poetry—the final lines of the elegiac poem, "Bivouac of the Dead":

> *Nor wreck, nor change, nor winter's blight*
> *Nor time's remorseless doom*
> *Shall dim one ray of glory's light*
> *That gilds your glorious tomb.*

The verse was especially appropriate for a Confederate monument because the poem's author, the Kentucky-born Theodore O'Hara, had served as colonel of an Alabama regiment. Given O'Hara's allegiance, there is some irony—and perhaps a subtle touch of reunification—in that the poem's first stanza is today engraved on cast-aluminum tablets in Knoxville and all other national cemeteries.[16]

Speakers at the memorial's dedication—held on a rainy November 28, a day before the anniversary of the battle—emphasized the courage of Confederate soldiers, dozens of whom were buried in Bethel Cemetery; but they also acknowledged the bravery of the fort's defenders. Wesley T. Kennerly, a Knoxville attorney, historian of the Henry M. Ashby Camp of the Sons of Confederate Veterans, a University of Tennessee graduate, and a Spanish-American War veteran, summed up the ceremony. He said he hoped the memorial would stand as "a perpetual monument both to the bravery of the Confederate soldier, engaged in this battle, and to the loyalty and devotion of the women of the south." Miss Missie Ault, a founder of both Knoxville's LMA and UDC, summed up the assault and its aftermath with an emotional speech. "Many of us have vivid recollections of that November morning," she recalled. "Oh! the sadness of that time." Describing the response of the assemblage, the *Knoxville Sentinel* observed, "tears came into the eyes of those who wore the gray and of those who wore the blue."[17]

More than a century later, some Knoxvillians view the Confederate Fort Sanders memorial the way its creators saw it: as a tribute to soldiers who died in battle. Others see it as a memorial to a discredited ideology that supported slavery and secession, and later segregation and oppression. These views increasingly are incompatible, especially when white supremacists join the defenders of Confederate heritage. Violence has

Epilogue

occurred elsewhere when similar opinions have clashed. In the summer of 2017, white supremacists and neo–Nazis marched in favor of maintaining Confederate monuments in Charlottesville, Virginia. One of their supporters drove his car into a group of counter-protesters, killing one and injuring nineteen. In one of many reactions throughout the

Veterans of the Seventy-ninth New York Regiment, the "Highlanders," dedicated a monument near the Fort Sanders battlefield in 1918. The regiment bore the brunt of the attack on the fort and several of its members were among the first burials in Knoxville National Cemetery. Central to the conciliatory monument is a bas relief of Union and Confederate soldiers shaking hands (courtesy Alan Sims, InsideofKnoxville.com).

Knoxville, Tennessee (Memorial Day, 1899)

country, groups vandalized and protested the Fort Sanders memorial. In the spring of 2020, a police officer in Minneapolis, Minnesota, suffocated George Floyd, a black man, by kneeling on his neck. In response, vandals spray-painted the monument and cars in the Fort Sanders area as part of a nationwide protest against systemic racism in American society. These protests accelerated efforts to remove Confederate monuments throughout the South. Results have varied.

The future of the Confederate memorial at Fort Sanders remains uncertain, even given Tennessee's targeted strengthening of its preservation laws. But the modest marble monument seems considerably less threatening than hundreds of other memorials erected as more obvious manifestations of white supremacy. The monument's relatively obscure location at the edge of a battlefield that no longer exists may preserve it from the fate of ostentatious Confederate memorials in other cities.[18]

No one is likely to suggest removing Knoxville's other Fort Sanders memorial from the corner of Sixteenth Street and Clinch Avenue. On September 23, 1918, seven veterans of the Seventy-ninth New York Regiment, who had camped near that place during the battle, dedicated the sixteen-foot-tall monument—more than twice the size of the nearby Confederate memorial—to the memory of the Highlanders who had defended the fort's northwest bastion.

Designed to look to the present and future more than the past, the Highlanders' memorial, also made of local pink marble, echoes the more elaborate New York Peace Monument dedicated on Lookout Mountain at Chattanooga in 1910. Engraved beneath a bas relief of Union and Confederate soldiers shaking hands is a poignant poem by Joseph Clarke, a New York newspaper writer, emphasizing the reunification of one-time enemies:

> *The hands that once were raised in strife*
> *Now clasp a brother's hand*
> *And long as flows the tide of life—*
> *In peace, in toil, when war is rife—*
> *We shall as brothers stand*
> *One heart, one soul, for our fine land*

Seven veterans of the Seventy-ninth, bearing the ragged flag they had flown in the fort, traveled from New York for the dedication. The local UDC chapter contributed a wreath of flowers. Union and Confederate veterans gave speeches emphasizing reconciliation and supporting America's role in World War I.[19]

Epilogue

William Rule, who seems to have represented the Knoxville GAR on nearly every occasion observing the Civil War until his death in 1928, walked from his nearby house to deliver a speech. "I do not recall within the range of my acquaintance a veteran of the Civil War, in either the Confederate or the Union armies, who is not a hundred per cent American," he said. "And their sons or grandsons are now standing shoulder to shoulder in the present big war against hateful autocracy."[20]

No speaker at the dedications of either of these monuments overtly mentioned secession or slavery or any other element of sectional friction that had provoked war. The ceremonies clearly emphasized the bravery of young soldiers and marked their disappearing field of battle.

Over the past century, reunification of North and South, so eloquently portrayed by the New York monument and so clearly ignored by the Confederate memorial, has proved to be both enduring and vulnerable. When national interests are at stake, as Mayor Rule noted well over a century ago, most people are "a hundred per cent American." But when the subject of "Southern heritage" arises—whether supported by dedicated historians or white supremacists—old wounds quickly reopen.

While many Americans embraced the Civil War Centennial Commission-sponsored battle reenactments and other commemorative events between 1961 and 1965, some Southerners worried that the national focus undercut their sectional heritage. Many black leaders felt that the commission did little to emphasize the significance of emancipation and nothing to advance civil rights. As a result of these disputes, no national commission was formed to coordinate sesquicentennial events; state and local organizations sponsored most activities between 2011 and 2015.[21]

In May 2015, Tennessee's Civil War Sesquicentennial Commission concluded statewide commemorative activities in Knoxville. The commission recognized East Tennessee's political leaders for the part they played at the end of the war and emphasized the exceptional reunions of Union and Confederate soldiers at Fort Sanders in 1890 and 1895. The program's title, "Blue & Gray Reunion and Freedom Jubilee," was designed to refer not only to reunion and reconciliation, but also to emancipation and the continuing struggle for civil rights.

As part of four days of exhibits, tours, and lectures throughout the city, First Presbyterian Church—the Knoxville church of Jack Bernard and, possibly, Henry McCorkle—devoted its Sunday service to a theme of "Remembrance, Reunion, and Reconciliation in a Divided Nation." In

Knoxville, Tennessee (Memorial Day, 1899)

her sermon, the Rev. Renee Kesler, a black minister at Mt. Calvary Baptist Church who promotes Knoxville's black history as president of the Beck Cultural Exchange Center, encouraged unity. "Today we are not remembering black people. Today we are not remembering white people," she told the congregation. "Today we are not here to remember yellow people or brown people or poor people or rich people, enslaved people or blue people or gray people. Today we are here, oh God, to remember all of God's people, who are all children of God."[22]

Delivered in one of the few sections of the country where "blue" and "gray" could be listed equally and intelligibly among types of human beings, this sermon concluded the sesquicentennial. With historical zeal, East Tennesseans had commemorated the end of a war. They had lamented the separation of states and celebrated the reunification of the war's white warriors. They had recognized that black Americans, South and North, had been largely barred from the reconciliation process, not only in the nineteenth century but through the present. And so they had acknowledged that the often painful and sometimes violent process of racial and sectional reconciliation continues.

Chapter Notes

Prologue

1. Historian Caroline E. Janney fleetingly mentions this graveside ceremony in *Remembering the Civil War: Reunion and the Limits of Reconciliation* (Chapel Hill: University of North Carolina Press, 2013), 228. Her end note (368 *n*158) cites an account of William Rule's Memorial Day speech from the United Confederate Veterans' Nashville-based magazine, *Confederate Veteran*, June 1899, 272 (actually 273). The *Confederate Veteran's* version of Rule's speech differs substantially from a May 31, 1899, account in the *Tennessean*, a daily newspaper also published in Nashville. Most material quoted here is drawn from the *Confederate Veteran* text.

2. The morning *Knoxville Journal and Tribune* and the evening *Knoxville Sentinel* commented at length on the deaths of the two soldiers in early July 1898. Other newspapers, including the *New York Times*, *Washington Evening Times*, *Richmond Dispatch*, and *Louisville Courier Journal*, reported the deaths, sometimes mentioning one or both fathers.

3. Paul H. Buck, *The Road to Reunion: 1865–1900* (Boston: Little, Brown, 1937), 256. Buck cites a May 31, 1892, *Boston Globe* article.

4. *New York Times*, July 24, 1885.

5. Thomas J. Fleming, *West Point: The Men and Times of the United States Military Academy* (New York: William Morrow, 1969), 210.

6. *Century*, July 1888, 440–42.

7. Janney, *Remembering the Civil War*, 9.

8. *Nashville Tennessean*, May 30, 1898. Writers and orators regularly employed the image of Union and Confederate veterans weeping, or "mingling their tears," to describe sectional reconciliation at military funerals and in other war-related commentary in the late nineteenth century. For example, an account of the 1885 funeral of President and General U.S. Grant mentioned that "the leading generals of the living Union and of the dead Confederacy stood shoulder to shoulder and mingled their tears in a common grief—this marked the virtual conclusion of sectional animosity in America—let us hope for all time to come." (*Century*, October 1885, 965).

9. Nina Silber, *The Romance of Reunion: Northerners and the South, 1865–1900* (Chapel Hill: University of North Carolina Press, 1993), 306.

10. *Knoxville Sentinel*, May 30, 1898.

11. Walter Hines Page, "The End of the War, and After," *Atlantic Monthly*, September 1898, 432.

12. William McKinley, "Speech Before the Legislature in Joint Assembly at the State Capitol, Atlanta, Georgia, December 14, 1898," in *Speeches and Addresses of William McKinley from March 1, 1897 to May 30, 1900* (New York: Doubleday & McClure, 1900), 158–59.

13. *Confederate Veteran*, June 1899, 246.

14. John R. Neff, *Honoring the Civil War Dead: Commemoration and the Problem of Reconciliation* (Lawrence: University Press of Kansas, 2005), 221.

Notes—Chapter 1

Chapter 1

1. Biographical information for Reuben Bernard comes chiefly from Don Russell's reverential *One Hundred and Three Fights and Scrimmages: The Story of General Reuben F. Bernard* (Washington, D.C.: United States Cavalry Association, 1936; reprint, Mechanicsburg, Pennsylvania: Stackpole Books, 2003) and a more objective introduction written by Edwin Sweeney, historian of the Apaches, for the reprint. Russell cited among his principal sources Bernard's official reports, correspondence, diaries, and journals collected by Brigadier General William Carey Brown, who succeeded Bernard as commander of the Order of Indian Wars of the United States and wrote the original introduction to Russell's biography. Many Order of Indian Wars materials are now held in the archives of the U.S. Army Military History Institute at Carlisle, Pennsylvania, and in the archives of the University of Colorado at Boulder. The National Archives' military service record consists merely of Bernard's enlistment and reenlistment forms for 1855 and 1859 and other incidental forms.

2. Major General Beaumont Bonaparte Buck to Brigadier General W. C. Brown, December 3, 1933, *William Carey Brown Papers*, University of Colorado Boulder Library Archives.

3. *Rogersville Review*, March 12, 1953.

4. William J. MacArthur, Jr., "Knoxville's History: An Interpretation," in *Heart of the Valley: A History of Knoxville, Tennessee*, ed. Lucille Deaderick (Knoxville: East Tennessee Historical Society, 1976), 20; William Rule, *Standard History of Knoxville, Tennessee* (Chicago: Lewis Publishing, 1900), 102–03; William B. Wheeler, *Knoxville, Tennessee: A Mountain City in the New South* (Knoxville: University of Tennessee Press, 2005), 3.

5. Russell, *One Hundred and Three Fights*, 7.

6. Gregory Michno, *Encyclopedia of Indian Wars: Western Battles and Skirmishes, 1850–1890* (Missoula, Montana: Mountain Press Publishing, 2003), 358; Don Russell, "Reuben Frank Bernard," *Journal of the American Military Foundation*, 2, no. 2 (Summer, 1938): 90. Following Bernard's death, some newspapers inflated the number of his battles. The *Washington Evening Star* (November 17, 1903) and the *Annapolis (Md.) Evening Capital* (November 20, 1903) claimed he had participated in 121 battles during the Civil War alone.

7. Military Service Record, National Archives; Edwin Sweeney, "Introduction," in *One Hundred and Three Fights*, vi.

8. Russell, *One Hundred and Three Fights*, 11.

9. Buck to Brown, December 3, 1933; Russell, *One Hundred and Three Fights*, 12–13. The humorous statement that this was "the only Republican victory in Tennessee in 1860'" is somewhat misleading. The Tennessee Republican Party fielded no candidates.

10. Sweeney, "Introduction," in *One Hundred and Three Fights*, x.

11. Russell, 24–27; Sweeney, x–xii, in *One Hundred and Three Fights*. A popular 1952 film, *The Battle at Apache Pass*, confused the matter even more by combining the Bascom Affair of 1861 with the actual Battle of Apache Pass in 1862. The movie version of Reuben Bernard (played by the actor Richard Egan) understands the Apaches and has little respect for a villainous Bascom. It is a flattering portrayal of a man who, according to Edwin Sweeney, was not there.

12. Russell, 33–35.

13. Reuben Bernard to Governor Andrew Johnson, *Papers of Andrew Johnson* (Knoxville: University of Tennessee Press, 1979), 5: 216–17. Most of Bernard's writing includes phonetic spelling, erratic punctuation, and other indications of rudimentary literacy. In "Reuben Frank Bernard": 93, Don Russell derided "a tendency to exaggerate Bernard's lack of learning." Despite technical errors, Bernard generally communicated clearly.

14. Russell, *One Hundred and Three Fights*, 47ff.

15. Russell, 53.

16. *History of the First U.S. Cavalry, 1833–1906* (Washington, D.C.: Regimental Press, 1906), 11.

17. Russell, *One Hundred and Three Fights*, 53–54.

Notes—Chapter 2

18. Herman J. Viola, ed., *The Memoirs of Charles Henry Veil: A Soldier's Recollections of the Civil War and the Arizona Territory* (Thorndike, Maine: Thorndike Press, 1994), 26–27; Russell, 55.

19. Viola, 160–61.

Chapter 2

1. Information about Reuben Bernard's brothers comes from service records held by the Tennessee State Library and Archives. Although several printed sources, including Bernard's biographer, Don Russell, claim that three brothers died during the war, no wartime deaths are documented. An afternoon's search found none of the brothers buried in cemeteries in the rocky fields and beech forests along Beech Creek near Van Hill, Hawkins County. Several Bernards living in the Beech Creek area said they knew little about General Bernard and nothing about his brothers.

2. Samuel Bernard took his amnesty oath four months after the U.S. War Department established conditions for amnesty. Deserters were permitted to go home if they signed a required oath of allegiance to the United States and if their homes were within Union lines. By 1864, all of Tennessee was Union territory.

3. John N. Fain, ed., *Sanctified Trial: The Diary of Eliza Rhea Anderson Fain, a Confederate Woman in East Tennessee* (Knoxville: University of Tennessee Press, 2004), lxiv.

4. Digby Gordon Seymour, *Divided Loyalties: Fort Sanders and the Civil War in East Tennessee* (Knoxville: East Tennessee Historical Society, 1903), 267–68.

5. Amy Murrell Taylor, *The Divided Family in Civil War America* (Chapel Hill: University of North Carolina Press, 2005), 74.

6. Robert T. McKenzie, *Lincolnites and Rebels: A Divided Town in the American Civil War* (New York: Oxford University Press, 2006), 127.

7. McKenzie, 203–04.

8. McKenzie, 128, 6.

9. Sheila Weems Johnston, *The Blue and Gray from Hawkins County Tennessee 1861–1865: The Battles* (Rogersville, Tennessee: Hawkins County Genealogical and Historical Society, 1995), 60.

10. All Confederate states contended with substantial opposition within their borders. For example, Newton Knight and like-minded Union supporters overthrew the Confederate authorities in Jones County, Mississippi, in the spring of 1864 and established the Free State of Jones. David Williams' *Bitterly Divided: The South's Inner Civil War* (New York: The New Press, 2008) is a comprehensive study of Southerners who remained loyal to the Union.

11. McKenzie, *Lincolnites and Rebels*, 80; Bryan, Charles Jr., "A Gathering of Tories: The East Tennessee Convention of 1861, *Tennessee Historical Quarterly* 39 no. 1 (1980): 43–45.

12. Blake Fontenay, "The Curious History of the 'Free and Independent State of Scott,'" Tri-Star Chronicles (Tennessee State Library and Archives), https://sos.tn.gov/tsla/tri-star-chronicles-scott-county.

13. Noel C. Fisher, *War at Every Door: Partisan Politics & Guerrilla Violence in East Tennessee, 1860–1869* (Chapel Hill: University of North Carolina Press, 1997), 180; "Map showing the distribution of the slave population of the southern states of the United States. Compiled from the census of 1860," Library of Congress, loc.gov/resource/g3861e.cw0013200/.

14. Oliver P. Temple, *East Tennessee and the Civil War* (Cincinnati: Robert Clarke, 1899), 135.

15. McKenzie, *Lincolnites and Rebels*, 71.

16. Seymour, *Divided Loyalties*, 11–12.

17. McKenzie, Lincolnites and Rebels, 226.

18. Seymour, *Divided Loyalties*, 10; McKenzie, *Lincolnites and Rebels*, 4.

19. Todd W. Groce, *Mountain Rebels: East Tennessee Confederates and the Civil War, 1860–1870* (Knoxville: University of Tennessee Press, 1999), 75–76; Fisher, *War at Every Door*, 68.

20. Thomas L. Connelly, *Civil War Tennessee: Battles and Leaders* (Knoxville: University of Tennessee Press, 1979), 8; A. James Fuller, *Chaplain to the*

Notes—Chapter 3

Confederacy: Basil Manly and Baptist Life in the Old South (Baton Rouge: Louisiana State Press, 2000), 299.

21. McKenzie, *Lincolnites and Rebels*, 92; Fisher, *War at Every Door*, 58–59.

22. Donahue Bible, "The Hangings of the Greene County Bridge Burners," *Tennessee Ancestors* 21, no. 2 (August 2005): 130ff.

23. Alton Lee Greene, *Greene Family Tree of Jeremiah and Anne Hartley Greene [1700–1970]* (Pineville, LA: Claude Greene, 1970), 2. The "Greene-Jones War" has been called the second deadliest Appalachian Mountain feud, after Hatfield-McCoy. Alfred Greene's brothers, Union soldiers, came home after the war and killed the men who had killed him.

24. Williams, *Bitterly Divided*, 127–28.

25. Fisher, *War at Every Door*, 65.

26. William Rule, *The Loyalists of Tennessee in the Late War* (Chicago: Lewis Publishing, 1900), 15–16. Rule enlisted in his regiment and rose to first lieutenant by the end of the war. He typically was addressed later in life as "Captain" Rule.

27. Fisher, *War at Every Door*, 68–69.

28. Williams, *Bitterly Divided*, 149–50.

29. Groce, *Mountain Rebels*, 102–03.

30. *New York Times*, September 18, 1863.

31. Groce, *Mountain Rebels*, 109–10.

32. Earl J. Hess, *The Knoxville Campaign: Burnside and Longstreet in East Tennessee* (Knoxville: University of Tennessee, Press, 2012), 135–37.

33. Hess, 151ff.

34. Hess, 229–30.

35. Groce, *Mountain Rebels*, 130–31; MacArthur, "Knoxville's History," 26–27.

36. McKenzie, *Lincolnites and Rebels*, 178ff.

37. Groce, *Mountain Rebels*, 133; Johnston, *Blue and Gray*, 60ff.

38. Fain, *Sanctified Trial*, xxvii, 309.

39. McKenzie, *Lincolnites and Rebels*, 206.

Chapter 3

1. John A. McCorkle, U.S. Sons of the American Revolution Membership Applications, 1889–1970. Ancestry.com; "Rockbridge County, Virginia Genealogy Trails History Group: The MacCorkle Family," genealogytrails.com/vir/rockbridge/fam_maccorkle.html; "In Memoriam" in the *University of Tennessee Record*, 1, no. 6 (Knoxville: University of Tennessee, September 1898), 337. This citation claims Alexander McCorkle was killed in the Mexican War, but his Lexington gravestone says he died in 1851.

2. Oren F. Morton, "The McCorkle Family" in *A History of Rockbridge County, Virginia* (Staunton, VA: McClure, 1920), 287.

3. Morton, 287.

4. Enrollment records, Washington & Lee University Archives; *Catalogue of the Officers and Alumni of Washington & Lee University, 1749–1888*, Washington & Lee University Special Collections; Tribute by "J. P.", *Christian Observer*, June 22, 1910, 22.

5. H.D. Cunningham, *Doctors in Gray: The Confederate Medical Service* (Baton Rouge: Louisiana State University Press, 1958), 9–11, 17.

6. Military Records, roll 8 (Confederate), Tennessee State Library and Archives, Nashville; John D. Rigdon, *Historical Sketch and Roster of the Tennessee 2nd Cavalry (Ashby's)* (Cartersville, GA: Eastern Digital Resources, 2004), 223.

7. State of Tennessee Soldiers' Application for Pension, October 12, 1909, Tennessee State Library and Archives.

8. Military Records, roll 8 (Confederate).

9. Pat Talty, McCorkle's great-great-granddaughter, email to the author, July 11, 2016; Cunningham, *Doctors in Gray*, 130–32.

10. William H. Knauss, *The Story of Camp Chase* (Nashville: Publishing House of the Methodist Episcopal Church South, 1906), 113.

11. Cunningham, *Doctors in Gray*, 3. (Samuel Cooper, adjutant and inspector general of the Confederacy, agreed with Jones' estimate); Tennessee 4 Me (The Tennessee State Museum), www.tn4me.org/article.cfm/era_id/5/major_id/3/a_id/17; Drew Gilpin Faust, *This Republic of Suffering: Death and the American*

Notes—Chapter 4

Civil War (New York: Vintage Books, 2008), 4.

12. Dr. W. J. Worsham, *The Old Nineteenth Tennessee Regiment* (Knoxville: Paragon Printing, 1902), 198.

13. James L. Mohon, "Defending the Confederate Heartland: Company F of Henry Ashby's 2nd Tennessee Cavalry," *Civil War Regiments: A Journal of the American Civil War*, 4, no. 1 (1994): 34.

14. Cunningham, *Doctors in Gray*, 107–08.

15. Cunningham, 116–17.

16. Tony Horwitz, "Did Civil War Soldiers Have PTSD?" *Smithsonian*, January 2015, 44.

17. Cunningham, *Doctors in Gray*, 163.

18. Gustavus W. Dyer and John Trotwood Moore, comps, *The Tennessee Civil War Veterans Questionnaires* (Easley, South Carolina: Southern Historical Press, 1985). Nicely questionnaire, 4: 1640–41; Ireland, 3: 1204–05; Nail, 4: 1621–22. Between 1915 and 1923, state archivists Dyer and Moore collected information from 1,650 Civil War veterans, most of them former Confederates. Among them seventeen veterans of the Second Tennessee Cavalry created what amount to abbreviated wartime autobiographies. One of the questions concerned the quality of camp life.

19. Robert J. Driver, Jr., *The Confederate Soldiers of Rockbridge County, Virginia: A Roster* (Jefferson, NC: McFarland, 2016), 194; Military service records, National Archives, Washington, D.C.

20. Alfred McCorkle's military career is problematic. The Missouri State Archives list McCorkle as a Confederate surgeon in December 1861 at Carrollton, Missouri, but provide no military unit. The National Archives has no record.

21. Military service records, National Archives.

22. Military service records; Driver, *Confederate Soldiers*, 204

23. Military service records; Driver, 201.

24. Matt Atkinson, "First Rockbridge Artillery," *Encyclopedia Virginia*, www.encyclopediavirginia.org/First_Rockbridge_Artillery.

25. Edmond Pendleton Tomkins, *Rockbridge County, Virginia: An Informal History* (Richmond, VA: Whittet & Shepperson, 1952), 141–43.

26. Ota Larmer, "Revival of Confederate Flag Recalls War Division of Mooresburg Family," *Hawkins County News*, January 20, 1960.

Chapter 4

1. Dyer, *Veterans Questionnaires*, Wetzel, 5: 2164–65; Taylor, 5: 2040–42.

2. James Marten, *Sing Not War: The Lives of Union & Confederate Veterans in Gilded Age America* (Chapel Hill: University of North Carolina Press, 2011), 42; Fisher, *War at Every Door*, 157.

3. Marten, *Sing Not War*, 44.

4. Anna Mary Moon, ed., "A Southern Woman, in 1897, Remembers the Civil War," *The East Tennessee Historical Society's Publications*, 21 (1949): 111–12; Dyer, *Veterans Questionnaires*, McCarty, 4: 1415–16.

5. Jeffrey McClurken, *Take Care of the Living* (Charlottesville: University of Virginia Press, 2009), 42–43.

6. Rule, *Loyalists of Tennessee*, 21; Temple, *East Tennessee and the Civil War*, 530.

7. Whitelaw Reid, *After the War: A Tour of the Southern States, 1865–1866* (London: Sampson Low, Son & Marston, 1866), 351–52.

8. Groce, *Mountain Rebels*, 127–28.

9. Fisher, *War at Every Door*, 159.

10. Fisher, 164.

11. Fisher, 155–156.

12. McKenzie, *Lincolnites and Rebels*, 213.

13. Groce, *Mountain Rebels*, 134.

14. Groce, 135.

15. Donald E. Sutherland, ed. *A Very Violent Rebel: The Civil War Diary of Ellen Renshaw House* (Knoxville: University of Tennessee Press, 1996), 181.

16. McKenzie, *Lincolnites and Rebels*, 200–02.

17. Groce, 139.

18. McKenzie, 207; 198ff.

19. Groce, *Mountain Rebels*, 132–133.

20. Groce, 150.

Notes—Chapters 5 and 6

21. Sutherland, *Very Violent Rebel*, 190.
22. Fain, *Sanctified Trial*, 349–50.
23. McKenzie, *Lincolnites and Rebels*, 217–19.
24. Johnston, *Blue and Gray*, 69–71.
25. Mohon, "Defending the Tennessee Heartland," 35; Groce, *Mountain Rebels*, 145.
26. *Knoxville Whig; Knoxville Press and Herald*, July 15, 1865.
27. Mohon, "Defending the Tennessee Heartland," 37.

Chapter 5

1. Neff, *Honoring Civil War Dead*, 132–33.
2. Hess, *Knoxville Campaign*, 292.
3. Faust, *Republic of Suffering*, 71–74; Hess, 168–69.
4. Neff, *Honoring Civil War Dead*, 29–30.
5. Faust, *Republic of Suffering*, 71.
6. Neff, *Honoring Civil War Dead*, 56; Meg Groeling, *The Aftermath of Battle: The Burial of the Civil War Dead* (El Dorado Hills, California: Savas Beatie, 2015), 18–19.
7. Faust, *Republic of Suffering*, 73; Janney, *Remembering the Civil War*, 78.
8. Kelly Merrifield, "From Necessity to Honor: The Evolution of National Cemeteries in the United States," https://www.nps.gov/nr/travel/national_cemeteries/Development.html.
9. Neff, *Honoring Civil War Dead*, 112.
10. Faust, *Republic of Suffering*, 212–13.
11. Merrifield, "From Necessity to Honor."
12. Faust, *Republic of Suffering*, 219–20, 234.
13. Neff, *Honoring Civil War Dead*, 126–27.
14. Neff, 130; Faust, *Republic of Suffering*, 235.
15. Neff, 128; July 24, 1866, diary entry, Edmund Whitman papers (1830–1881), James S. Schoff Civil War Collection, William L. Clements Library, University of Michigan.
16. Jack Neely, "Knoxville's National Cemetery: A Short History—Part I," https://knoxvillehistoryproject.org/national-cemetery.
17. *Army Mail Bag*, September 17, 1864; *Knoxville Whig*, May 8, 1867; Neely, "Knoxville's National Cemetery—Parts I, II."
18. *Knoxville Whig*, July 17, 1867; November 11, 1868.
19. Faust, *Republic of Suffering*, 238; William Blair, *Cities of the Dead: Contesting the Memory of the Civil War in the South, 1865–1914* (Chapel Hill: University of North Carolina Press, 2004), 53.
20. Faust, 239–43.
21. Neff, *Honoring Civil War Dead*, 146–47.
22. Caroline Janney, *Burying the Dead but not the Past: Ladies' Memorial Associations & the Lost Cause* (Chapel Hill: University of North Carolina Press, 2008), 88.
23. Janney, *Burying the Dead*, 90–92.
24. Faust, *Republic of Suffering*, 244.
25. Jack Neely, *The Marble City: A Photographic Tour of Knoxville's Graveyards* (Knoxville: University of Tennessee Press, 1999), 46.
26. *Knoxville Whig*, April 3, 1867.
27. *Knoxville Press and Herald*, May 5, 1868.
28. *Knoxville Press*, September 4, October 29, 1868.

Chapter 6

1. Keith M. Harris, *Across the Blood Chasm: The Culture of Commemoration among Civil War Veterans* (Baton Rouge: Louisiana State University Press, 2014), 50.
2. Janney, *Remembering the Civil War*, 93; David W. Blight, *Race and Reunion: The Civil War in American Memory* (Cambridge, MA: Harvard University Press, 2001), 65ff.
3. *Knoxville Press and Messenger*, June 4, 1868.
4. *Knoxville Press and Herald*, June 11, 1870.
5. *Knoxville Chronicle*, June 14, 1870.
6. Janney, *Remembering the Civil War*, 100.

Notes—Chapter 7

7. *Philadelphia Evening Telegraph*, May 28, 1869.
8. Janney, *Remembering the Civil War*, 102.
9. Harris, *Across the Bloody Chasm*, 50–51.
10. Janney, *Burying the Dead*, 93, 80; Gaines Foster. *Ghosts of the Confederacy: Defeat, the Lost Cause, and the Emergence of New South*. (New York: Oxford University Press, 1987), 42.
11. Blair, *Cities of the Dead*, 52.
12. Janney, *Remembering the Civil War*, 94–96. Edward Alfred Pollard, a Richmond newspaper editor and author of several books on the Civil War, coined the term "Lost Cause" in his 1866 history of the war. Pollard emphasized, among other things, the bravery of Confederate soldiers in the face of greater Northern firepower.
13. Buck, *Road to Reunion*, 120–21.
14. Blight, *Race and Reunion*, 86, 208–10.
15. *Knoxville Press and Messenger*, June 2, 1869.
16. Rule, *Standard History of Knoxville*, 586.
17. Neely, "Knoxville's National Cemetery—Part II."
18. *Knoxville Press and Herald*, June 2, 3, 1874; *Knoxville Weekly Chronicle*, June 10, 1874.
19. *Knoxville Whig and Chronicle*, June 2, 1875.
20. *Knoxville Journal*, May 30, 1886.
21. *Knoxville Tribune*, May 31, 1889.
22. *Knoxville Journal*, May 31, 1892.
23. *Knoxville Journal*, May 31, 1896.
24. *Knoxville Tribune*, May 31, 1898.
25. Neff, *Honoring Civil War Dead*, 136.
26. *Knoxville Press and Herald*, May 18, 1871.
27. *Knoxville Press*, May 16, 1872.
28. *Knoxville Journal*, May 26, 1886.
29. *Knoxville Journal*, May 19, 1893.
30. *Knoxville Tribune*, May 21, 1893.
31. *Knoxville Tribune*, May 20, 1898.

Chapter 7

1. MacArthur, "Knoxville's History," 30.
2. Jack Neely, *Market Square: A History of the Most Democratic Place on Earth* (Knoxville: Market Square District Association, 2009), 36–37.
3. Harris, *Across the Bloody Chasm*, 2.
4. Groce, *Mountain Rebels*, 155–56.
5. Groce, 151.
6. Merton E. Coulter, *William G. Brownlow: Fighting Parson of the Southern Highlands* (Chapel Hill: University of North Carolina Press, 1937), 395.
7. Thomas E. Wise, "The Day President Rutherford B. Hayes Came to Town, Knoxville, 21 September 1877," *Tennessee Ancestors* 18, no. 1 (April 2000): 66.
8. David L. Eubanks, "Dr. J. G. M. Ramsey of East Tennessee: A Career of Public Service" (Ph. D. diss., University of Tennessee, 1965), 32.
9. Temple, *East Tennessee and the Civil War*, 531; *New York Tribune*, April 29, 1874, as quoted in Buck, *Road to Reunion*, 115.
10. Blight, *Race and Reunion*, 194; Barbara A. Gannon, *The Won Cause: Black and White Comradeship in the Grand Army of the Republic* (Chapel Hill: University of North Carolina Press, 2014), Appendices 1, 2.
11. David W. Blight, *Beyond the Battlefield: Race, Memory, and the American Civil War* (Amherst: University of Massachusetts Press, 2002), 173.
12. Silber, *Romance of Reunion*, 143ff.
13. *New York Times*, June 13, 1865.
14. *Oration of the Honorable Oliver P. Morton, Address of Major General George G. Meade ... at the Dedication of the Monument in the Soldiers' National Cemetery at Gettysburg, July 1st, 1869.* (Gettysburg, PA: Wible Printers, 1870), 20.
15. John H. Brubaker, III, "Confederate Memorial Rests in Cemetery Here, Not on Typical Courthouse Lawn," *Danville* (VA) *Register*, August 6, 1972.
16. F. Sheffield Hale, "Challenging Historical Remembrance, Myth, and Identity: The Confederate Monuments Debate," in *Controversial Monuments and Memorials: A Guide for Community Leaders*, ed. David B. Allison (Lanham, MD: Rowman & Littlefield, 2018), 93–94.
17. *Knoxville Journal*, May 20, 1892.
18. Hazen Historical Museum at Bethel Cemetery, Knoxville.

Notes—Chapter 8

19. *Knoxville Sentinel,* May 19, 1892.
20. *Knoxville Sentinel,* October 15, 1896.
21. Buck, *Road to Reunion,* 160–61.
22. Janney, *Remembering the Civil War,* 166, 354 n20.
23. Marten, *Sing Not War,* 252.
24. Samuel McGuire, "East Tennessee's Grand Army: Union Veterans Confront Race, Reconciliation, and Civil War Memory, 1884–1913," (PhD diss., University of Georgia, 2015), 136.
25. Hess, *Knoxville Campaign,* 275–76; Joan L. Markel, *Knoxville in the Civil War* (Charleston, SC: Arcadia Publishing, 2013), 122.
26. *Knoxville Tribune,* October 7, 9, 1890.
27. *Knoxville Tribune,* October 8, 1890.
28. *Knoxville Journal,* September 18, 1895.
29. Henry Van Ness Boynton, comp., *Dedication of the Chickamauga and Chattanooga National Military Park, September 18–20, 1895; Report of the Joint Committee to Represent the Congress at the Dedication of the Chickamauga and Chattanooga Military Park* (Washington, D.C.: Government Printing Office, 1896), 25.
30. Boynton, *Dedication of Chickamauga,* 82, 181–84, 239–40.
31. Herman Justi, ed. *Official History of the Tennessee Centennial Exposition* (Nashville: Brandon Printing, 1898), 232.

Chapter 8

1. Cecelia Elizabeth O'Leary, *To Die For: The Paradox of American Patriotism* (Princeton, NJ: Princeton University Press, 1999), 116.
2. Frederick Jackson Turner, "The Significance of the Frontier in American History" in *Frederick Jackson Turner: Wisconsin's Historian of the Frontier,* ed. Martin Ridge (Madison: Wisconsin Historical Society Press, 2016), 42.
3. Russell, *One Hundred and Three Fights,* 60.
4. Sweeney, "Introduction," in *One Hundred and Three Fights,* xiii–xiv.
5. Russell, Don. "Reuben Frank Bernard" *Journal of the American Military History Foundation* 2, no. 2 (Summer, 1938): 91.
6. Russell, *One Hundred and Three Fights,* 72–73.
7. Sweeney, "Introduction," in *One Hundred and Three Fights,* xvi–xvii.
8. Russell, *One Hundred and Three Fights,* 84.
9. Russell, 103.
10. *Jonesborough Herald and Tribune,* November 25, 1903.
11. Sweeney, "Introduction," in *One Hundred and Three Fights,* xviii; additional details: O'Neal, Bill, *Fighting Men of the Indian Wars: A Biographical Encyclopedia of the Mountain Men, Soldiers, Cowboys, and Pioneers Who Took up Arms During America's Westward Expansion* (Stillwater, OK: Barbed Wire Press, 1991), 44ff.
12. Russell, *One Hundred and Three Fights,* 87–88.
13. *Knoxville Journal,* February 6, 1887.
14. Russell, "Reuben Frank Bernard," 91, 93.
15. Reuben F. Bernard to Ruth Lavinia Simpson Bernard's unnamed father, January 9, 1893, Bernard family papers.
16. *Knoxville Journal,* January 2, 1896.
17. Priscilla Rogers and other McCorkle family descendants, interview by the author, Mooresburg, Tennessee, June 2, 2016.
18. *Hawkins County News,* January 30, 1960; R. S. McCarty to Guy A. McCorkle, July 14, 1938, McCorkle family papers.
19. *Jonesborough Herald and Tribune,* October 5, 1871.
20. Fain, *Sanctified Trial,* xiv; MacArthur, "Knoxville's History," 35.
21. Tennessee Department of Health. tn.gov/health/history-of-public-health-in-tennessee/pre-1900.
22. Emma Deane Smith Trent, *Faces, Places, and Things of Early East Tennessee* (Whitesburg, TN: Emma Deane Smith Trent, 1989), 267.
23. State of Tennessee Soldiers' Application for Pension, October 12, 1909.

206

Chapter 9

1. William McCorkle to Margaret Elizabeth McCorkle Montgomery, August 15, 1898; Henry McCorkle to William McCorkle, April 13, 1896, McCorkle family papers.
2. "In Memoriam" in *University of Tennessee Record*, 1, no. 6 (September 1898): 333.
3. James Riley Montgomery, Stanley J. Folmsbee, and Lee Seifert Greene, *To Foster Knowledge: A History of the University of Tennessee, 1794–1970* (Knoxville: University of Tennessee Press, 1984), 71–72.
4. Montgomery, 139–41.
5. Montgomery, 145, 125.
6. McCorkle transcripts, 1885–86, 1886–87, University of Tennessee Archives; "In Memoriam," 333.
7. "In Memoriam," 334.
8. *Knoxville Journal*, June 6, 1889.
9. "In Memoriam," 334; Letter from William McCorkle to the *Morristown Gazette*, November 9, 1898.
10. *Knoxville Journal*, September 13, 1891.
11. John H. Nankivell, *Buffalo Soldier Regiment: History of the Twenty-Fifth United States Infantry, 1879–1926* (Reprint, Lincoln: University of Nebraska Press, 2001), 48ff.
12. Nankivell, 53–54.
13. Nankivel, 60–62; U.S. Returns from Military Posts, Fort Missoula, Montana, January 1894.
14. Henry McCorkle to Jennie Sterritt McCorkle, January 24, 1895, McCorkle family papers.
15. Henry McCorkle to William McCorkle, April 13, 1896.
16. T. G. Steward, *Buffalo Soldiers: The Colored Regulars in the United States Army* (Philadelphia: A.M.E. Book Concern, 1904; reprint, Mineola, New York: Dover, 2014), 96.
17. Steward, 100.
18. William McCorkle to Margaret Montgomery, August 15, 1898; *Knoxville Sentinel*, November 14, 1898.
19. "In Memoriam," 338.
20. The university's full-time undergraduate and graduate enrollment totaled just over 200 students from McCorkle's matriculation in 1885 until Bernard graduated in 1893, when enrollment rose to 266. (University of Tennessee Archives); *Knoxville Sentinel*, November 14, 1898.
21. "In Memoriam," 338; *Knoxville Sentinel*, November 14, 1898; Bernard transcript, 1890–91, University of Tennessee Archives.
22. Montgomery, *To Foster Knowledge*, 147–48.
23. *The Caduceus of Kappa Sigma* 13, no. 1 (January 1898): 342.
24. Jack Neely email to the author, November 5, 2018.
25. "In Memoriam," 338.
26. *General Orders and Circulars* (Washington: Adjutant General's Office, 1897), 162–64; *Salt Lake City Tribune*, November 23, 1897.
27. Robert M. Travis, "The Adventures of a Company of Regular Soldiers in Our War with Spain." http://www.spanamwar.com/4thUSTravis.htm. Travis, a soldier from Henry County, Tennessee, in Company B, Fourth Infantry, maintained a diary and scrapbook from April to December 1898. He concentrated particularly on the battle of El Caney.

Chapter 10

1. *New York Sun*, April 23, 1898.
2. U.S. Secretary of State John Hay called the conflict "a splendid little war" in a letter to Lieutenant Colonel Theodore Roosevelt, July 27, 1898.
3. *Knoxville Sentinel*, April 22, 1898; *Maryville Times*, April 23, 1898.
4. Stephen Kinzer, *The True Flag: Theodore Roosevelt, Mark Twain, and the Birth of American Empire* (New York: Henry Holt, 2017), 2.
5. Janney, *Remembering the Civil War*, 367 *n*126.
6. Jack McCallam, *Leonard Wood: Rough Rider, Surgeon, Architect of American Imperialism* (New York: NYU Press, 2005), 55.
7. William Stanco, "Speaker Thomas Brackett Reed and the Will of the Majority," *Capitol Dome* (Fall 2007): 13.
8. *Nashville American*, February 18,

Notes—Chapter 11

1898; *Knoxville Sentinel*, February 19, 1898.

9. *Maryville Times*, March 12, 1898. "Capt. Gibson" presumably is Henry Gibson, a popular Republican congressman representing Knoxville. The reference to Gibson's military prowess may be satiric; he was not a Civil War veteran.

10. *Knoxville Sentinel*, April 12, 1898.

11. Rule, *Standard History*, 185.

12. William Allen White, "When Johnny Went Marching," *McClure's Magazine*, October 1898, 199.

13. Mark Lee Gardner, *Rough Riders: Theodore Roosevelt, His Cowboy Regiment, and the Immortal Charge Up San Juan Hill* (New York: William Morrow, 2017), 60; "The Rough Riders" in *The Works of Theodore Roosevelt*, vol. 11 (New York, Scribner's, 1923–26), 54.

14. *Knoxville Sentinel*, February 28, March 29, 1898.

15. L. Ridley Bromfield, *Battles and Sketches of the History of the Army of Tennessee* (Mexico, Missouri: Missouri Printing & Publishing, 1906), 618–19.

16. Patrick McSherry, "A Brief History of the 4th Tennessee Volunteer Infantry," The Spanish-American War Centennial Website. spanamwar.com/4thtennessee.html; Rule, 187.

17. Colin F. Baxter, "Spanish-American War," Tennessee Encyclopedia of History and Culture. http://tennesseeencyclopedia.net/entries/spanish-american-war/.

18. *University of Tennessee Record*, 1, no. 6 (September 1898): 328; *Knoxville Sentinel*, June 4, 1898; Charles Dabney to Dandridge Spotswood, July 6, 1898, University of Tennessee Archives.

19. Silber, *Romance of Reunion*, 162–63.

20. Janney, *Remembering the Civil War*, 223.

21. Wood, "The South and Reunion," *Historian* 31 (1969): 420; *Nashville American*, March 27, 1898.

22. Foster, *Ghosts of the Confederacy*, 146.

23. *Confederate Veteran* 6, July 1898, 304.

24. Quoted in *Chattanooga Times*, May 7, 1898.

25. Wood, "The South and Reunion," 427.

26. Silber, *Romance of Reunion*, 178–79; Congressional Record (Washington: Government Printing Office, 1898), Appendix 33, part 8, 320.

27. Wood, "The South and Reunion," 425; *Knoxville Sentinel*, May 19, 1898; Wood, 426; Bonnie M. Miller, *From Liberation to Conquest: The Visual and Popular Cultures of the Spanish-American War of 1898* (Amherst: University of Massachusetts Press, 2011), 118.

28. David Traxel, *1898: The Birth of the American Century* (New York: Macmillan, 1998), 64–65.

Chapter 11

1. Travis, "Adventures of a Company"; Nankivell, *Buffalo Soldier Regiment*, 66, 68.

2. Traxel, *1898*, 163; Addeo, Alicia, "Tampa is a Bum Place: The Letters of First Sergeant Henry A. Dobson in 1898," *Tampa Bay History*, 20, no. 1 (Spring/Summer 1998): 55. Dobson returned to the United States in late August 1898 and died of typhoid two weeks later.

3. Angus Konstam, *San Juan Hill 1898: America's Emergence as a World Power* (Oxford, England: Osprey, 1998), 17, 19.

4. Richard Harding Davis, *The Cuban and Porto Rican Campaigns* (New York: Scribner's Monthly*, 1898), 49–50.

5. Willard B. Gatewood, "Black Troops in Florida during the Spanish-American War," *Tampa Bay History*, 20, no. 1 (Spring/Summer 1998): 25–26.

6. Henry McCorkle to Mildred McCorkle, then staying with McCorkle's parents in Mooresburg, June 13, 1898, McCorkle family papers. McCorkle wrote his Cuban campaign letters in a rush with a pencil on pages torn from a pocket notebook. His thoughts jumped from one subject to another. Punctuation is haphazard.

7. Henry McCorkle to Mildred McCorkle, June 13, 1898; Browne, Jefferson B., *Key West: The Old and New* (Gainesville: University of Florida Press, 1912), 146.

8. Henry McCorkle to Mildred McCorkle, June 15, 1898.

Notes—Chapter 12

9. Steward, *Buffalo Soldiers*, 116.
10. Travis, "Adventures of a Company"; Traxel, *1898*, 169; Gardner, *Rough Riders*, 79.
11. *Knoxville Sentinel*, April 3, 1899.
12. Henry McCorkle to Mildred McCorkle, June 21, 1898.
13. Charles H. Brown, *The Correspondents' War: Journalists in the Spanish-American War* (New York: Scribner's, 1967), 300–01.
14. Burr McIntosh, *The Little I Saw of Cuba* (New York: F. Tennyson Neely, 1899), 61; Steward, *Buffalo Soldiers*, 122; Moss, James A., *Memories of the Campaign of Santiago, June 6, 1898–Aug. 18, 1898* (San Francisco: Mysell-Rollins, 1899), 15.
15. Moss, *Memories of the Campaign*, 17.
16. Traxel, *1898*, 178.
17. Peter M. MacQueen, "With Wheeler and Roosevelt at Santiago." *Leslie's Illustrated Newspaper*, November 1898, 19.
18. Henry McCorkle to Mildred McCorkle, June 26, 1898.
19. Moss, *Memories of the Campaign*, 17ff.
20. Henry McCorkle to Mildred McCorkle, June 26, 1898.
21. Moss, *Memories of the Campaign*, 27; Robert Turley, "Diary of the war went through by Robert Turley," http://www.spanamwar.com/4thUS.htm. Turley, of Company E, Fourth Infantry, maintained a diary from April 19 to November 20, 1898, including notes on the battle of El Caney.
22. Henry McCorkle to Mildred McCorkle, June 29, 1898.
23. *Knoxville Journal and Tribune*, July 23, 1898.
24. Konstam, *San Juan Hill*, 21.

Chapter 12

1. McIntosh, *Little I Saw of Cuba*, 98; Gardner, *Rough Riders*, 142. The senior Capron would become a war casualty himself, dying of typhoid soon after returning to his Virginia home that September.
2. *Washington Times*, September 19, 1898.
3. The description of the battle at El Caney in this chapter has been drawn largely from participants and other contemporary accounts. Major sources: "General Lawton's Report" (July 3, 1898) in *Annual Reports of the War Department for the Fiscal Year Ended June 30, 1898* (Washington: Government Printing Office, 1898), 1, pt. 2: 37ff; J. A. Moss's colorful *Memories of the Campaign*; and T. G. Steward's detailed account in *Buffalo Soldiers*.
4. Richard Harding Davis, "The Battle of San Juan," *Scribner's Monthly*, October 1898, 397; Frank Norris, "With Lawton at El Caney," *Century*, June 1899, 305.
5. Norris, "With Lawton at El Caney," 305.
6. Arthur H. Lee, "The Regulars at El Caney," *Scribner's Monthly*, October 1898, 403.
7. Caspar Whitney, "The Santiago Campaign," *Harper's Weekly*, October 1898, 810.
8. Moss, *Memories of the Campaign*, 33.
9. Moss, 35.
10. Steward, *Buffalo Soldiers*, 164.
11. *Knoxville Journal and Tribune*, April 3, 1899. Quoted by University of Tennessee President Charles W. Dabney in remarks at the reburial of Henry McCorkle and Jack Bernard in Knoxville; Dr. William A. McCorkle to Margaret Montgomery, August 15, 1898, McCorkle family papers.
12. Moss, *Memories of the Campaign*, 37.
13. *Knoxville Journal and Tribune*, November 14, 1899. University of Tennessee President Charles W. Dabney described Bernard's wound during a memorial service.
14. *Knoxville Journal and Tribune*, April 3, 1899; *Chicago Tribune*, July 19, 1898; Travis, "Adventures of a Company."
15. *Chicago Tribune*, July 19, 1898.
16. "Lawton's Report," 381.
17. Frank Pullen, "Sergeant-Major Pullen of the 25th Infantry Describes the Conduct of the Negro Soldiers Around El Caney" in Edward A. Johnson, *History of*

Notes—Chapter 13

Negro Soldiers in the Spanish-American War (Raleigh: Capital Printing, 1899), 29.

18. Moss, *Memories of the Campaign*, 39.

19. "Lawton's Report," 379; Lee, "The Regulars at El Caney," 410; Brown, *Correspondents' War*, 349.

20. "Lawton's Report," 388; Moss, *Memories of the Campaign*, 39; Johnson, *History of Negro Soldiers*, 30.

21. Moss, *Memories of the Campaign*, 41.

22. Travis, "Adventures of a Company."

23. Joseph Edgar Chamberlin, "How the Spaniards Fought at Caney," *Scribner's Monthly*, September 1898, 278.

24. Michael Clodfelter, *Warfare and Armed Conflict: A Statistical Reference to Casualty Figures, 1500–2000* (Jefferson, NC: McFarland, 2002), 286.

25. Dedication of the Battle Monument at El Caney (Baltimore: John S. Bridges, 1906), 23–24.

26. "Lawton's Report," 384–86.

27. Pat Talty email to the author, February 10, 2018.

28. Nankivell, *Buffalo Soldier Regiment*, 84; "Lawton's Report," 385.

Chapter 13

1. *Knoxville Journal and Tribune*, July 23, 1898. A copy of Bernard's letter was provided to the newspaper by "a friend of the dead lieutenant residing in this city."

2. C. L. Hodges to Mildred McCorkle, July 26, 1898; William McCorkle to Margaret Montgomery, August 15, 1898, McCorkle family papers.

3. S. C. Staunton to Mildred McCorkle, January 18, 1899, McCorkle family papers. Why this item was found on a field of battle well removed from El Caney is unclear.

4. Henry C. McCook, *The Martial Graves of Our Fallen Heroes* (Philadelphia: J. W. Jacobs, 1899), 210–11. Several newspapers nationwide published McCook's sketches of the two "monument trees" in mid-January 1899. (Frank N. Schubert, editor of *On the Trail of the Buffalo Soldier: Biographies of African Americans in the U.S. Army, 1866–1917* [Wilmington, DE: Scarecrow Press, 1995], cites a Twenty-fifth Infantry scrapbook that claims Leftwich was buried in a separate grave with his "name in tightly corked bottle, buried at head of grave.")

5. McCook, *Martial Graves*, 209; Faust, *Republic of Suffering*, 103.

6. Moss, *Memories of the Campaign*, 43; Travis, "Adventures of a Company."

7. Norris, "With Lawton at El Caney," 309.

8. Charles W. Dabney to Dr. W. A. McCorkle, July 6, 1898, University of Tennessee Archives.

9. "In Memoriam," 334.

10. *University of Tennessee Record*, 1, no. 6 (September 1898): 328.

11. *Knoxville Journal and Tribune*, July 23, 1898.

12. *Knoxville Sentinel*, November 14, 1898.

13. Mildred McCorkle to Jennie McCorkle, November 14, 1898, McCorkle family papers.

14. Hodges to McCorkle, July 26, 1898.

15. Unknown Knoxville writer to William McCorkle, July 14, 1898, McCorkle family papers.

16. McCorkle to Montgomery, August 15, 1898.

17. Mildred McCorkle to Henry Ritzius, December 19, 1898, McCorkle family papers.

18. The Spanish-American War Centennial Website. http://www.spanamwar.com/casualties.htm.; Travis, "Adventures of a Company."

19. Arlington National Cemetery Website. www.arlingtoncemetery.net/jhaskell.htm.

20. O'Leary, *To Die For*, 146.

21. *Knoxville Sentinel*, July 14, 1898.

22. *Confederate Veteran*, July 1898, 324–25.

23. Foster, *Ghosts of the Confederacy*, 147–48.

24. Lawrence I. Berkove, ed., *Skepticism and Dissent: Selected Journalism, 1898–1901: by Ambrose Bierce* (Ann Arbor, MI: UMI Research Press, 1986), 98.

25. Noyalis, *Civil War Legacy in the*

Notes—Chapter 14 and Epilogue

Shenandoah: Remembrance, Reunion and Reconstruction (Charleston, SC: History Press, 2015), 113–15.

26. William McKinley, "Speech before the Legislature in Joint Assembly at the State Capitol, Atlanta, Georgia, December 14, 1898," in *Speeches and Addresses of William McKinley, from March 1, 1897, to May 30, 1900* (New York: Doubleday & McClure, 1900), 159.

27. *Confederate Veteran*, February 1899, 76, quoted in Neff, *Honoring the Civil War Dead*, 223. In fact, Union tombstones never were made to fit Confederate graves. In all national cemeteries, Union stones are rounded on top; Confederate stones are pointed.

28. Michelle A. Krowl, "'In the Spirit of Fraternity': The United States Government and the Burial of Confederate Dead at Arlington National Cemetery, 1864–1914," *Virginia Magazine of History and Biography* 3, no. 2 (2003): 152; Blair, *Cities of the Dead*, 182–84.

Chapter 14

1. McCook, *Martial Graves*, 10.
2. McCook, 202. In a letter to the *Morristown Gazette* dated November 9, 1898, William McCorkle said Brigadier General Chambers McKibbin, formerly a major in the Twenty-fifth Regiment, obtained the railing. Amelia Scherrer, Henry McCorkle's sister-in-law, thought the railing came from the windows of Morro Castle, which dominated the entrance to Santiago's harbor. (Amelia Scherrer to Guy and Phyllis McCorkle, April 27, 1959, McCorkle family papers.)
3. McCook, 34–35.
4. Faust, *Republic of Suffering*, 9.
5. McCook, *Martial Graves*, 18; Edward Steere, "National Cemeteries and Memorials in Global Conflict," *Quartermaster Review*, November–December 1953. http://old.quartermasterfoundation.org/national_cemeteries_and_memorials_in_global_conflict.htm; Charles Dabney to William McCorkle, November 14, 1898, University of Tennessee Archives; Mildred McCorkle to Henry Ritzius, December 19, 1898.
6. McCook, *Martial Graves*, 19. (Neither McCook nor Edward Steere explained why the government waited so long to ship the bodies to the United States.)
7. *Knoxville Journal and Tribune*, April 7, 1899.
8. *Knoxville Journal and Tribune*, April 3, 1899.
9. MacArthur, "Knoxville's History," 29–30; Wheeler, *Knoxville, Tennessee*, 29–30.
10. Mark T. Banker, *Appalachians All: East Tennesseans and the Elusive History of an American Region* (Knoxville: University of Tennessee Press, 2011), 99–101; Neely, *Market Square*, 96–97.
11. Montgomery, *To Foster Knowledge*, 153–54.
12. *Knoxville Journal and Tribune*, April 2, 3, 1899.
13. *Knoxville Journal and Tribune*, April 3, 1899.
14. *Knoxville Sentinel*, April 3, 1899.
15. *Knoxville Journal and Tribune*, April 3, 1899; *Knoxville Sentinel*, April 2, 3, 1899.
16. *Knoxville Journal and Tribune*, April 4, 1899.
17. Neely, *Knoxville's National Cemetery: A History—Parts I, III*.
18. *Knoxville Journal and Tribune*, November 13, 1898; *Knoxville Sentinel*, December 6, 1898.
19. *Knoxville Sentinel*, April 3, 1899.
20. Blight, *Race and Reunion*, 76.
21. *Knoxville Sentinel*; *Knoxville Journal and Tribune*, April 3, 1899.

Epilogue

1. *Knoxville Sentinel*, May 28, 1899.
2. *Knoxville Sentinel*, May 18, 1899.
3. *Knoxville Sentinel*, May 31, 1899.
4. *Knoxville Journal and Tribune*, May 31, 1899.
5. *Cincinnati Post*, May 31, 1899. The "swords of anger" imagery is vivid, but surgeon William McCorkle more likely would have drawn a scalpel.
6. *University of Tennessee Volunteer*, 1899, 9, 11; *University of Tennessee Record*, 3, no. 17 (October 1900): 27–28.

Notes—Epilogue

7. *University of Tennessee Record*, 7, no. 5 (August 1904): 296.

8. At some point, the McCorkle-Bernard tablet moved to the landing between the first and second floors of the University Administrative Building, according to the September 9, 1951, *Knoxville Journal*. From there, it may have disappeared. University Archives does not list it among its holdings. Several university officials contacted in 2018 and 2020 said they are uncertain about its location.

9. Buck, *Road to Reunion*, 307. Buck's pioneering commentary on the reunion of white veterans has lost standing because the historian virtually dismissed race relations while documenting the process of reconciliation. Referencing "the Negro problem," in the North and the South, Buck concluded, "Once a people admits that a major problem is basically insoluble they have taken the first step in learning how to live with it." (Buck, 297).

10. Harris, *Across the Bloody Chasm*, 144.

11. Markel, *Knoxville in the Civil War*, 113; Guy, Joe, *The Hidden History of East Tennessee* (Charleston, SC: History Press, 2008), 25–26.

12. Timothy S. Sedore. *Tennessee Civil War Monuments: An Illustrated Field Guide*. Bloomington: Indiana University Press, 2020, 230–70; Megan Boehnke, *Knoxville News Sentinel*, August 14, 2017.

13. Sedore, *Tennessee Monuments*, 230, 236ff, 242–243; Kelli B. Nelson, "On the Imperishable Face of Granite: Civil War Monuments and the Evolution of Historical Memory in East Tennessee, 1878–1931" (master's thesis, East Tennessee State University, 2011), 82–83, 87.

14. Jack Neely, "Time's Remorseless Doom: Two Monuments in Fort Sanders," *Knoxville Mercury*, August 25, 2017. http://www.knoxmercury.com/2017/08/25/times-remorseless-doom-two-monuments-fort-sanders/.

15. Hess, *Knoxville Campaign*, 279.

16. "Theodore O'Hara's Bivouac of the Dead," National Cemetery Administration. https://www.cem.va.gov/history/bivouac.asp.

17. *Knoxville Sentinel*, November 28, 1914.

18. Tyler Whetstone, "Knoxville's Fort Sanders Confederate Statue Likely to Stay," *Knoxville News Sentinel*, December 21, 2017.

19. *Report of the New York Monuments Commission on the Dedication of Monument to the Seventy-Ninth Regiment Highlanders New York Volunteers: Knoxville Tenn., September 23, 1918* (Albany, New York: L. B. Lyon, 1919), 5–6.

20. *Report of Monuments Commission*, 29–30. As Rule spoke, Lieutenant Guy McCorkle was serving with a New York infantry regiment in France. He represented the sixth generation of his family to serve in the military.

21. Janney, *Remembering the Civil War*, 306ff.

22. From "O Praise the Lord," a sermon delivered at Knoxville's First Presbyterian Church by the Reverend Renee Kesler, May 3, 2015.

Bibliography

Archival Collections

Bernard, John Jay. Student transcripts. Betsey B. Creekmore Special Collections and University Archives, University of Tennessee Libraries, Knoxville.
Bernard, Reuben. Military service records. National Archives, Washington, D.C.
Bernard family. Papers. Private collection.
Brown, William Carey. Papers. Order of American Indian Wars Collection. U.S. Army Military History Institute, Carlisle, PA.
Brown, William Carey. Papers. University of Colorado Archives, Boulder, CO.
Dabney, Charles W., Jr. Presidential correspondence. Betsey B. Creekmore Special Collections and University Archives, University of Tennessee Libraries, Knoxville.
Deaderick, David Anderson. Manuscript, "Register of Events and Facts Recorded Annually." Calvin M. McClung Historical Collection, Knox County Public Library, Knoxville.
McCorkle, Henry. Student transcripts. Betsey B. Creekmore Special Collections and University Archives, University of Tennessee Libraries, Knoxville.
McCorkle, William. Enrollment records. Washington & Lee University Special Collections and Archives, Lexington, VA.
McCorkle, William. Military service records, pension application. Tennessee State Library and Archives, Nashville.
McCorkle family. Papers. Private collections.
Rule, William. Papers. Calvin M. McClung Historical Collection, Knox County Public Library, Knoxville.
Whitman, Edmund. Papers. James S. Schoff Civil War Collection, William L. Clements Library, University of Michigan, Ann Arbor.

Published Primary Sources

Addeo, Alicia. "Tampa Is a Bum Place: The Letters of First Sergeant Henry A. Dobson in 1898." *Tampa Bay History* 20, no.1 (Spring/Summer 1998): 48–60.
Alger, Russell A. *The Spanish-American-War*. New York: Harper & Brothers, 1901.
Berkove, Lawrence I, ed. *Ambrose Bierce: Skepticism and Dissent: Selected Journalism, 1898–1901*. Ann Arbor, MI: UMI Research Press, 1986.
Bonsal, Stephen. *The Fight for Santiago: The Story of the Soldier in the Cuban Campaign, from Tampa to the Surrender*. New York: Doubleday & McClure, 1899.
Boynton, Henry Van Ness, comp. *Dedication of the Chickamauga and Chattanooga National Military Park, September 18–20, 1895; Report of the Joint Committee to Represent the Congress at the Dedication of the Chickamauga and Chattanooga National Military Park*. Washington, D.C.: Government Printing Office, 1896.

Bibliography

Bromfield, L. Ridley. *Battles and Sketches of the History of the Army of the Tennessee.* Mexico, MO: Missouri Printing & Publishing, 1906.

Browne, Jefferson B. *Key West: The Old and New.* Gainesville: University of Florida Press, 1973 facsimile of 1912 edition.

Buck, Beaumont B. *Memories of Peace and War.* San Antonio, TX: Naylor, 1935.

Chamberlin, Joseph Edgar. "How the Spanish Fought at Caney." *Scribner's Monthly*, September 1898, 278–82.

Davis, Richard Harding. "The Battle of San Juan." *Scribner's Monthly*, October 1898, 387–403.

Davis, Richard Harding. *The Cuban and Porto Rican Campaigns.* New York: Scribner's, 1898.

Dedication of the Battle Monument at El Caney. Baltimore: John S. Bridges, 1906.

Dyer, Gustavus W., and John Trotwood Moore, comps. *The Tennessee Civil War Veterans Questionnaires.* Easley, SC: Southern Historical Press, 1985.

Fain, John N., ed. *Sanctified Trial: The Diary of Eliza Rhea Anderson Fain, a Confederate Woman in East Tennessee.* Knoxville: University of Tennessee Press, 2004.

"General Lawton's Report." In *Annual Reports of the War Department for the Fiscal Year Ended June 30, 1898; Report of the Major-General Commanding the Army*, 1, pt. 2, 378–88. Washington, D.C.: Government Printing Office, 1898

Graf, LeRoy P., and Ralph W. Haskins, eds. *The Papers of Andrew Johnson*, 5: 1861–62. Knoxville: University of Tennessee Press, 1979.

Hagemann, E. R., ed. *Fighting Rebels and Redskins: Experiences in Army Life of Colonel George B. Sanford, 1861–1892.* Norman: University of Oklahoma Press, 1969.

History of the First U.S. Cavalry, 1833–1906. Washington, D.C.: Regimental Press, 1906.

Johnson, Edward A. *History of Negro Soldiers in the Spanish-American War and Other Items of Interest.* Raleigh, NC: Capital Printing, 1899.

Justi, Herman. *Official History of the Tennessee Centennial Exposition.* Nashville: Brandon Printing, 1898.

Kennan, George. *Campaigning in Cuba.* New York: Century Co., 1899.

Knauss, William H. *The Story of Camp Chase.* Nashville: Publishing House of the Methodist Episcopal Church South, 1906.

Lee, Captain Arthur H. "The Regulars at El Caney." *Scribner's Monthly*, October 1898, 403–13.

MacQueen, Peter M. "With Wheeler and Roosevelt at Santiago." *Leslie's Illustrated Newspaper*, November 1898, 18–31.

McCook, Henry C. *The Martial Graves of Our Fallen Heroes in Santiago de Cuba.* Philadelphia: J. W. Jacobs, 1899.

McIntosh, Burr. *The Little I Saw of Cuba.* New York: F. Tennyson Neely, 1899.

McKinley, William. "Speeches Before the Legislature in Joint Assembly at the State Capital, Atlanta, Georgia, December 14, 1898." In *Speeches and Addresses of William McKinley, from March 1, 1897 to May 30, 1900*, 158–59. New York: Doubleday & McClure, 1900.

Moon, Anna Mary, ed. "A Southern Woman, in 1897, Remembers the Civil War." *East Tennessee Historical Society's Publications* 21 (1949): 111–15.

Moss, James A. *Memories of the Campaign of Santiago; June 6, 1898–Aug. 18, 1898.* San Francisco: Mysell-Rollins, 1899.

Norris, Frank. "With Lawton at El Caney." *Century*, June 1899, 304–09.

Oration of the Honorable Oliver P. Morton, Address of Major General George G. Meade. at the Dedication of the Monument in the Soldier's National Cemetery at Gettysburg, July 1st, 1869. Gettysburg: Wible Printers, 1870.

Page, Walter Hines. "The End of the War and After." *Atlantic Monthly*, September 1898, 430–32.

"Patriotism in the South." *Confederate Veteran*, July 1898, 324–25.

Pullen, Frank. "Sergeant-Major Pullen of the 25th Infantry Describes the Conduct of

Bibliography

the Negro Soldiers Around El Caney." In chapter 3, *History of Negro Soldiers in the Spanish-American War*, author Edward A. Johnson, 29–32. Raleigh, NC: Capital Printing, 1899.

Reid, Whitelaw. *After the War: A Tour of the Southern States, 1865–66*. London: Sampson Low, Son & Marston, 1866.

Report of the New York Monuments Commission on the Dedication of Monument to the Seventy-Ninth Regiment Highlanders New York Volunteers, Knoxville, Tenn., September 23, 1918. Albany: J. B. Lyon, 1919.

Roosevelt, Theodore. *The Rough Riders and Men of Action* in *The Works of Theodore Roosevelt*, 11. New York: Scribner's, 1926.

Rule, William. *The Loyalists of Tennessee in the Late War*. Cincinnati: H. C. Sherick, 1887.

Rule, William and George Frederick Mellen. *Standard History of Knoxville, Tennessee*. Chicago: Lewis Publishing, 1906.

St. Claire, Edward D. W. "Three Years in a Frontier Military Post Forty-Five Years Ago and Some Soldiers I Met There." *The American Oldtimer*, February 1939, 18–25.

Steward, T. G. *Buffalo Soldiers: The Colored Regulars in the United States Army*. Philadelphia: A. M. E. Book Concern, 1904; reprint Mineola, NY: Dover, 2014.

Sutherland, Daniel E. ed. *A Very Violent Rebel: The Civil War Diary of Ellen Renshaw House*. Knoxville: University of Tennessee Press, 1996.

Temple, Oliver P. *East Tennessee and the Civil War*. Cincinnati: Robert Clarke, 1899.

Travis, Robert M. "The Adventures of a Company of Regular Soldiers in Our War with Spain." http://www.spanamwar.com/4thUSTravis.htm.

Turley, Robert. "Diary of the War Went Through by Robert Turley." http://www.spanamwar.com/4thUS.htm.

Turner, Frederick Jackson. "The Significance of the Frontier in American History." In *Frederick Jackson Turner: Wisconsin's Historian of the Frontier*, edited by Martin Ridge. Madison: Wisconsin Historical Society Press, 2016, 26–47.

University of Tennessee Record. Knoxville: University of Tennessee, 1 no. 6 (September 1898), 328, 333–40; 3 no. 17 (October 1900), 27–28; 7 no. 5 (August 1904), 296.

Viola, Herman J., ed. *The Memoirs of Charles Henry Veil*. Thorndike, ME: Thorndike Press, 1994.

Volunteer, University of Tennessee yearbook. Knoxville: University of Tennessee, 1899.

White, William Allen. "When Johnny Went Marching." *McClure's Magazine*, June 1898, 199–205.

Whitney, Caspar. "The Santiago Campaign." *Harper's Weekly*, October 1898, 795–818.

Worsham, Dr. D. J. *The Old Nineteenth Tennessee Regiment*. Knoxville, TN: Paragon Printing, 1902.

Periodicals

Anaconda (Missoula, MT) *Standard*
Army Mail Bag
Atlantic Monthly
Century
Chattanooga Times
Chicago Tribune
Cincinnati Post
Confederate Veteran
Danville (VA) *Register*
Evening Capital (Annapolis, MD)
Harper's Weekly
Hawkins County (TN) *News*
Jonesborough (TN) *Herald and Tribune*
Knoxville Chronicle
Knoxville Journal
Knoxville Journal and Tribune
Knoxville Mercury
Knoxville News Sentinel
Knoxville Press and Herald
Knoxville Press and Messenger
Knoxville Sentinel
Knoxville Tribune
Knoxville Whig
Knoxville Whig and Chronicle
Leslie's Illustrated Newspaper
Lexington (VA) *Gazette*

Bibliography

Maryville (TN) *Times*
McClure's *Magazine*
Morristown (TN) *Gazette*
Nashville *Tennessean*
New York Sun
New York Times
Richmond *Dispatch*
Rogersville (TN) *Review*
Salt Lake City *Tribune*
Scribner's *Monthly*
Washington *Evening Star*
Washington *Times*

Secondary Sources

Atkinson, Matt. "First Rockbridge Artillery." *Encyclopedia Virginia*. www.encyclopedia virginia.org/First_Rockbridge_Artillery.

Ayers, Edward L. *The Promise of the New South: Life after Reconstruction*. New York: Oxford University Press, 1992.

Banker, Mark T. *Appalachians All: East Tennessee and the Elusive History of an American Empire*. Knoxville: University of Tennessee Press, 2011.

Baxter, Colin F. "Spanish-American War." *Tennessee Encyclopedia of History and Culture*. http://tennesseeencyclopedia.net/entries/spanish-american-war/.

Bergeron Paul. H., Steven V. Ash, and Jeanette Keith. *Tennesseans and Their History*. Knoxville: University of Tennessee Press, 1996.

Berkove, Lawrence I, ed. *Skepticism and Dissent: Selected Journalism, 1898–1901: by Ambrose Bierce*. Ann Arbor, MI: UMI Research Press, 1986.

Bible, Donahue. "The Hanging of the Greene County Bridge Burners." *Tennessee Ancestors* 21, no. 2 (August 2005): 130–38.

Blair, William A. *Cities of the Dead: Contesting the Memory of the Civil War in the South, 1865–1914*. Chapel Hill: University of North Carolina Press, 2004.

Blight, David W. *Beyond the Battlefield: Race, Memory, and the American Civil War*. Amherst: University of Massachusetts Press, 2002.

Blight, David W., *Race and Reunion: The Civil War in American Memory*. Cambridge: Harvard University Press, 2001.

Brown, Charles H. *The Correspondents' War: Journalists in the Spanish-American War*. New York: Scribner's, 1967.

Bryan, Charles F., Jr. "A Gathering of Tories: The East Tennessee Convention of 1861." *Tennessee Historical Quarterly* 39, no. 1 (1980): 27–48.

Buck, Paul H. *The Road to Reunion*. Boston: Little, Brown. 1937.

Byerly, David J. *History of the Twenty Fifth Infantry Regiment, United States Army, 1896–1947*. Fort Benning, Ga.: HQ, 25th Infantry Regiment, 1947.

Clodfelter, Michael. *Warfare and Armed Conflicts: A Statistical Reference to Casualty and Other Figures, 1500–2000*. Jefferson, NC: McFarland, 2002.

Connelly, Thomas L. *Civil War Tennessee*. Knoxville: University of Tennessee Press, 1979.

Coulter, E. Merton, *William G. Brownlow: Fighting Parson of the Southern Highlands*. Chapel Hill: University of North Carolina Press, 1937.

Cunningham, H. H. *Doctors in Gray: The Confederate Medical Service*. Baton Rouge: Louisiana State University Press, 1958.

Driver, Robert J., Jr. *The Confederate Soldiers of Rockbridge County, Virginia: A Roster*. Jefferson, NC: McFarland, 2016.

Ebel. Lt. Col. Wilfred L. "The Amnesty Issue: A Historical Perspective." U.S. Army War College *Parameters* 4, no. 1 (1974): 67–77.

Eubanks, David L. "Dr. J. G. M. Ramsey of East Tennessee: A Career of Public Service." PhD. Diss., University of Tennessee, 1965.

Fahs, Alice, and Joan Waugh, eds. *The Memory of the Civil War in American Culture*. Chapel Hill: University of North Carolina Press, 2004.

Faust, Drew Gilpin. *This Republic of Suffering: Death and the American Civil War*. New York: Vintage Books, 2008.

Bibliography

Fisher, Noel C. *War at Every Door: Partisan Politics & Guerrilla Violence in East Tennessee, 1860–1869*. Chapel Hill: University of North Carolina Press, 1997.
Fleming, Thomas J. *West Point: The Men and the Times of the United States Military Academy*. New York: William Morrow, 1969.
Fontenay, Blake. "The Curious History of the 'Free and Independent State of Scott.'" *Tri-Star Chronicles* (Tennessee State Library and Archives). https://sos.tn.gov/tsla/tri-star-chronicles-scott-county.
Foster, Gaines. *Ghosts of the Confederacy: Defeat, the Lost Cause, and the Emergence of the New South*. New York: Oxford University Press, 1987.
Freidel, Frank. *The Splendid Little War*. Boston: Burford Books, 1958.
Fuller, A. James. *Chaplain of the Confederacy: Basil Manly and Baptist Life in the Old South*. Baton Rouge: Louisiana State University Press, 2000.
Gannon, Barbara A. *The Won Cause: Black and White Comradeship in the Grand Army of the Republic*. Chapel Hill: University of North Carolina Press, 2014.
Gardner, Mark Lee. *Rough Riders: Theodore Roosevelt, His Cowboy Regiment, and the Immortal Charge Up San Juan Hill*. New York: William Morrow, 2017.
Gatewood, Willard B. "Black Troops in Florida during the Spanish-American War." *Tampa Bay History* 20, no. 1 (1998): 17–31.
Greene, Alton Lee. *Greene Family Tree of Jeremiah and Anne Hartley Greene (1700–1970)*. Pineville, LA: Claude Greene, 1970.
Groce, Todd W. *Mountain Rebels: East Tennessee Confederates and the Civil War, 1860–1870*. Knoxville: University of Tennessee Press, 1999.
Groeling, Meg. *The Aftermath of Battle: The Burial of the Civil War Dead*. El Dorado Hills, CA: Savas Beatie, 2015.
Guy, Joe. *The Hidden History of East Tennessee*. Charleston, SC: History Press, 2008.
Hale, F. Sheffield. "Challenging Historical Remembrance, Myth, and Identity: The Confederate Monuments Debate." In *Controversial Monuments and Memorials: A Guide for Community Leaders*, edited by David B. Allison, 93–94. Lanham, MD: Rowman & Littlefield, 2018.
Harris, M. Keith. *Across the Bloody Chasm: The Culture of Commemoration among Civil War Veterans*. Baton Rouge: Louisiana State University Press, 2014.
Harris, M. Keith. "Slavery, Emancipation, and Veterans of the Union Cause: Commemorating Freedom in the Era of Reconciliation, 1885–1915." *Civil War History* 53 (September 2007): 264–90.
Hess, Earl T. *The Knoxville Campaign: Burnside and Longstreet in East Tennessee*. Knoxville: University of Tennessee Press, 2012.
Hocking, Doug. "The Alleged Bascom Affair." *True West*, July 21, 2015. truewestmagazine.com/the-alleged-bascom-affair/.
Horwitz, Tony. "Did Civil War Soldiers Have PTSD?" *Smithsonian*, January 2015, 44–49.
Janney, Caroline E. *Burying the Dead but Not the Past: Ladies' Memorial Associations & the Lost Cause*. Chapel Hill: University of North Carolina Press, 2008.
Janney, Caroline E. "The Civil War at 150." *Common-Place: the Interactive Journal of Early American Life* 14, no. 2 (Winter 2014). commonplace.online/article/civil-war-150-afterword/.
Janney, Caroline E. *Remembering the Civil War: Reunion and the Limits of Reconciliation*. Chapel Hill: University of North Carolina Press, 2013.
Johnston, Sheila Weems. *The Blue and Gray from Hawkins County, Tennessee, 1861–1865: The Battles*. Rogersville, TN: Hawkins County Genealogical and Historical Society, 1995.
Kelley, Lucas P. "A Divided State in a Divided Nation: An Exploration of East Tennessee's Support of the Union in the Secession Crisis of 1860–1861." *Journal of East Tennessee History* 84 (2012): 3–22.
Kinzer, Stephen. *The True Flag: Theodore Roosevelt, Mark Twain, and the Birth of American Empire*. New York: Henry Holt, 2017.

Bibliography

Konstam, Angus. *San Juan Hill 1898: America's Emergence as a World Power.* Oxford, England: Osprey, 1998.

Krowl, Michelle A. "'In the Spirit of Fraternity': The United States Government and the Burial of Confederate Dead at Arlington National Cemetery, 1864–1914." *Virginia Magazine of History and Biography* 3, no. 2 (2003): 151–86.

Lonn, Ella. "Reconciliation Between the North and the South." *Journal of Southern History* 13, no. 1 (February 1947): 3–26.

MacArthur, William J., Jr. "Knoxville's History: An Interpretation." In *Heart of the Valley: A History of Knoxville Tennessee*, edited by Lucille Deaderick, 1–67. Knoxville: East Tennessee Historical Society, 1976.

"MacCorkle Family." Rockbridge County, Virginia Genealogy Trails History Group. genealogytrails.com/vir/rockbridge/fam_maccorkle.html.

Markel, Joan L. *Knoxville in the Civil War.* Charleston, SC: Arcadia, 2013.

Marten, James Alan. *Sing Not War: The Lives of Union and Confederate Veterans in Gilded Age America.* Chapel Hill: University of North Carolina Press, 2011.

McCallam, Jack. *Leonard Wood: Rough Rider, Surgeon, Architect of American Imperialism.* New York: New York University Press, 2005.

McClurken, Jeffrey W. *Take Care of the Living: Reconstructing Confederate Veteran Families in Virginia.* Charlottesville, VA: University of Virginia Press., 2009.

McGuire, Samuel. "East Tennessee's Grand Army: Union Veterans Confront Race, Reconciliation, and Civil War Memory, 1884–1913." PhD diss., University of Chicago, 2013.

McKenzie, Robert Tracy. *Lincolnites and Rebels: A Divided Town in the American Civil War.* New York: Oxford University Press, 2006.

McKinney, Gordon B. "Civil War and Reconstruction." In *High Mountains Rising: Appalachia in Time and Place*, edited by Richard A. Straw and H. Tyler Blethen, 46–56. Champaign: University of Illinois Press, 2004.

McSherry, Patrick. "A Brief History of the 4th Tennessee Volunteer Infantry." Spanish-American War Centennial Website. www.spanamwar.com/4thtennessee.html.

Merrifield, Kelly, "From Necessity to Honor: The Evolution of National Cemeteries." In "Civil War Era National Cemeteries: Honoring Those Who Served." https://www.nps.gov/nr/travel/national_cemeteries/Development.html.

Michno, Gregory. *Encyclopedia of Indian Wars: Western Battles and Skirmishes, 1850–1890.* Missoula, MT: Mountain Press, 2003.

Miller, Bonnie M. *From Liberation to Conquest: The Visual and Popular Cultures of the Spanish-American War of 1898.* Amherst: University of Massachusetts Press, 2011.

Mills, Cynthia and Pamela H. Simpson, eds. *Monuments to the Lost Cause: Women, Art, and the Landscape of Southern Memory.* Knoxville: University of Tennessee Press, 2019.

Mohon, James L. "Defending the Tennessee Heartland: Company F. of Henry Ashby's 2nd Tennessee Cavalry." *Civil War Regiments: A Journal of the American Civil War* 4, no. 1 (1994): 1–43.

Montgomery, James Riley, Stanley J. Folmsbee, and Lee Seifert Greene. *To Foster Knowledge: A History of The University of Tennessee, 1794–1970.* Knoxville: University of Tennessee Press, 1984.

Morten, Oren F. "The MacCorkle Family." In *A History of Rockbridge County, Va.*, 278–92. Staunton, VA: McClure, 1920.

Nankivell, John H. *Buffalo Soldier Regiment: History of the Twenty-Fifth United States Infantry, 1869–1926.* Lincoln: University of Nebraska Press, 2001.

National Cemetery Administration. *Federal Stewardship of Confederate Dead.* Washington, D.C.: U.S. Department of Veterans Affairs, 2016.

National Cemetery Administration. "Theodore O'Hara's Bivouac of the Dead." https://www.cem.va.gov/history/bivouac.asp.

Bibliography

Neely, Jack. "Knoxville's National Cemetery: A Short History." https://knoxville historyproject.org/national-cemetery-2/.

Neely, Jack. *The Marble City: A Photographic Tour of Knoxville's Graveyards*. Knoxville: University of Tennessee Press, 1999.

Neely, Jack. *Market Square: A History of the Most Democratic Place on Earth*. Knoxville: Market Square District Association, 2009.

Neely, Jack. "Time's Remorseless Doom: Two Monuments in Fort Sanders." *Knoxville Mercury*, August 25, 2017. http//www.knoxmercury.com/2017/08/25/times-remorseless-doom-two-monuments-in-fort-sanders/.

Neff, John R. *Honoring the Civil War Dead: Commemoration and the Problem of Reconciliation*. Lawrence: University Press of Kansas, 2005.

Nelson, Kelli B. "On the Imperishable Face of Granite: Civil War Monuments and the Evolution of Historical Memory in East Tennessee, 1878–1931." Master's thesis, East Tennessee State University, 2011.

Noyales, Jonathan A. *Civil War Legacy in the Shenandoah: Remembrance, Reunion & Reconciliation*. Charleston, SC: History Press, 2015.

O'Leary, Cecelia Elizabeth. *To Die For: The Paradox of American Patriotism*. Princeton, NJ: Princeton University Press, 1999.

O'Neal, Bill. "Bernard, Reuben Frank." In *Fighting Men of the Indian Wars: A Biographical Encyclopedia of the Mountain Men, Soldiers, Cowboys, and Pioneers Who Took Up Arms During America's Westward Expansion*. Stillwater, OK: Barbed Wire Press, 1991.

O'Neill, Connor Towne. *Down Along with that Devil's Bones: A Reckoning with Monuments, Memory, and the Legacy of White Supremacy*. Chapel Hill, NC: Algonquin Books, 2020.

Pettegrew, John. "'The Soldier's Faith': Turn-of-the-Century Memory of the Civil War and the Emergence of Modern American Nationalism." *Journal of Contemporary History* 31, no. 1 (January 1996): 49–73.

Price, Henry R. *Hawkins County, Tennessee: A Pictorial History*. Brookfield, MO: Donning, 1996.

Queener, Verton M. "East Tennessee Sentiment and the Secession Movement, November 1860–June 1861," East Tennessee Historical Society's *Publications* 20 (1948): 59–83.

Reynolds, Patrick H., III. *I Could Almost Hear the Guns: The Battle of Big Creek, Hawkins County, Tennessee, November 4, 1863*. Surgoinsville, TN: Old Stage Printing, 1994.

Rigdon, John C. *Historical Sketch and Roster of the Tennessee 2nd Cavalry Regiment (Ashby's)*. Cartersville, GA: Eastern Digital Resources, 2004.

Russell, Don. *One Hundred and Three Fights and Scrimmages: The Story of General Reuben F. Bernard*. Mechanicsburg, PA: Stackpole, 2003. Reprint of 1936 United States Cavalry Association edition.

Russell, Don. "Reuben Frank Bernard." *Journal of the American Military History Foundation* 2, no. 2 (Summer 1938): 90–93.

Schubert, Frank N. "Leftwich, Aaron." In *On the Trail of the Buffalo Soldier: Biographies of African Americans in the U.S. Army, 1866–1917*. Wilmington, DE: Scarecrow Press, 1995, 262.

Schubert, Frank N. "Buffalo Soldiers at San Juan Hill." Paper delivered at the 1998 Conference of Army Historians, Bethesda, MD. history.army.mil/documents/spanam/BSSJH/Shbrt-BSSJH.htm.

Sedore, Timothy S. *Tennessee Civil War Monuments: An Illustrated Field Guide*. Bloomington: Indiana University Press, 2020.

Seymour, Digby Gordon. *Divided Loyalties: Fort Sanders and the Civil War in East Tennessee*. Knoxville: East Tennessee Historical Society, 1963.

Silber, Nina. *The Romance of Reunion: Northerners and the South, 1865–1900*. Chapel Hill: University of North Carolina Press, 1993.

Smith, Timothy B. *The Golden Age of Battlefield Preservation: The Decade of the 1890s*

Bibliography

and the Establishment of America's First Five Military Parks. Knoxville: University of Tennessee Press, 2008.

Stanco, William. "Speaker Thomas Brackett Reed and the Will of the Majority." *The Capitol Dome*, Fall, 2007, 9–15.

Steere, Edward. "National Cemeteries and Memorials in Global Conflict." *Quartermaster Review* (November–December 1953). http://old.quartermasterfoundation.org/national_cemeteries_and_memorials_in_global_conflict.htm.

Taylor, Amy Murrell. *The Divided Family in Civil War America*. Chapel Hill: University of North Carolina Press, 2005.

Taylor, Robert. "The New South Mind of a Mountain Editor: William Rule, 1877–1898." *East Tennessee Historical Society* 47 (1995): 100–17.

Tennesseans in the Civil War, Part 1: A Military History of Confederate and Union Units with Available Rosters and Personnel. Nashville: Tennessee Civil War Centennial Commission, 1964.

Tomkins, Edward Pendleton. *Rockbridge County, Virginia: An Informal History*. Richmond, VA: Whittet & Shepperson, 1952.

Trask, David F. *The War with Spain in 1898*. New York: Macmillan, 1981.

Traxel, David. *The Birth of the American Century*. New York: Macmillan, 1998.

Trent, Emma Deane Smith. *Faces, Places, and Things of Early East Tennessee*. Whitesburg, TN: Emma Deane Smith Trent, 1989.

Warren, Robert Penn. *The Legacy of the Civil War*. New York: Random House, 1961.

Wheeler, William Bruce. *Knoxville, Tennessee: A Mountain City in the New South*. Knoxville: University of Tennessee Press, 2005.

Williams, David. *Bitterly Divided: The South's Inner Civil War*. New York: The New Press, 2008.

Wise, Thomas E. "The Day President Rutherford B. Hayes Came to Town, Knoxville, 21 September 1877." *Tennessee Ancestors* 18, no. 1 (April 2002): 57–73.

Wood, Richard E. "The South and Reunion, 1898." *Historian* 31 (1969): 415–30.

Woodward, C. Vann. *Origins of the New South, 1877–1913*. Baton Rouge: Louisiana State University Press, 1951.

Websites

Ancestry.com

Arlington National Cemetery (https://www.arlingtoncemetery.mil/Explore/History-of-Arlington-National-Cemetery)

Cuban Battlefields of the Spanish-Cuban-American War (http://cubanbattlefields.unl.edu/)

National Park Service: "Civil War Era National Cemeteries: Honoring Those Who Served" (nps.gov/nr/travel/national_cemeteries)

Newspapers.com

Spanish-American War Centennial Website (http://www.spanamwar.com)

Tennessee Encyclopedia of History and Culture (tennesseeencyclopedia.net)

Index

Numbers in ***bold italics*** indicate pages with illustrations

Academy of Rogersville (TN) 115
African Americans 121, 132, 160, 193, 195; as "Buffalo Soldiers" 119; excluded from white veteran reconciliation 8, 91–93, 197; and reaction to Confederate monuments 95; and segregation 92–93, 118–19, 140, 143; and Spanish-American War record 159; and "Tampa Riot" 140
Alger, Russell 134, 135, 181–82
Alley, Isham 59
American Flag Association 103
Anaconda (Missoula, MT) *Standard* 120
Anderson, Dee 60
Antietam, battle of 69
Apache Indians 24–25, 105–7, 110–11, 124
Apache Pass, battle of 25, 27
Appomattox Court House 30, 54
Archer, Henry 39
Arlington National Cemetery 79, 176–***77***
Army of Northern Virginia (CS) 30
Army of Tennessee (CS) 40, 42, 47–49
Army of the Ohio (US) 40
Army of the Potomac (US) 27, 31
Ashby, Henry 47–48, 64–***65***, 66
Association of Graduates of the United States Military Academy 15
Astor, Aaron 191
Atgeld, John P. 103
Atlanta 49
Atlanta Constitution 136
Atlanta Peace Jubilee 172–73
Ault, Missie 193
"Azalia" (Joel Chandler Harris) ***92***

Bagley, Worth 136
Baker, Abner 62–63

Baker, Harvey 62
Baker, Stephen 161
Baker family 102
Ball's Bluff, battle of 69
Bannock Indians 109–10
Bartol, Cyrus Augustus 81
Barton, Clara 70
Barton, R.M., Jr. 173
Bascom, George N. 25
Bate, William 96
Bates, John 152, 157
Battery McCorkle 188
The Battle at Apache Pass (film) 200*n*11
Battles and Leaders of the Civil War 91
Bean's Station, battle of 44
Beecher, Henry Ward 183
Bernard, Alice Virginia Frank (first wife of Reuben Bernard) 105, 109, 111
Bernard, Eleanor Light (sister-in-law of Reuben Bernard) 31
Bernard, Elsie May Camp (third wife) 179
Bernard, George (son) 112
Bernard, Henry (son) 105, 111
Bernard, John (brother) 32
Bernard, John (father) 21
Bernard, John Jay "Jack" (son) 14, 107, 115, ***122***, 134, 166, ***180***; commendation 161, 167–68, 187–88; Cuban grave ***165***, 175; death 156; early life 122–23; at El Caney 155–56; funeral 179–83; Knoxville grave 2, 184, 185, ***186***; landing in Cuba 145; letters 144, 147, 162; memorial services 13, 168, 179–81, 186–88; memorial tablet 188, 212*n*8; military career 124–25; obituary 167; in Tampa 138; at University of Tennessee 123–24
Bernard, Jonathan (brother) 31, 40, 51
Bernard, May Morelock (mother) 21

221

Index

Bernard, Reuben Frank 14, 16, **26**, 31, 63, 66, **106**, 122, 162, 176; attends son's funeral 179–83; brevetted brigadier general 111; characteristics 21–22, 24–25, 28, 107–8, 110; Civil War battles 25–30; with Confederate veterans on frontier 104–5; death 190; early years 21–23; and Indian wars 24–25, 104–12; learns of son's death 166–67; letters 27, 111; limited literacy 200n13; promotes Indian reservation 105–6; retires 112; wounded at Todd's Tavern 28–29
Bernard, Robert Simpson (son) 111–12
Bernard, Ruth Lavinia Simpson (second wife) 111
Bernard, Samuel (brother) 32, 40
Bernard Avenue 188
Bethel Cemetery 67, 75–76, 86–88, **95**, 96, 184, 191
Bierce, Ambrose 172
"Bill Bailey" (song) 142
Billings (MT) 120
Birch Creek, battle at 109–10, 111
Birmingham News 135
Blair, William: *Cities of the Dead* 7
Blevins, John 39
Blight, David 93
Blount County (TN) 56
"Blue & Gray Reunion and Freedom Jubilee" 196
Boise Barracks 109
Bridge Burners Monument (Greene County, TN) 191
Brooke, John Rutter 132
Brown, George Leroy 133
Brownlow, John Bell 192
Brownlow, William G. 37, 44, 59, 60, 64, 73, 90
Brownsville (TX) 122
Buck, Beaumont Bonaparte 21–22
Buck, Paul 81, 190, 212n9
Buckner, Simon Bolivar 40
Buena Ventura (Spanish freighter) 126–27
"Buffalo Soldiers" **119**, 140
Burial and Disinterment Corps (US) 175
Burnett, Henry L. 79
Burnside, Ambrose 3, 40, **41**, 42, 71, 181
Burrows, J.C. 85
Butler, T.C. 159

Caldwell, Joshua 101
Camp, Eldad Cicero 64–65, 66
Camp Chase 49
Camp Poland (Knoxville) 133

Canby, Edward R.S. 26, 109
Cantrell, Charles 133
Capron, Allyn, Jr. 149
Capron, Allyn, Sr. 149, **150**, 152, 155, 157
Captain Jack *see* Kintpuash
Carlisle (PA) 26
Carlisle Barracks 105
Carrollton (MO) 53–54
Caswell, Mrs. E.C. 59
cemeteries 81, 94, 172–73, 181–82; Confederate 73–76; National 69–73; separation of Confederate and Union burials in 6–7, 66–70, 86; *see also* graves, individual cemeteries
Century 91
Cervero y Topete, Pascual 142
Chaffee, Adna 151, 152, 153, 157
Chamberlin, Joseph Edgar 159
Charlotte 49
Charlottesville 194
Chattanooga 121
Chattanooga National Cemetery 69, 86, 173
Chickamauga and Chattanooga National Military Park 102, 121
Chickamauga battlefield 132
Chiricahua Pass, battle of 106–7
Churchman, Caleb 175
Churchman, Clarke 175
Cincinnati Post 187
Cities of the Dead (Blair) 7
Civil War 5, 11, 15–16, 25, 27–30, 36–45, 47–53, 104; casualties 67; cemeteries (Confederate) 73–76; cemeteries (Union) 69–73; centennial 196; digging graves during, literature 91; divided families 32–34; medical care 50, **51**, 52–53; monuments 83–97, 190–96; sesquicentennial 196; *see also* cemeteries and individual armies, regiments, battles, monuments
Civil War Centennial Commission 196
Clarke, Joseph 195
Cleveland, Grover 112
Cochise 25, 105–7
Coeur D'Alene mining district (ID) 119–20
Cold Harbor, battle of 29
Committee on the Conduct of the War 68–69
Concho (transport ship) 141
Confederate Decoration Day *see* Memorial Day (Confederate)
Confederate flag 190

Index

Confederate Monument (Bethel Cemetery, Knoxville) **95**, 96
Confederate tombstones 211*n*27
Confederate Veteran 173, 199*n*1
Confederates, as deserters 40; divided by war 32–37, 201*n*10; as guerrillas 39; and harsh treatment by Unionists 58–61; and home guard 39, 41; and hostility to Unionists 61–62; and military draft 37–38
Coxey, Jacob 120
Coxey, Jesse 120
Coxey's Army 120
Creelman, James 157–58
Crook (transport ship) 176
Cuba 127, 169; challenges of island climate 174–75; debate over invasion 127–30; description of jungle 146; diseases 170, 174; invasion 144–45; Spanish rule over 127
"Cuba Libre" (Fritz Guerin tableau) *171*
Culliny, Michael 102
Culpeper, battle of 28
Cunningham, S.A. 135
Curtis, George William 134

Dabney, Charles W., Jr. 4, 116, 118, 123, 167, 168, 178, 182, 188; letters 134, 166, 176
Daggett, A.S. 157, 158–59, 160–61
Daiquiri (Cuba) 144, *145*
Dalton (NC) 49
Danville (VA) 94
Davis, Richard Harding 140, 151
Dawson, Simeon 37
Deaton, Spencer 39
Decoration Day *see* Memorial Day
Democrats 34, 90
Dewey, George 131, 136
Dickinson, Walter 153
"Disaster of 1898" 126
disease 113; in Civil War 50–52; in Cuba 170, 174
Dobson, Henry A. 139
Douglass, Charles 35
Dragoon Mountains (AZ) 111

East Tennessee 6; Anglo-Saxon heritage 93; characteristics 34–35; detested by Confederate soldiers 37; divided by war 19, 32, 37, **38**; opposes secession 34–35, **36**; political divisions in 90; slavery in 34–35; valued by both sides 36; violence after Civil War in 56–65

Eighth Cavalry Regiment 111
El Caney 149; defenses 149–51, 152, 159
El Caney, battle 152–61; casualties 159–60
El Pozo 147, 151
El Viso 149, **154**, 155–157, **158**; debate on who captured 157–59
Etheridge, Emerson 63–64

Fain, Eliza 44–45, 62, 113
Fain, Richard 113
Felix Zollicoffer brigade (Confederate veterans) 89
Fentress County (TN) 40
Field, Charles 165
Fifth Army Corps (in Cuba) 138
First Artillery Regiment **149**, 150, 152, 155, 157
First Cavalry Regiment 24–30, 105, 109–10, 124; casualties 29; and medals of honor 107
First Dragoons *see* First Cavalry Regiment
First Manassas, battle of 69, 97–98
First Presbyterian Church (Knoxville) 63, 123, 196
First Tennessee Cavalry Regiment (CS) *see* Second Tennessee Cavalry
First Tennessee Volunteer Regiment 132
First U.S. Volunteer Cavalry *see* Rough Riders
Fishing Creek, battle of 49
Fisk University Glee Club 13
Five Forks, battle of 29
Florida Times Union 136
Floyd, George 195
Fordyce, S.S. 171–72
Fort Bayard 124
Fort Bidwell 107, 122
Fort Bowie 106, 107
Fort Buchanan 24
Fort Craig 24
Fort Fillmore 24
Fort Huachuca 124
Fort Lowell 105
Fort McHenry 49
Fort McIntosh 111
Fort Meade 122
Fort Missoula 119–20
Fort Moultrie 188
Fort Norfolk 49
Fort Robinson 111, 112
Fort Sanders 42, 75, 191

223

Index

Fort Sanders, battle of 32, 42, *43*, 67, 100, 191
Fort Sanders Monument 191, *192*, 195
Fort Sheridan 124, 156, 169
Fort Union 27
Fort Walla Walla 110
Foster, R.B. 128
Fourth Infantry Regiment 124, 125, 143, 145, 147, 153, 157, 165, 169; casualties 160; at El Caney 155–56; in Philippines 178; in Tampa 138; on transport ship to Cuba 141–44
Fourth Tennessee Volunteer Regiment 132, *133*, 168
Fred Ault Bivouac (UCV) 88
"Free and Independent State of Scott" (TN) 34, 40
French, H.W. 155
Frierson, J.W.S. 88
Fry, David *38*
Fulerton, J.S. 102

Galbraith, Joseph 113
Galbraith Springs 113–14
"General Lawton's Report" (on battle of El Caney) 157, 161
Georgia Memorial Association 75
Gettysburg National Cemetery 69–70, 183
Gettysburg National Cemetery Association 93
Gibson, Capt. 130
Gilmore, James 46
Glorietta (Pigeon's Ranch), battle of 27
Gordon, John 30, 172
Grainger County 56
Grand Army of the Republic (GAR) 79 85, 88, 89, 96, 134; Post 19 (Philadelphia) 79
Grant, Ulysses S. 15–16; funeral 199*n*8
graves: decorating 77–79, *80*, 82, *83*, 86, 184; desecration 69; digging 67, *68*, 70, 162; marking 67, 71, 72–73, 163–66, 175, 181–82, 184–85; reburial of bodies 71–76, 175–77, 182–83; searching for 70–71, 74–76; *see also* cemeteries
Green Hill Cemetery 94
Greene, Alfred 39, 202*n*23
Greene County (TN) 44
Greene County Courthouse 191
Greeneville (TN) 113, 191
Greeneville New Era 61
Griffin, J.M. 181
Griffin, John 37

Griffin, Joseph C. 181
Guerin, Fritz *171*

Hall, Will 63
Hamilton County (TN) 61
Hammond, Charles 124
Hardee, William J. 49
Hardin, Charles 107–8
Harris, Isham G. 37, 118
Harris, James 56
Harris, Joel Chandler 91, *92*
Harris, M. Keith 190
Haskell, Joseph T. 153, 170
Havana 131
Havana harbor 127
Hawkins County (TN) 14, 21, 56, 102; "disputed land" in 33–34, 47; divided by war 44–45, 54–55
Hawn, A.C. 60
Hayes, Rutherford B. 90
Hazen, Gideon Morgan 33
Hazen, William Cogswell 33
Hearst, William Randolph 130, 157–58
Heiskell, Frederick S. 33
Heiskell, Joseph P. 33
Henderson, Samuel 52
Hess, Earl 66–67
"Highlanders" *see* Seventy-ninth New York Regiment
"Highlanders" Monument (Knoxville) *194*, 195–96
"Hiker" statue (Knoxville) 188, *189*
Hodges, Charles 162–63; letter 168–69
Hollywood Cemetery 74
Hollywood Memorial Association of the Ladies of Richmond 74
Holmes, Oliver Wendell, Jr. 81
Holston River 33–34, 112
Honoring the Civil War Dead (Neff) 18
Hosford, Orville 72
Hoss, Elijah Embree Jr. 87, 179–81
"Hot Time in the Old Town Tonight" (song) 143
Houk, L.C. 90
House, Ellen Renshaw 60, 62
Howard, Oliver O. 15, 107
Humes, Thomas W. 33, 78
Humes, William Young Conn 33

"I Don't Like No Cheap Man" (song) 143
Indian wars 104–5
Indiana (transport ship) 142
Ingersoll, H.H. 130
Ireland, Rufus 53

Index

Jack Bernard Camp No. 1 (Spanish-American War veterans) 188
Janney, Caroline E.: *Remembering the Civil War* 5–6, 16, 199*n*1
Jefferson County (TN) 56
John Hunt Morgan monument (Greeneville) 191
Johnson, Andrew 27, 35, 83, **84**
Johnson, Robert 58
Johnston, Joseph E. 16
Jones, Joseph 50
Jonesborough (TN) 62, 109, 113, 123

Kappa Sigma fraternity 123
Kennerly, Wesley T. 193
Kesler, Renee 197
Kettle Hill 147, 149, 151, 166
Kettle Hill, battle of 161
Key West 126, 142
Kincaid, John 59
Kinnison, Henry 156
Kintpuash (Captain Jack) **108**, 109
Kinzer, Stephen 127–28
Kirk, George W. 57
Knox County 62
Knox County Courthouse 63
Knoxville **22**, 40–42, 45, 59, 62, 64–65, 66–67, 196; and blue-gray reunions 98, **99**, **100**, **101**, 102; descriptions 3, 23, 89, 123–24, 178; divided by war 32–33
Knoxville Chronicle 78, 84
Knoxville Journal 101, 102, 118, 166, 187
Knoxville Journal and Tribune 166, 168, 181, 183
Knoxville Ladies' Memorial Association *see* Ladies' Memorial Association (LMA)
Knoxville National Cemetery 1, 18, 67, 69, 96–97, 191; acquisition of land for 71–72; burial of Spanish-American War veterans in 181–82; decorating with flags 82, **83**; Memorial Day ceremonies in 77–78, 82–86, 184–87; not segregated by race 73
Knoxville Press and Herald 65, 75, 84
Knoxville Press and Messenger 78, 83
Knoxville Sentinel 126, 130, 132, 134, 136, 166, 167, 178, 181, 183, 184, 193
Knoxville Tribune 86, 88
Knoxville Whig 45, 61, 65, 73
Knoxville YMCA 115, 123
Krag Jorgensen rifles 139, 153
Ku Klux Klan 58

Ladies' Memorial Association (LMA) 74–76, 78, 88, 96, 184
Ladies' Memorial Association for the Confederate Dead of Oakland 74
Laredo (TX) 111
Las Guasimas 146, 149
Lava Beds (CA) 109
Lawton, Henry 135, 151, 152, 153, 157
"Lawton's Report" *see* "General Lawton's Report"
Leahy, John 102
Ledgerwood, Washington 85
Lee, Arthur H. 153, 157
Lee, Fitzhugh 135
Lee, Stephen D. 18–19
Leftwich, Aaron 27, 165
Lick Creek Bridge 37
Lieutenant H.L. McCorkle Camp No. 2 (Spanish-American War veterans) 188
Light Battery E, First Artillery Regiment *see* First Artillery Regiment
Linares y Pombo, Arsenio 152
Lincolnites and Rebels (McKenzie) 33–36
Little Rock (AR) 81
Lodge, Henry Cabot 129
Logan, John A. 77
Longstreet, James 16, 42, 43–44, 101
Lord, Richard S.C. 24, 26–27
"Lost Cause" 81, 95, 132, 190, 205*ch*6*n*12
Louisville & Nashville Railroad 12
Lovering, Leonard 124, 156–57
Ludlow, William 151–53
Luttrell, James C. 33

Mabry, Joseph, Jr. 40–41
Mabry, Joseph, Sr. 66
USS *Maine* 127, **129**, 130, 157
Manila Bay 131
Manly, Basil 37
Marietta National Cemetery 71, 75
Marten, James Alan 98
The Martial Graves of Our Fallen Heroes (McCook) 175, 176
Maryville Times 126, 130
Mauser rifles 139, 153
Maxwell, John 156
Maynard, Horace 64, 127
Maynard, T. Washburn 126, **127**, 131, 134
McAdoo, William 35
McCarty, J.C. 57
McClure's Magazine 91
McCook, Henry Christopher 174–75, 176

225

Index

McCorkle, Alexander (grandfather) 46
McCorkle, Alfred Leyburn (brother) 53
McCorkle, Guy Alexander (grandson) 120, 121–22, 162, 168, 179
McCorkle, Henry Leftwich (son) 14, 112, **116**, 134, 166, **180**; battlefield wallet 162, **163**; commendations 160–61, 167, 187–88; Cuban grave markers 163, **164**, 165, 175; death 156; description 118; early life 115; at El Caney 155–56; funeral 179–83; Knoxville grave 2, 184, **185**; landing in Cuba 145; letters 120–21, 141, 142, 143, 144, 146–47, 208n6; memorial services for 13, 168, 179–81, 186–88; memorial tablet for 188, 212n8; military career 118–22; obituary 167; in Tampa 138; at University of Tennessee 115–18
McCorkle, Jennie (sister) 120, 168
McCorkle, John (great-grandfather) 46
McCorkle, John Baxter (brother) 53
McCorkle, Margaret (sister) 169
McCorkle, Mildred Ritzius (daughter-in-law) 120, 121–22, 162, 168, 179, 188; letters 168, 169, 176
McCorkle, Susan Alexander (mother) 46
McCorkle, Susan Leftwich (wife) 47, 112, 115, 160
McCorkle, Thomas Edward (brother) 54
McCorkle, Thomas J. (father) 46
McCorkle, William Alexander 14, 16, 63, 64, 66, 104, 115; attends son's funeral 179–83; civilian medical practice 47, 112–14; as Confederate surgeon 47–50, **51**, 52–53; death 190; description 48; early years 46–47; illness 114; letters 115, 121–22, 163, 169; medical education 47; as prisoner of war 49–50; at Washington College 46–47
McCorkle-Bernard Camp of Spanish-American War Veterans 188
McIntosh, Burr 144, 149
McKenzie, George W. 57
McKenzie, Robert, Jr.: *Lincolnites and Rebels* 33–36
McKinley, William 18, 128–29, 130, 134, 135, 136, 140, 175; at Arlington National Cemetery 176–77; at Atlanta Peace Jubilee 172–73; and tour of the South 172
McLain, Thomas 51
McMillan, Benton 135
McNutt, John Rice 54
McNutt, Sarah McCorkle 54

Meigs, Montgomery 70
Memorial Day 77; Confederate observance 77–78, 79, **80**, 81–82, 86–88, 184; Federal observance 11–13, 77–78, 81–82, **83**, 84–86, 184–87; joint observance 81–82; separate observance 79–81
Merrimon, James Peyton 32
Merrimon, William 32
Michno, Gregory 23
Miles, Evan 140, 152, 153, 157
Miles, Nelson 135
Mill Bend (TN) 44
Missoula (MT) 121
Modoc Indians **108**, 109
monuments *see* Civil War, individual monuments
A Moon for the Misbegotten (O'Neill) 8
Moore family 55
Mooresburg (TN) 14, 47, 55, 112, 115, 121
Mooresburg Presbyterian Church 115
Morgan, John Hunt 191
Morgan, Washington 35
Morgan County (TN) 40
Morton, Levi 129
Morton, Oliver P. 94
Moss, James A. 120, 145, 146, 147, 154–55, 157, 159, 166
Murdock, J.S. 155
Murfreesboro (Stones River), battle of **48**, 49
Museum of East Tennessee History 39

Naiche _ **110**, 111
Nail, James 53
Nashville 103
USS *Nashville* 126–27, **128**, 131
Nashville American 130, 136
Nashville National Cemetery 11, **12**, 171
Nashville Tennessean 16, 199n1
National Cemetery Act 70
National Chickamauga Park Commission 132
National Relief Commission 174
National Tribune 91
Native Americans *see* Indian wars and individual Indian tribes: Apache, Bannock, Modoc, Sheepeater, Snake
"Nearer My God to Thee" (song) 176
Neary, William C. 160, 161
Neff, John R.: *Honoring the Civil War Dead* 19
Nelson, T.A.R. 82
Nelson, Valentine S. 188

Index

New Orleans 31
New Town, battle of 29
New York Journal 136, 158
New York Peace Memorial 195
New York Sun 126
New York Times 40, 93, 166
New York Tribune 91, 136
Nicely, James 52–53
Ninth Cavalry Regiment 118–19, 132
Norris, Frank 151, 152, 166
Northern Pacific Railroad 120

Ochs, Milton B. 162
Office of Correspondence with the Friends of the Missing Men of the United States Army 70
Official History of the Tennessee Centennial Exposition (Justi, ed.) 103
O'Hara, Theodore 193
Old Grey Cemetery 66, 71, 184
O'Leary, Cecelia 104
One Hundred and Three Fights and Scrimmages (Russell) 23, 25, 28, 111, 200n1
O'Neill, Eugene: *A Moon for the Misbegotten* 8
The Order of Indian Wars of the United States 112
Overton County (TN) 40

Page, Thomas Nelson 91
Page, Walter Hines 18
Palmer, Samuel Bell 36
Park, James 87
partisan politicians 91
Passmore, J.C. 73
Patterson, David T. 59
Patterson, John 152
Petersburg national cemeteries 74
Philippine Insurrection 132
Philippine Islands 169, 170
Philomathesian Literary Society 118, 123
Pi Kappa Alpha fraternity 118
Pine Ridge Campaign 119
Pioneer Corps 162, 165
Plant, Henry B. 138
Plessy v. Ferguson 86
Poindexter, Johnny 112
Pulitzer, Joseph 130
Pullen, Frank 157, 159
Puerto Rico 170

Quartermaster Burial Corps 176

Ramsey, J.G.M. 90–91
Ramsey, John Crozier 59
Rattlesnake Creek, campaign 105
Ray, Alfred 134
reconciliation 3–4, 7–8, 15–16, *17*, 18, 79, 84–85, 103, 136–37, 172–73, 179–80, 187; exclusion of black veterans from 8, 91–93, 197; President Hayes' Southern Reconciliation Tour and 90; produces "mingling of tears" 6, 13, 184, 199n8; and unresolved sectional conflicts 190, 196–97; veteran support for 61, 93, 98–99; *see also* reunification
Reconstruction 63, 80–81, 90–91
Reed, Thomas 129
Reid, Whitelaw 58
Remembering the Civil War (Janney) 5–6, 16, 199n1
Republicans 34, 63–64, 90
reunification 7, 11, 13, 15–19, 90, 136, 170–72, 186–87, 195, 196; and Indian wars 104–105; as Tennessee rejoins union 63; *see also* reconciliation
Rhea County (TN) 56–57
Rhodes, David H. 175, 176
Richardson, Laura Caitlin 82–83
Richmond Examiner 73
Rifle and Light Infantry Tactics (Hardee) 49
Ringgold, Samuel 182
Rio Grande (transport ship) **142**
Ritzius, Amelia 120
Ritzius, Henry 120, 140, 163
Robert E. Lee Camp No. 1 (Richmond) 16
Rockbridge County (VA) 46, 54
Rockbridge County "Rifles" 46
Rogersville (TN) 22, 58–59
The Romance of Reunion (Silber) 18
Romney (WV) 94
Roosevelt, Theodore 128, 161
Rosser, Thomas Lafayette 132
Rough Riders (First U.S. Volunteer Cavalry) 129, 131, 134, 143, 146, 161
Rule, William 11–13, *14*, 39, 57–58, 66, 76, 82, 97, 131, 186, 196
Russell, Don: *One Hundred and Three Fights and Scrimmages* 23, 25, 28, 111, 200n1
Rutledge (TN) 59

Sailor's Creek, battle of 29
Sampson, William 131, 136, 142, 144
Sanders, William P. 30, 40, 42, 62

Index

San Francisco Examiner 172
San Juan Hill 147, 149, 151, 166
San Juan Hill, battle of 161
Santiago 131, 144, 152, 161, 169
Santiago Harbor 142
Scherrer, Elmer 162
Schley, Winfield Scott 136
Scott County (TN) *see* "Free and Independent State of Scott"
secession 6, 34–36, 44, 54, 81, 96, 98, 103, 193
Second Manassas, battle of 53
Second Massachusetts Volunteer Regiment 141, 143, 152, 154, 165
Second Tennessee Cavalry Regiment (CS) 47, 49, 51–52, 56, 62
Sedore, Timothy S. 191
segregation 92–93, 118–19, 140, 143
Seguranca (transport ship) 143
Seventeenth Infantry Regiment 153, 159
Seventh Infantry Regiment 153, 160
Seventy-ninth New York Regiment, the "Highlanders" 42, 72–73, 82, 100–101, ***194***, 195–96
Sevilla 146, 151
Seymour, Digby Gordon, 32
Shafter, William 135, 139–40, 142, 144, 147, 148, 151
Sharpe, Alfred C. 160
Sharpshooters 149, 150–51, 153, 155, 156
Sheepeater Indians 110
Sheridan, Philip 29
Sherman, William T. 16
Shiloh, battle of 69, 71
Shiloh National Cemetery 71
Siboney 145
"The Significance of the Frontier in American History" (Turner) 104–5
Silber, Nina: *The Romance of Reunion* 18
Silbey, Henry H. 26
Silver Creek, battle of 109, 111
Sixth U.S. Volunteer Infantry 178, 179
Sizemore, William O. 44–45
slavery 34–35, 85, 93–94, 96, 98, 103
Slocum, H.W. 16
Slough, John P. 27
Smith, Edmund Kirby 37, 40, 96
Smith, John 39
Smithfield, battle of 29
"Smoked Yankees" 119
Snake Indians 105
Society of the Army of the Potomac 16
"The Soldier's Faith" 81, 168
"soldier's heart" 52

Soldiers' Home 112
"The Soldier's Motive" 81
Sons of Union Veterans 102
Southern Railway Depot (Knoxville) 179
Spanish-American War 7, 11, 130–32, 139, 181, 182, 184; black troops and 132, 159; casualties in 159–60, 166, 174; debate preceding 127–30; and reconciliation 18–19, 103–4, 136–37, 170–72; Southerners role in 134–36
"splendid little war" 126, 170
Spottsylvania Court House, battle of 29
Spring Grove Cemetery 79
Springfield rifle 139
"The Star Spangled Banner" (song) 143, 170
states' rights 94, 103
Staunton, Edwin M. 28
Staunton, S.C. 163
Sterrett, Susan McCorkle 54
Sterrett, William Madison 54
Steward, T.G. 121, 134
Stewart, Alexander P. 132
Stones River National Cemetery 69
Stuart, J.E.B. 29
Sullins, David D. 87
Sullivan County (TN) 61–62
Sweeney, Edwin 24, 25

Tampa 122, 125, 138–41
Tampa Bay ***141***
Tampa Bay Hotel 138–40
"Tampa Riot" 140
"Taps" (song) 166, 177, 182, 187
Tate, Allen S. 86
Taylor, H.H. 98, 100
Taylor, H.T. 78
Taylor, Robert L. 136
Taylor, William G. 56
Tejaras Pass, battle of 27
Temple, Oliver P. 35, 57–58, 78, 91
Tennessee Civil War Sesquicentennial Commission 196
The Tennessee Civil War Veterans Questionnaires (Dyer, comp.) 203*ch*3*n*18
"Tennessee Day" 132
Tennessee Exposition 103
Tennessee monument preservation laws 195
Tenth Cavalry Regiment 118–19, 132
Third Tennessee Volunteer Regiment 178–79
Thruston, Gates 12
Tillman, George N. 12–13, 16

228

Index

Todd's Tavern, battle at _ **28**, 29
transport ships 142–44
Travis, Robert 125, 143, 156, 159, 166, 170
Traxel, David 136–37
Treaty of Paris 169
Tucson 24
Turner, C.W. 188
Turner, Frederick Jackson 104–5
Turney, Peter 102
Twelfth Infantry Regiment 153, 157–59
Twenty-fifth Infantry Regiment 118–19, 121, 132, 143, 145, 147, 163–65; and Bicycle Corps 120; casualties 160; dispute with Twelfth Regiment 157–59; at El Caney 153–54, 155–56; and leading role in Spanish-American War 159; in Philippines 169; in Tampa 122, 138–40; on transport ship to Cuba, 141–44
Twenty-fourth Infantry Regiment 119, 132, 140
Twenty-ninth Constitutional Regiment 152

Union Flag 62
Unionists 39, 40, 44, 61; as army recruiters 39; and attacks on Confederate civilians 58–59; and attacks on Confederate veterans 56–61; as bridge burners 37, **38**, 60; as bushwhackers and guerrillas 44–45; and lawsuits against former Confederates 60
United Confederate Veterans (UCV) 18–19, 85, 172
United Daughters of the Confederacy (UDC) 179, 191
Union Soldiers Monument (Greeneville) 191
Union Soldiers Monument (Knoxville) 96, **97**
U.S. National Cemetery System 69–71, 73, 181–82
U.S. Naval Board of Inquiry 130
University Cotillion Club 123
University of Pennsylvania Medical School 47, 53
University of Tennessee 15, 115–16, **117**, 118, 123, 168, 178–81; and Spanish-American War alumni 134, 187–88
University of Tennessee Alumni Association 167–68
University of Tennessee Record 123
University of Tennessee *Volunteer* (yearbook) 187

University of Virginia Medical School 47, 53
Van Dyke, W.D. 57
Van Hill (TN) 21
Vara de Rey y Rubio, Joaquin 159
Vaughn, John C. 57, 60
veterans 81–82, 188; diverse opinions 89–90; and exclusion of blacks from reconciliation process 8, 91–93, 197; and reunions 98, **99, 100, 101**, 102; *see also* Grand Army of the Republic, United Confederate Veterans and other veterans' groups
Vicksburg, battle of 31, 40
"Voices of the Land" 39

Warner, Thomas C. 85
Warren, Robert Penn 5
Washington, George 87
Washington (College) Literary Society 47
Washington County (TN) 56, 58
Watkins, Kathleen Blake 139
Watterson, Henry 136
Weaver, Samuel 69
Weissert, Augustus G. 87
West, Robert 59
West Point Military Academy 15
Wetzel, W.H. 56
Wheeler, Joseph 3, 135, 146, 172
Wheeler, Xen 84
White, William Allen 131
white supremacy 35, 95, 190, 194
Whitman, Edward Burke 70–71, 73
Whitney, Caspar 144, 153
Wilder, John T. 18, 88, 90
Wilderness, battle of **28**, 29
Wilkinson, "Captain" 170–71
Williams, Henry 145
Wilson, S.F. 88
Winchester, battle of 29
Winchester National Cemetery 172
Winslow (torpedo boat) 136
Winstead, George 186–87
Winters, Edwin E. 100
Women's Relief Corps (Knoxville) 184
Wood, Leonard 129, 131
Wounded Knee 119

"Yankee Doodle" (song) 143
Yellow Tavern, battle of 29
Young, Hugh 72

Ziegler, Isaac 85

229

www.ingramcontent.com/pod-product-compliance
Ingram Content Group UK Ltd.
Pitfield, Milton Keynes, MK11 3LW, UK
UKHW041947140426
5217IPUK00014B/687